ALASTAIR SAWDAY'S
SPECIAL PLACES TO STAY

£11.99

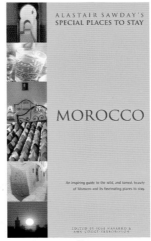

£11.99/$21.95

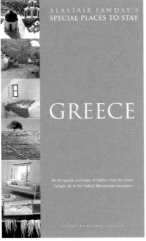

£11.99/$21.95

£10.99/$21.95

Credit card orders (free p&tp) 01275 3?5431

www.sawdays.co.uk

Second edition
Copyright © July 2006
Alastair Sawday Publishing Co. Ltd

Published in 2006
Reprinted in 2008

Alastair Sawday Publishing,
The Old Farmyard,
Yanley Lane, Long Ashton
Bristol BS41 9LR
Tel: +44 (0)1275 395430
Fax: +44 (0)1275 393388
Email: info@sawdays.co.uk
Web: www.sawdays.co.uk

Design:
Caroline King

Maps & Mapping:
Maidenhead Cartographic Services Ltd

Printing:
Multivista Global, Chennai, India

UK Distribution:
Penguin UK, 80 Strand, London

ISBN-10: 1-901970-64-7
ISBN-13: 978-1-901970-64-7

ALASTAIR SAWDAY'S
SPECIAL PLACES TO STAY

INDIA

Contents

Back

Photo Sara Allan

Alastair Sawday Publishing

Our main aim is to publish beautiful guidebooks but, for us, the question of who we are and how we inter-react is also important. For who we are shapes the books, the books shape your holidays, and thus are shaped the lives of people who own these 'special places'. So we are trying to be a little more than 'just a publishing company'.

New eco offices
In January 2006 we moved into our new eco offices. By introducing super-insulation, underfloor heating, a wood-pellet boiler, solar panels and a rainwater tank, we have a working environment benign to ourselves and to the environment. Lighting is low-energy, dark corners are lit by sun-pipes and one building is of green oak. Carpet tiles are from Herdwick sheep in the Lake District. We will sail through our environmental audit.

Environmental & ethical policies
We make many other, smaller, gestures: company cars run on gas or recycled cooking oil; kitchen waste is composted and other waste recycled; cycling and car-sharing are encouraged; the company only buys organic or local food; we don't accept web links with companies we consider unethical; we use the ethical Triodos Bank for our deposit account.

We have used recycled paper for some books but have settled on selecting paper and printing for their low energy use. Our printer is British and ISO14001-certified and together we will work to reduce our environmental impact.

In 2005 we won a Business Commitment to the Environment Award and in April 2006 we won a Queen's Award for Enterprise in the Sustainable Development category. All this has boosted our resolve to promote our green policies. Our flagship gesture, however, is carbon offsetting; we calculate our carbon emissions and plant trees to compensate. In future we will support projects overseas that plant trees or reduce carbon use.

Ethics
But why, you may ask, take these things so seriously? You are just a little publishing company, for heaven's sake! Well, is there any good argument for not taking them seriously? The world, by the admission of the vast majority of scientists, is in trouble. If we do not change our ways urgently we will doom the planet and all its creatures – whether innocent or not – to a variety of possible catastrophes. To maintain the status quo is unacceptable. Business does much of the damage and should undo it, and provide new models.

Who are we?

Pressure on companies to produce Corporate Social Responsibility policies is mounting. We are trying to keep ahead of it all, yet still to be as informal and human as possible – the antithesis of 'corporate'.

The books – and a dilemma
So, we have created fine books that do good work. They promote authenticity, individuality and high quality, local and organic food – a far cry from the now-dominant corporate culture. Rural economies, pubs, small farms, villages and hamlets all benefit. However, people use fossil fuel to get there. Should we aim to get our readers to offset their own carbon emissions, and the B&B and hotel owners too? That might have been a hopeless task a year or so ago, but less so now that the media has taken on board the enormity of the work ahead of us all.

We are gradually introducing green ideas into the books: the Fine Breakfast scheme that highlights British and Irish B&B owners who use local and organic food; celebrating those who make an extra effort; gently encouraging the use of public transport, cycling and walking. This year we are publishing a book focusing on responsible travel and eco-projects around the globe.

Our Fragile Earth series
The 'hard' side of our environmental publishing is the Fragile Earth series: *The Little Earth Book*, *The Little Food Book* and *The Little Money Book*. They consist of bite-sized essays, polemical, hard-hitting and well researched. They are a 'must have' for anyone who is confused and needs clarity about some of the key issues of our time.

This year we are also publishing *One Planet Living* and extracts from *The Little Earth Book* under the title *Earth, Air, Fire and Water*.

Lastly – what is special?
The notion of 'special' is at the heart of what we do, and highly subjective. We discuss this in the introduction. We take huge pleasure from finding people and places that do their own thing – brilliantly; places that are unusual and follow no trends; places of peace and beauty; people who are kind and interesting – and genuine.

We seem to have touched a raw nerve with thousands of readers; they obviously want to stay in special places rather than the dull corporate monstrosities that have disfigured so many of our cities and towns. Life is too short to be wasted in the wrong places. A night in a special place can be a transforming experience.

Alastair Sawday

Acknowledgements

In the best traditions of redoubtable lady explorers, Laura Kinch criss-crossed the continent with indomitable spirit, undaunted by tales of hassle and woe. The rewards were great, and she has fallen more deeply than ever for the charms of India. She deserved every moment of pleasure, for it was hard work. A whole day spent bumping along rough roads to reach a rumoured 'Special Place' is not everybody's idea of fun. So we salute Laura's achievement in taking this now-popular guide to new places and new heights. It has been a hard act and she has performed superbly, with huge independence of spirit.

Laura had a strong supporting cast of inspectors, whose names we have writ large opposite. They too have done a superb job, often in trying conditions, and I thank them all. Also in support has been a strong home team, notably Maria Serrano and Rebecca Stephens in Editorial and Rachel Coe and Allys Williams in Production. Behind the scenes have been many others in this office, to all of whom I offer my very real gratitude. This second edition, three years after the ground-breaking first edition, pays even richer tribute to the many fascinating, generous and original people whose special places we celebrate.

Alastair Sawday

Series Editor Alastair Sawday

Editor Laura Kinch

Editorial Director Annie Shillito

Writing Laura Kinch, Jo Boissevain, Viv Cripps, Richard Hammond, Matthew Hilton-Dennis, Helen Pickles

Inspections Laura Kinch, Callum Chiverton, Mel Clarkson, Matthew Hilton-Dennis, Anna Lamplough, Piers Moore Ede, Trish Thomas

Accounts Bridget Bishop, Christine Buxton, Hannah Greaves, Sandra Hassell, Sally Ranahan

Editorial Jackie King, Jo Boissevain, Florence Oldfield, Maria Serrano, Rebecca Stevens, Danielle Williams

Production Julia Richardson, Rachel Coe, Tom Germain, Rebecca Thomas, Allys Williams

Sales & Marketing & PR Siobhán Flynn, Andreea Petre Goncalves, Sarah Bolton

Web & IT Russell Wilkinson, Chris Banks, Brian Kimberling, Sarah Mark

Previous editor Toby Sawday

Thanks to: Ravi Sunder Kabir, the best driver in Southern India

It is a fleeting moment, your first tentative glimpse of the 'essence' of India. You may never have it. Or you will experience it time and again as you are jolted out of one reverie into another by extraordinary minor events.

It may be yellow paint powder thrown gaily over you during Holi. You may smile with those around you while deep in a tangle of rickshaws. A traveller interrogates you minutely. A monkey neatly purloins your sandwich. Statues and carvings collide and cavort over the face of an austere temple. Elephants and cows preside over chaotic street scenes. Nothing, and everything, is to be expected.

Whatever the commercial success of corners of India, the bulk of Indians live in a separate world, where survival requires the utmost ingenuity – and sheer hard work. Poverty remains deep; malnutrition among the under-fives is 45%. The middle-class minority, about 150 million people, lives, or tries to, in a separate world. To meet a deep variety of these people, of whatever class, is the real pleasure of India. It is even possible, in one's wonder, to put aside political and social judgement – for a while.

We immerse you in the most colourful and vital aspects of India.

You will be seduced by sounds you have never heard before, tastes that transport you. You will sleep in places that, majestically dignified, would be condemned at home. You will have tea with a maharaja one day and a communist the next. You may dine on the roof of a church, under the spreading antlers of a slaughtered beast, on a palm leaf by the waves' edge or around the pool of a boutique fortress.

'Special Places' have gathered a uniquely colourful reputation in India, for their exotic variety and utter dependability. This guide is your servant: it will introduce you to the most delightful and welcoming denizens of this great and many-layered civilisation. You need nothing else.

Alastair Sawday

Introduction

INDIA'S DIVERSITY IS BREATHTAKING – AS IF 20 COUNTRIES WERE ROLLED INTO ONE

A changing India

India throws one's senses into a frenzy – and touches me so deeply I find it hard to stay away. What is it that makes this country so special? Everyone's experience is personal but I can tell you why I love it and recommend a trip to India to anyone.

I have travelled thousands of miles by road, rail, water and air and everywhere found that people smile easily and are generous, respectful and kind. On my arrival in Jaipur during 'Diwali', the Hindu New Year festival, a beaming young Indian invited me to spend the party with the family. The town was packed with beautiful women in shimmering dresses jostling to buy gold and fireworks. At his home, the women whisked me off to envelop me in hugs, smiles and an exquisite sari. A simple 'puja' was performed; then the sky exploded with a million bright lights and the children ran through the streets with their home-crafted 'bangers'.

Memories of my trip to those majestic snow-peaked mountains on the border of Tibet, where Kinnaur Kailash rises to 6,050m, are vivid enough for a lifetime. Chanting, twinkly-eyed monks, an iridescent river that flows from the glacial melt, a monastery with 1,000 golden-painted buddhas on every inch of wall, prayer flags fluttering in the breeze. It's easy to see why this is called 'the land of the Gods'. And the tranquillity is extraordinary.

Recalled images are powerful: a ten-year old boy, galloping out of the desert dusk on a camel, singing a hauntingly melodic tune; stopping at a bus station, being surrounded by a hundred curious, smiling people all wanting to say "hello madam, what is your good name?"; acres of palm trees, lime green paddy fields and a pink sari-clad lady tip-toeing elegantly through the shallows; ten brown and black stripy wild boar skirting along a roadside; a saffron-robed Sadhu meditating on the banks of the Ganges under a red umbrella; a baby daubed with black eyeliner to ward off evil spirits; a small boy learning how to hold a pencil on a train platform.

Photo right Sara Allan
Photo left Laura Kinch

Introduction

India's diversity is breathtaking – as if 20 countries were rolled into one. Most regions have different religions, cultures and languages from the ones next door. It is also a rapidly changing country. When I first visited, internet connections were slow and telephone lines poor. But the influx of cheap mobile phones and low call costs has transformed rural communities in particular. Everyone shouts down their phones to be heard over the cacophony of street sounds.

Globalisation and the introduction of international call centres to cities such as Mumbai, Delhi and Bangalore, and the IT revolution in cities like Hyderabad, have brought a new wealth to certain sectors of society. Globalisation is also affecting the prices in many hotels and homestays. In fact prices in many areas are rising fast, encouraged by the growth both of the middle class and luxury long-haul tourism. With this come western trappings: boutiques, stylish hotels, classy restaurants, mobile phones, designer clothing.

The effect on the environment is significant. With an affluent car culture come harmful emissions as millions of cars, rickshaws and trucks belch out their fumes daily. However, a change of attitude is in the air. India may be one of the most polluted countries on the planet yet recycling is now commonplace, as are simple solar panels for hot water.

Ten years ago India was perceived by many to be a dirty, third-world country where a bout of Delhi-belly was inevitable – a place you'd be brave to visit. India today is an exciting nation that is developing rapidly, and travelling around is easier than it once was. Of course, some areas are more difficult to reach, and some have higher standards of luxury and hygiene than others, but an easy acceptance of simplicity, and a chance to visit some of the lesser-known regions, can bring the greatest rewards.

So, India is a complex country teeming with paradoxes. That is the fascination of the place. Just as you think you've got to grips with one particular aspect, something else comes along to astonish you. Nobody travels to India without

Photo Ben Ross

being impressed, challenged and delighted. This book gives you the independence to get close to it all, to capture a small part of a vibrant, magical and diverse country that is in the process of joining the modern world.

How to use this book
Choosing your special place

We try to make this as easy as possible, by giving you an honest and first-hand description of each and every place. You should be able to tell whether you'll find the privacy you seek or whether you are likely to be drawn into family life; whether a place is formal or relaxed; whether the bathrooms have deep Victorian tubs or open-air showers. Although we have tried to avoid plastic furniture, shiny curtains and embossed wallpaper, you must expect small flurries of kitsch in modern Indian interior design.

Two photos of a property cannot tell the whole story so if you take a peek at web sites – most of our entries have them – you will get a fuller picture. As for price, there is a massive range in this book.

Map

On the map pages at the front of the book each property is labelled with an entry number. The maps show the rough location of properties and are not accurate for journey planning.

Photo Sara Allen

Rooms

We give the total number of single, double, twin or triple rooms, suites, apartments and cottages. (Extra beds are often available for children.) We avoid the more exotic room descriptions that some hotels use, eg. 'luxury double', 'maharani', 'maharaja', even 'vice-regal'. Rooms vary enormously; in one you may find thin mattresses on top of each other in *The Princess and the Pea* style, while some of the pricier rooms will have luxurious orthopaedic bedding. Pillows tend to be hard or foam-filled.

Bathrooms

Rooms have their own bathrooms unless we say otherwise. Only those with 'separate' or 'shared' bathrooms are not en suite. The vast majority of places now have en suite western loos. Occasionally you may find the term 'bucket' shower – so expect a bucket and a jug in your bathroom.

Introduction

You may also find open-air showers – a joy during the day, less appealing at night when insects are attracted by lights. Good bathroom toiletries are a bit of a treat in India and only to be expected in the swishest places.

Prices

We give the double room price based on two people sharing. Prices for solo travellers are also given. If the property has a single room, the single price is for this room' otherwise it is for the single occupancy of a double. Although we have asked owners to give us their prices for 2006-2008, many have been able to give us their prices up to 2007 only. Check when booking.

Price bands

Owners have given us their prices in sterling, US dollars, euros or Indian rupees. To save confusion, we have added a price band that ranges from A (under £25) to G (over £250). The letter code is printed at the bottom of each entry and the breakdown is shown on the inside back page.

Seasonal prices and special deals

Be aware of price differences in low and high season – they can change dramatically. We mention the high season period in the price section, so if you are going out of season, prices may be lower. Don't be afraid to ask for special deals for longer stays.

Taxes

We normally show the % tax charged on top of the room price – otherwise you may presume it is included in the price. However, things change: check when booking.

Booking

You can book direct by fax, phone, email, via the owner's web site or through our web site. Emails are not necessarily received immediately so be patient and plan your trip well in advance. It is normal for places to take a non-refundable deposit by credit card or international transfer.

Cancellations

Try to give plenty of notice when cancelling a booking. Ask for the owner's cancellation policy when you book.

Payment

If owners have the ✉ symbol you should be able to pay by credit card. Otherwise you must pay in cash, so make sure you have the right currency if going to a remote hotel.

Photo right Laura Kinch
Photo left Harriet Richardson

Introduction

Meals

Where meals are available, prices are given per person. Breakfast is included in the price, unless otherwise stated. Lunch and/or dinner may be included in the overall price: look for 'full-board' or 'half-board'. Taxes on meals can add a further 8%.

Food is generally wholesome, delicious and cheap, with vegetarians well catered for. Dishes change as you pass from state to state reflecting the dizzying array of regional produce. Coconut and fish dominate the dishes of the southern coastal areas while the influences in the Himalayan areas are Tibetan and Chinese. The deserts of Rajasthan may deliver some pretty fiery curries, but not all Indian food is spicy. Note

Photo Sara Allen

that it is culturally acceptable to use only your right hand for eating.

Tipping

In a standard hotel, Rs50 (65p) per day is about right. Or, 10% of the bill to spread between various people should be OK Bear in mind that a 2km rickshaw ride will be about Rs25, so a tip to a rail porter of Rs15 for carting your luggage should be more than enough. Drivers rely on tips; between Rs750 and Rs1,000 for a week is reasonable.

Directions

We give details of the nearest airport and train station. Brief directions from the nearest main road may also be described. Further details can be given on booking, or can be found on the owner's web site.

Types of Properties

It is not easy to place properties into fixed categories in India – a palace is not always a palace and some guest houses call themselves resorts. You may even find a tent called a 'hotel'.

Hotels This category covers everything from 'heritage' to 'boutique' hotels. They vary – some are lavishly decorated palaces teeming with dusty antiques, others may be surprisingly contemporary.

Resorts – and eco resorts – are places of varying size that cater for individuals and small groups. They generally consist of huts, tree houses and cottages throughout the grounds, may put on evening entertainments, have an ayurvedic or a beauty spa, and arrange activities and trips.

Homestays These are the equivalent of B&B and make up a rapidly growing sector. They tend to be family homes where you get a taste of (mostly middle-class) home life. Although many of the host families have moved away from a strictly traditional lifestyle, it is important to respect the customs of the family. Homestay owners adore having guests to stay and friendships are easily formed over sociable dinners.

Guest houses tend to be smaller and less anonymous than hotels, but less intimate than homestays. They are often private houses that have been partially converted and may or may not have a restaurant, room service or telephones in the rooms.

Catered cottages Private cottages, possibly by the sea, where someone comes in daily to cook and clean.

Safari camps Rooms or tents or both, in India's national parks. Meals and safaris are often included in the price.

Under canvas The standard of luxury varies – some tents have four-poster

Photo Harriet Richardson

beds and en suite showers, others are very simple. Be warmed by camp fires and dine by candlelight.

Water scarcity & responsible tourism
India is suffering. Rainfall is declining, monsoons are failing, water tables are falling and crops and livestock are suffering.
It is a problem exacerbated by deforestation, by extravagant use of water and poor conservation practices. Although Indian communities have coped with poor rains and semi-arid climates for generations, the Indian population growns apace and the introduction of western technologies and tastes have stretched resources to breaking point.

The growth of tourism in India is also playing its part. Hotels in the desert of Rajasthan, embellished with water

Introduction

around religious sites.
Communities visited by tourists
sometimes complain that their
children are abandoning school
to hound tourists for money.
So, although it may go against your
instincts, please do not give money,
sweets or trinkets to school children.
Leave donations with established
Indian charities instead.

Getting involved

There are hundreds of charitable
organisations needing help. We are
keen to endorse the work done
by SCAD (Social Change and
Development) which dedicates itself
to helping the poor, neglected,
marginalized and under-privileged
eg. the landless agricultural workers,
saltpan workers, gypsies, lepers, the
physically disabled and rural women
and children. In the UK, SCAD is
supported by Salt of the Earth,
tel: 0116 276 6439
www.salt-of-the-earth.org.uk

Green entries

We have chosen, very subjectively,
half a dozen places which are making
a particular effort to be eco-friendly,
and have given them a 'Special Green
Entry' stamp. This does not mean
there are no other places in the guide
taking green initiatives – there are
many – but we have highlighted just
a few. A growing number of our
owners recycle, use solar energy, have
photo-voltaic panels for electricity,

gardens and infinity pools, are drilling
ever further into the ground to slake
their thirst, while nearby villages find
their communal taps running dry and
their animals dying.

It is a savage irony. India's tourism
brings in the foreign exchange
needed to fuel its growth, yet many
of her people are suffering as a result.
A more considered approach to
tourism is required. Be sensitive to
your surroundings – and do not run
baths in the desert!

Culture clashes

India's beaches are undeniably
beautiful but for fishing communities
they are both work place and home.
Scantily clad tourists cause offence to
traditional Indians of all religions, and
topless sunbathing is intolerable.
Indian women seldom bare their skin
and would certainly be grateful if you
followed their example – particularly

Photo above Toby Sawday
Photo right Sara Allan

Introduction

tend their land and animals organically, and use eco-building methods and local materials.

Practicalities
Time difference
India is five and a half hours ahead of GMT.

Where to go – regional differences
India is vast: there are so many contrasts and such diversity. With a billion people it can seem noisy and chaotic – and yet an immense serenity and peace can be found. Seventeen major regional languages, hundreds of dialects, a sophisticated civilisation that goes back 5,000 years and four major religions – Hinduism, Jaininsm, Sikkism and Buddhism – were founded here. Plus there are Muslims and Christians. Then there are the historical and colonial influences, the many cuisines, and the rich variety of landscape, vegetation and wildlife.

You can visit over 7,000km of stunning coastline, the volcanic area of the Deccan plateau, the tree-rich hills of the Western and Eastern Ghats, the vast plains where wheat, sugarcane, rice and pulses flourish... and desert, salt plains and snowcapped peaks. Caste-based divisions, sexual inequality, poverty and illiteracy are most noticeable in the countryside.

Some states are so large that one section is dramatically different from another. We tell you a little about the regions at the start of each section; a good travel guide will tell you far more.

You may notice that large swathes of the country do not include any of our Special Places, particularly the central and northern regions. The reasons vary: a lack of good accommodation; undeveloped tourism; extreme living conditions; a sparse terrain. Other regions we choose not to include because of political unrest.

We are delighted to include two new regions in this second edition: the Punjab and Ladakh. Amritsar is, deservedly, a popular destination on many north India itineraries, while exciting reports have come back from Ladakh, a friendly and visually stunning place, much of it simple, unspoilt and perfect for nature lovers.

Photo Laura Kinch

When to go

Please also see the introductory pages to the regions.

Himalayas – May to September

Himalayan foothills – March to September

Rajasthan, Gujarat and central northern India – October to March

Southern India – October to March

Monsoon

The main monsoon comes from the south-west, starts in the first week of June in the extreme south, then heads north, covering the whole country by mid-July. The north-east monsoon hits the south-east coast between mid-October and December.

Visas & health

Everyone needs a visa to enter India. Contact the Indian High Commission www.hcilondon.net for details. The easiest way to apply for a visa is by post; allow at least two weeks for its return. Do organise your visa before you book your holiday. You will also need immunisation before you go. This can be arranged via your local doctor or you can contact Masta www.masta.org for immunisation – and anti-malarial advice.

Communication

Email & fax   Communication within and to India is improving all the time. Almost all entries in this guide have an email address; most have a fax number.

Telephones   The numbers printed include the country code (+91)

Calling India from the UK

Dial 00 then the number (omitting the zero in brackets).

Calling internationally from India

Dial 00 then the country code and the area code (omitting the zero).

Calling within India

Land lines   No country code (+91) is needed. Simply dial the number printed starting with and including the zero in brackets.

Mobiles   All mobile numbers begin with a 9. Prefix the number with a zero if calling a different Indian state. If you are in the same state as the person you are calling, there is no need to use the zero. Given the high costs of using your own mobile phone in India, it is often more attractive to buy an Indian SIM card, available on almost every street corner for approximately Rs300 (£4). The rates are still somewhat higher than using the landline system and you need a photocopy of your passport and a photo to buy one. Generally, you need different SIM cards in different states.

Electricity

The current in India is 220/240 volts, 50 Hz. Virtually all hotel rooms will have at least one socket that takes a two-pin plug. For UK travellers, a European adaptor plug (available in airports) is ideal.

Introduction

Subscriptions

Owners pay to appear in this guide. Their fee goes towards the cost of inspections (every entry has been inspected by a member of our team before being selected), of producing an all-colour book and of maintaining a sophisticated web site. We only include places and owners that we find positively special. It is not possible for anyone to buy their way into our guides.

Internet

www.specialplacestostay.com has online pages for all of the places featured here and from all our other books – around 5,000 Special Places in Britain, Ireland, France, Italy, Spain, Portugal, India, Morocco, Turkey and Greece. There's a searchable database, a taster of the write-ups and colour photos.

Disclaimer

We make no claims to pure objectivity in choosing our Special Places to Stay. They are here because we like them. Our opinions and tastes are ours alone and this book is a statement of them; we hope that you will share them.

We have done our utmost to get our facts right but apologise unreservedly for any mistakes that may have crept in. Feedback from you is invaluable and we always act upon comments. With your help and our own inspections we can maintain our reputation for dependability.

You should know that we do not check such things as fire alarms, swimming pool security or any other regulation with which owners of properties receiving paying guests should comply. This is the responsibility of the owners.

Stay in touch

We love hearing about your experiences – good and bad – and your comments make a real contribution, be they on our report form, by letter or by email to info@sawdays.co.uk. Please also keep writing with your recommendations of new places for the next edition.

And finally

India can be a frustrating country to visit, and at times requires humour and patience, but it is an invigorating, complex and challenging place. Its people are passionate, spiritual and hospitable, its nature resplendent, its sights magnificent. One visit may change you forever.

Laura Kinch

Photo Laura Kinch

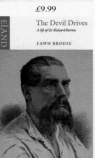

General map

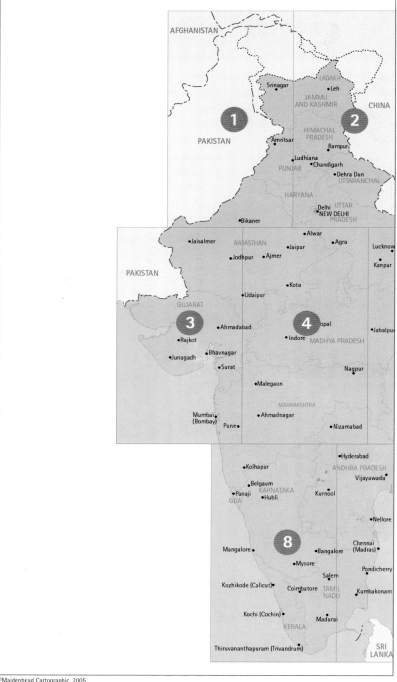

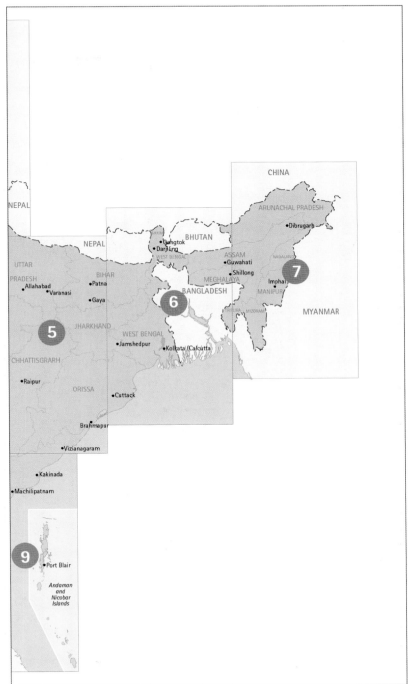

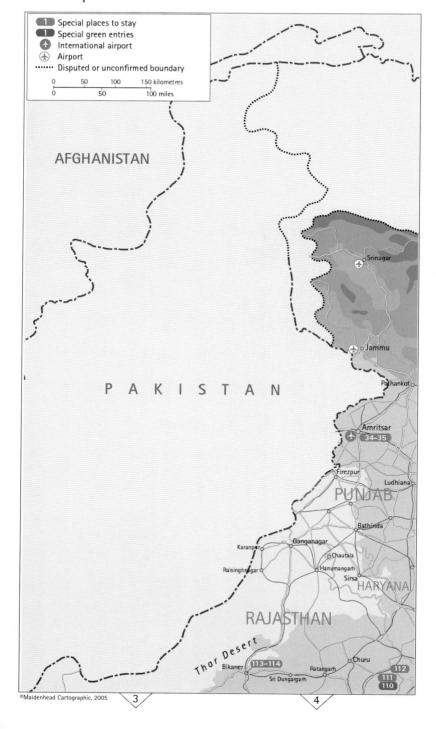

Special places to stay
Special green entries
International airport
Airport
Disputed or unconfirmed boundary

0   50   100   150 kilometres
0   50   100 miles

AFGHANISTAN

Srinagar

Jammu

PAKISTAN

Pathankot

Amritsar
34-35

Firezpur

Ludhiana

PUNJAB

Bathinda

Karanpur
Ganganagar

Chautala

Raisinghnagar
Hanumangarh

Sirsa

HARYANA

RAJASTHAN

Thar Desert
Bikaner
113-114
Ratangarh
Churu
112

Sri Dungargarh
111
110

Map 2

27

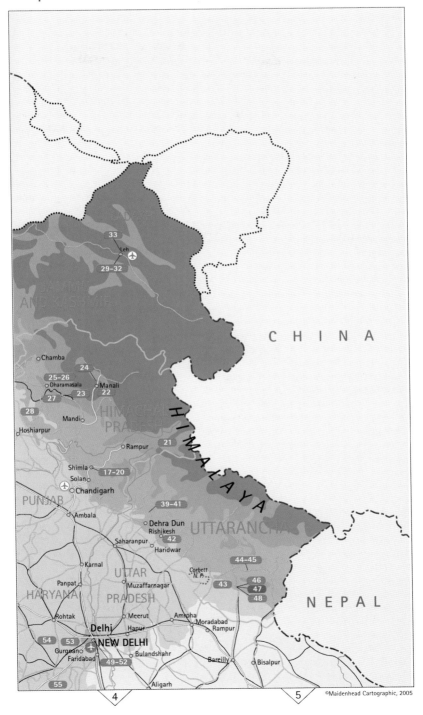

Map 3

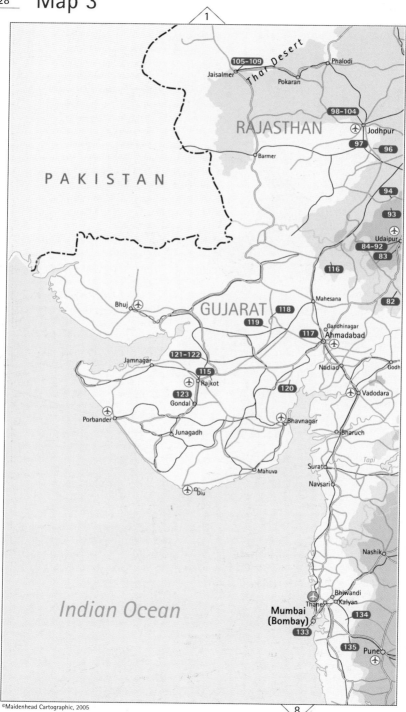

Map 4

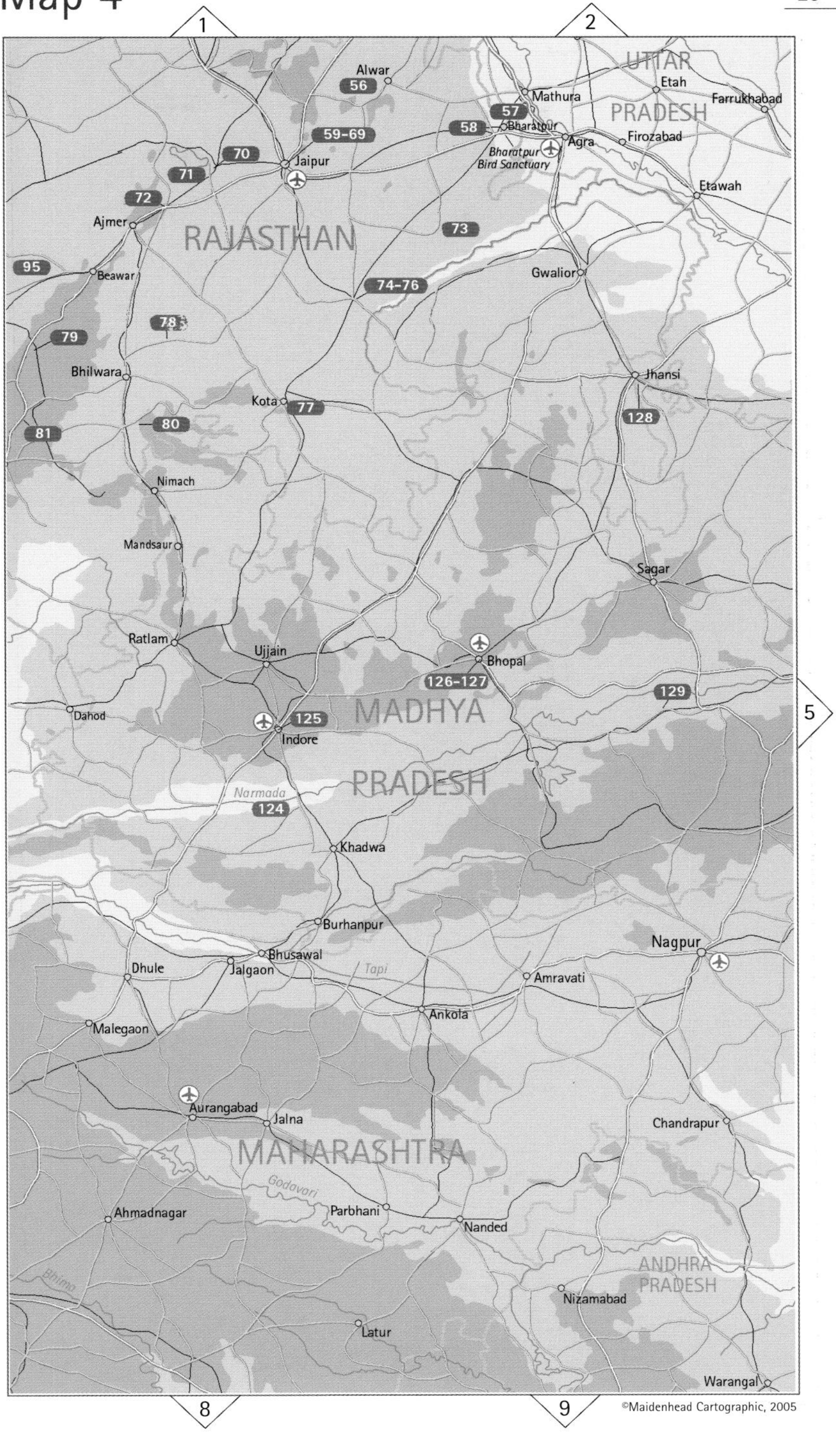

29

Alwar
56
Mathura
Etah
Farrukhabad
UTTAR
PRADESH
57
58
Bharatpur
Agra
Firozabad
59-69
Bharatpur
Bird Sanctuary
70
Jaipur
71
Etawah
72
73
Ajmer
RAJASTHAN
95
Beawar
74-76
Gwalior
79
78
Jhansi
Bhilwara
Kota
77
128
81
80
Nimach

Mandsaur
Sagar

Ratlam
Ujjain
Bhopal
Dahod
126-127
125
MADHYA
129
Indore
PRADESH
Narmada
124
Khadwa

Burhanpur
Nagpur
Dhule
Bhusawal
Tapi
Jalgaon
Amravati
Malegaon
Ankola

Aurangabad
Jalna
Chandrapur
MAHARASHTRA
Godavari
Ahmadnagar
Parbhani
Nanded
ANDHRA
Bhima
PRADESH
Nizamabad
Latur
Warangal

Map 5

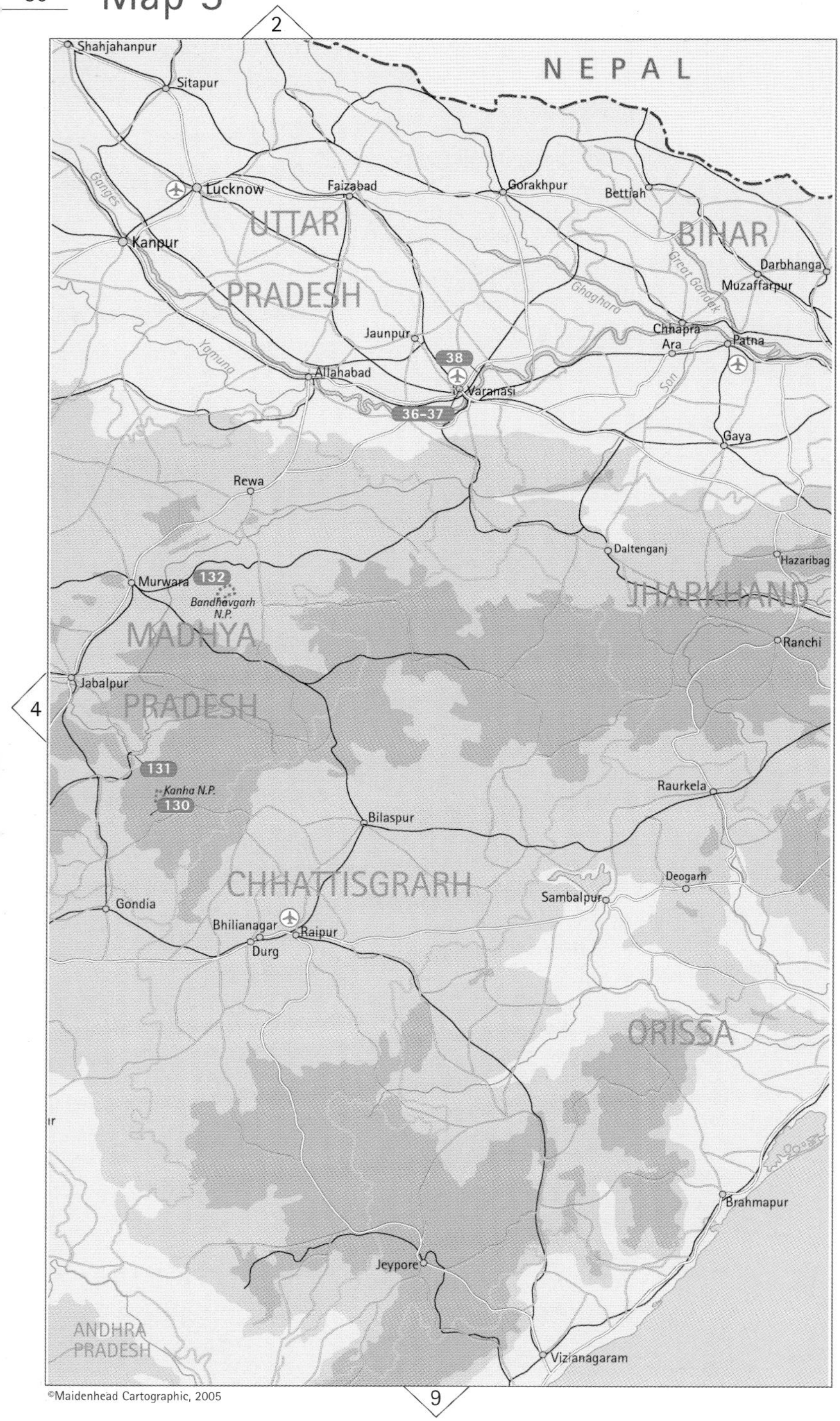

Shahjahanpur

Sitapur

NEPAL

Lucknow

Faizabad

Gorakhpur

Bettiah

BIHAR

UTTAR

Kanpur

Darbhanga

Muzaffarpur

PRADESH

Jaunpur

Chhapra

Ara

Patna

Allahabad

38

Varanasi

36-37

Gaya

Rewa

Son

Daltenganj

Hazaribag

JHARKHAND

Murwara

132

Bandhavgarh
N.P.

MADHYA

Ranchi

Jabalpur

4

PRADESH

131

Konha N.P.

130

Bilaspur

Raurkela

CHHATTISGRARH

Sambalpur

Deogarh

Gondia

Bhilianagar

Raipur

Durg

ORISSA

Brahmapur

Jeypore

ANDHRA
PRADESH

Vizianagaram

Map 6

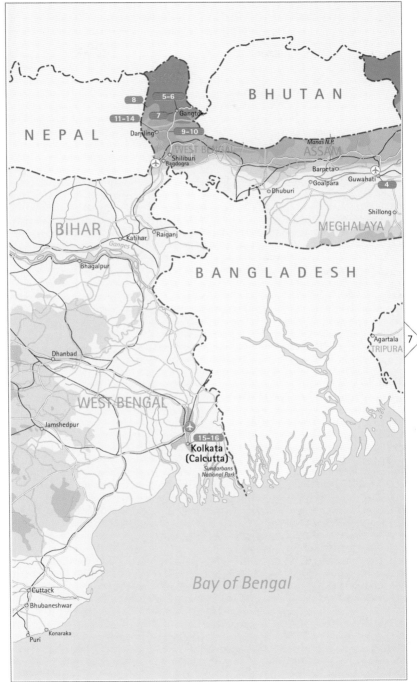

©Maidenhead Cartographic, 2005

Map 7

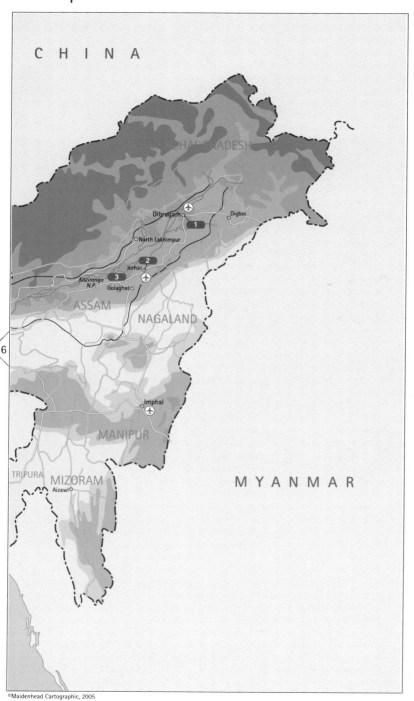

Map 8

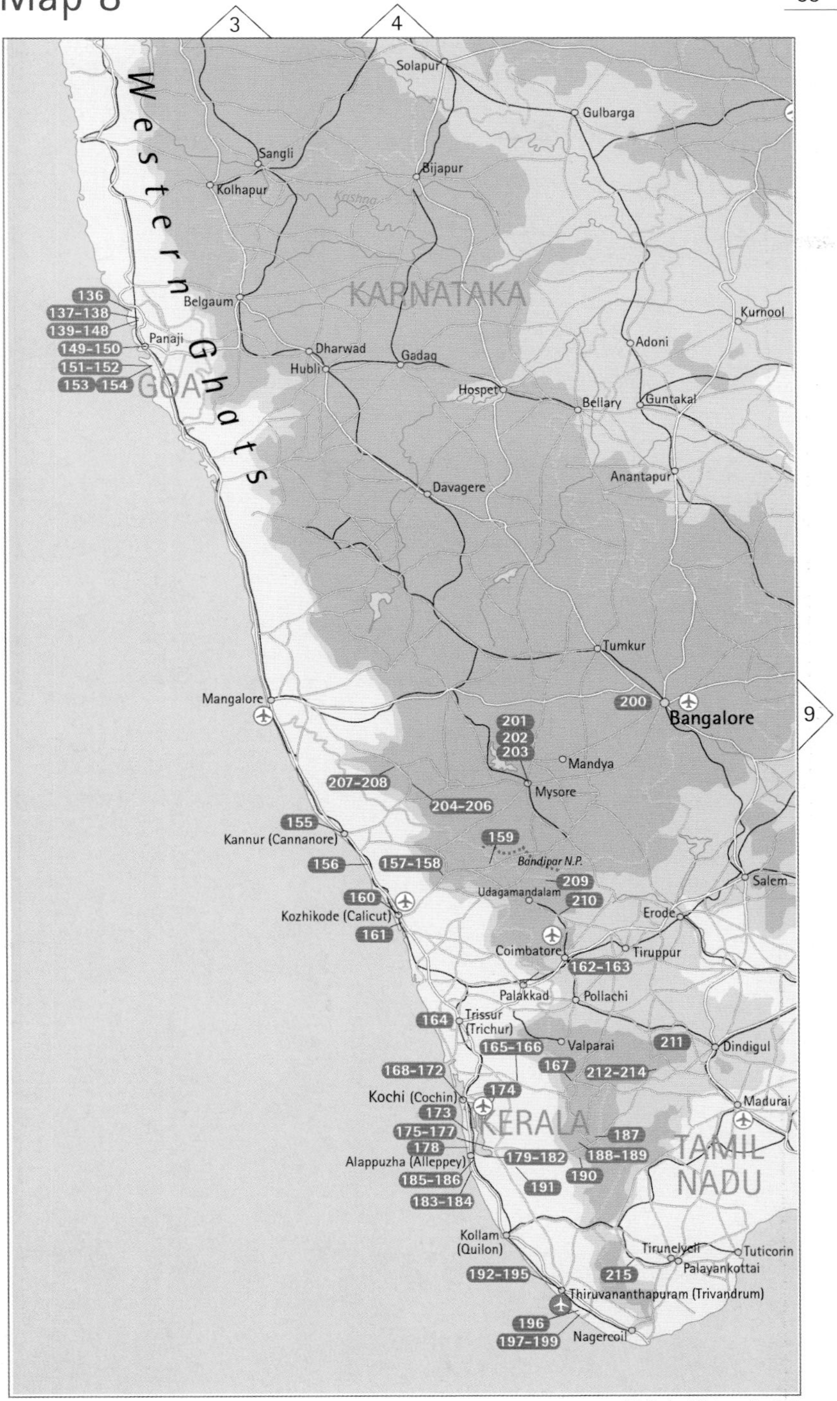

3 4

Western Ghats

Solapur

Gulbarga

Sangli

Kolhapur

Bijapur

KARNATAKA

Kurnool

136
137–138
139–148   Panaji
149–150
151–152
153 154   GOA

Belgaum

Dharwad

Hubli   Gadag

Adoni

Hospet

Bellary   Guntakal

Davagere

Anantapur

Mangalore

Tumkur

200   Bangalore   9

201
202
203   Mandya

207–208

204–206

Mysore

155   Kannur (Cannanore)

156   157–158

159
Bandipar N.P.

209
Udagamandalam   210

Salem

160   Kozhikode (Calicut)
161

Coimbatore   Tiruppur

162–163

Erode

Palakkad   Pollachi

164   Trissur
(Trichur)

165–166

Valparai

211   Dindigul

167   212–214

168–172

Kochi (Cochin)   174
173

Madurai

175–177
178   Alappuzha (Alleppey)

179–182

187

188–189

185–186

191   190

KERALA

TAMIL
NADU

183–184

Kollam
(Quilon)

Tirunelveli   Tuticorin

Palayankottai

192–195

215   Thiruvananthapuram (Trivandrum)

196
197–199   Nagercoil

Map 9

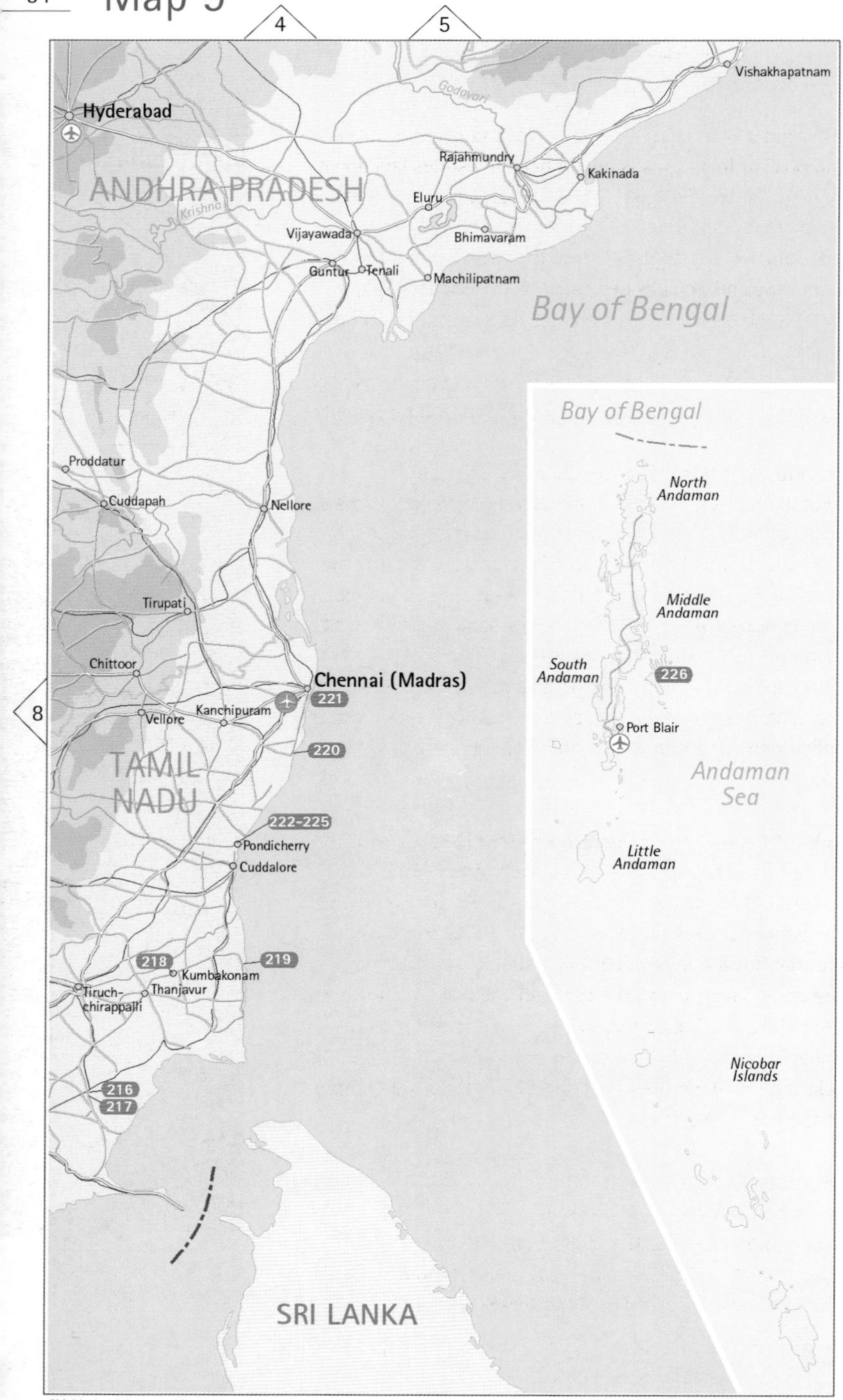

4 5

Vishakhapatnam

Godavari

Hyderabad

Rajahmundry

Kakinada

ANDHRA PRADESH

Eluru

Krishna

Vijayawada

Bhimavaram

Guntur Tenali

Machilipatnam

Bay of Bengal

Bay of Bengal

North
Andaman

Proddatur

Cuddapah

Nellore

Middle
Andaman

Tirupati

South
Andaman

226

Chittoor

Chennai (Madras)

8

Kanchipuram

221

Port Blair

Vellore

TAMIL
NADU

220

Andaman
Sea

222–225

Pondicherry

Cuddalore

Little
Andaman

218

219

Tiruch-
chirappalli

Kumbakonam

Thanjavur

216
217

Nicobar
Islands

SRI LANKA

Assam, Sikkim, Kolkata & West Bengal

The mighty Brahmaputra River feeds Assam's lush valleys and 60% of India's tea is grown here, in estates laid down by the British. The capital, Guwuhati, is the gateway to the more remote north-eastern states – home to many colourful, tribal groups. South of the town lies the Hindu Kamakahya hill temple, dedicated to the Goddess Kali, a splendid example of the distinctive Assamese architecture. In the stunning grasslands of the World Heritage Kaziranga National Park you may be lucky enough to see the one-horned rhino, Hoolock gibbons and wild elephants.

Peaceful Sikkim is influenced by its neighbours, Tibet, Bhutan and Nepal, and is dominated by the snow-capped peaks of India's highest mountain, Kanchendzongra (8,586m). In this tiny and beautiful state, there are richly decorated Buddhist monasteries, lime-green rice paddies, orange groves, mountain lakes and smiling, gentle people. Come to trek through the orchid-rich, view-filled landscape where snow leopards and red panda live – or for the Saga Dawa Festival in May to celebrate Buddha's birth, enlightenment and nirvana. You need a permit to visit Sikkim.

In West Bengal lie the famous, Raj-era hill stations of Darjeeling and Kalimpong and the World Heritage Sunderbans – the mangrove swamp area that's home to the gangetic dolphin, fiddler crabs, saltwater crocodiles and the Royal Bengal tiger. The state capital, Kolkata (formerly Calcutta), on the banks of the Hoogly River was once the capital of British India and home to the East India Company. It has been a communist state since 1978. Take a dawn drive from Kolkata to Tiger Hill for a glimpse of the ineffable Everest.

Best time to visit:
Assam: Nov-April
Sikkim: Mid-Oct-mid-Dec; March to late May
Kolkata & West Bengal Lower Plains: Oct-March
West Bengal Hills: Oct-Dec & March-May

Photo top Indian Tourist Board,
Photo bottom Laura Kinch

Mancotta Chang Bungalow

Purvi Discovery (P) Ltd, Jalan Nagar, Dibrugarh, 786 005 Assam

In the middle of a working Assam tea estate, this 157-year-old bungalow was built by British planters. Raised on wooden stilts to make it easier to stride your elephant – and for protection against floods and jungle beasts – it's a big, airy space with two levels of verandas. Varnished dark wooden floors, beds and writing desks give a clubby feel to the rooms, which are elegant and comfortable. Meals can be taken on a veranda, and the food alternates between Indian and continental; Indian wins every time. There's a place to watch videos and a small library of books. After the rain, take some time to sniff the air, sip some tea and enjoy the rich pea-green of the tea bushes. The Jalan family, who own the bungalow, have been in the area for five generations; Manoj and Vineeta will quickly make you feel at home and can arrange tours to Rukmini Island for birdwatching and adventure sports. The guides they use are exceptional, particularly Hemanta, who is full of stories. If you're a big party, there's a second, cosier bungalow a short drive away, though it is near a road. *Croquet, boating & tea-tasting.*

Guest house

rooms	9: 3 doubles, 4 twins, 2 singles, sharing bathrooms.
price	Full-board $89–$120. Singles $55. Plus 10% tax. Peak season: November–May.
meals	Full-board only.
closed	Rarely.
directions	In middle of Mancotta Tea Estate. Airport: Dibrugarh (15km). Train: Dibrugarh (5km).

Mr Ranjeet Das

tel	+91 (0)3732 301 120
mobile	+91 (0)9435 130 014
fax	+91 (0)3732 301 944
email	purvi@sancharnet.in
web	www.purviweb.com

B

Map 7 Entry 1

Thengal Manor
Jalukanibari, Na Ali, Jorhat, 785 001 Assam

A slice of another life – and, although the architecture is thoroughly colonial, the family that owns it is Assamese, and immensely distinguished. It is on a grand scale, almost opulent, though there is little hint of 'hotel'. The furniture is a handsome mix of antique and reproduction with original objects from all over the world: solidly upholstered and deeply comfortable furniture – perhaps a mahogany drum table or a Louis IV-style sideboard – heavy floral curtains, giant-chequered floor, white walls and old-fashioned ceiling fans. The bedrooms are magnificent: maybe a four-poster bed, dark but elegant wooden pieces, red polished floors with attractive rugs and plain walls; all are big enough to have their own sitting areas and dressing rooms. Somehow it is very European, despite the epic space and ceiling fans, but in the middle of a green sea of tea plantation. The colonial style re-emerges in the splendidly colonnaded quadrangular veranda, with polished red floors and white cane chairs. There are a sitting room, dining room and lounge – space galore.

rooms	5 doubles.
price	Rs2,350. Whole house Rs9,500. Plus 20% tax. Peak season: October-April.
meals	Breakfast Rs165. Lunch & dinner from Rs315 each. Plus 12% tax.
closed	Rarely.
directions	15km from Jorhat along the Na Ali (new road) towards Titabor. Signed.

	Mr Hemendra Prasad Barooah
tel	+91 (0)3762 339 519
res. no	+91 (0)3762 304 267
fax	+91 (0)3762 304 672
email	heritagenortheast@gmail.com
web	www.heritagetourismindia.com

Hotel

Map 7 Entry 2

Wild Grass Resort
Kaziranga, 785 109 Assam

If you are planning on making the journey to Assam, a path seldom trodden by the European traveller, seek this place out. Nature lovers come for wild elephants and the one-horned rhino, and the guides, whose knowledge is a wonder: your eyes and ears will be opened wide. Wild Grass is fully committed to the National Park and to ensuring that its eco and social structure is not damaged; not a sweet wrapper in sight and the locally employed staff supremely helpful and happy. Bedrooms in the rural-style lodge are airy and spacious with views over gorgeous gardens – not that you'll want to stay in for long. If not out on the jeep, there are endless big trees to rest under, a pool to swim and lunches to be lingered over in a dining room washed with light. You'll feast on authentic Assam cuisine accompanied by delicious fruity side dishes – plucked that day in the grounds. For your evening's entertainment, relax on the veranda and pick out your favourite birdsong: over 200 species dwell here, bathed in the firefly glow that floods the surrounding fields. *Cottages & tents peak season only.*

Safari lodge

rooms	26: 18 twins, 2 cottages for 2, 3 tents for 2; 3 lodges with separate showers.
price	Rs850-Rs2,200. Cottages from Rs950. Tents Rs450. Peak season November–April.
meals	Lunch Rs200. Dinner Rs300.
closed	Never.
directions	2km from the entrance to Kaziranga National Park, on the right towards Jorhat. Unsigned;ask for directions.

Manju Barua

tel	+91 (0)3776 262 085
res. no	+91 (0)3612 546 827
mobile	+91 (0)9954 16945
email	wildgrasskaziranga@gmail.com
web	www.oldassam.com

B 人 🏊

Map 7 Entry 3

Assam Bengal Navigation
Guwahati, Assam

Making stately progress along the Brahmaputra river, her shiny white and green hull and sparkling rails towering above the water, RV Charaidew is a throwback to the days when colonial tea-planters and forest officers went 'up country'. You will surely turn heads. This 38m boat is now the river's only passenger cruiser and gives a rare insight into Assam – history, adventure, wilderness. One day might be tea gardens and temples, another rickshaw rides and silk-weaving villages; on the next, you might glimpse Himalayan snows. The highlight is the wildlife: the one-horned rhinos of Kaziranga National Park, the tigers of Manas National Park, even the rare Gangetic dolphin. The boat's style is brisk and comfortable rather than cruise-ship glamorous and displays a fondness for stained pine, wicker furniture and checked cushions. Cabins are roomy, shipshape and on the upper deck, but you'll want to be in the saloon with its wraparound windows, or taking the air. Moustachioed Manu, the manager, joins guests for dinner – or finds a deserted river island for a barbecue. An off the tourist track experience.

rooms	12 cabins for 2.
price	Full-board $490. Airport/rail transfers included.
meals	Full-board only. Peak season: October-April.
closed	May-September.
directions	Directions given on booking.

Andrew & Grania Brock

tel	+91 (0)3612 602 186
res. no	+44 (0)208 995 3642 (UK)
fax	+44 (0)208 742 1066 (UK)
email	assambengal@aol.com
web	www.assambengalnavigation.com

Hotel

Map 6 Entry 4

The Hidden Forest Retreat

Lower Sichey Busty, Gangtok, 737 101 Sikkim

A three-year-old plant nursery with a guest house thrown in – this retreat has a fabulous, fresh, wholesome feel. It is a steep, half-hour walk up into bustling town but you are close enough not to feel isolated, and can be as private or as sociable as you like. Kesong, her family and dog Georgie are friendly, down-to-earth, green-fingered enthusiasts who will cheerfully join you for an interesting chat and a cup of tea. On these lush acres are cow sheds and greenhouses, a large organic vegetable patch for guava, kiwi and oranges, bonsai trees in the tea room and orchids and lilies galore. Birds chirrup, butterflies flutter, cicadas hum and the views reach across the valley to the Ranka Runtek hills; perch on a forest bench and admire. The guest accommodation is built into the terraced hillside on split levels, the two cottages (with bedroom and sitting room) being the newest and largest. The bright twin rooms have floors and ceilings of teak and alnus-wood, white and spotless shower rooms and a balcony each. Let the peace and the nature wash over you, and stay at least two nights.

Guest house

rooms	10: 8 twins, 2 cottages.
price	Rs1,700. Full-board option.
meals	Lunch & dinner available.
closed	Rarely.
directions	Short drive from Gangtok market; right past stadium, follow winding road, left at district court; opposite wide bend. Airport: Bagdora (124km, 4 hours). Train: New Jalpaiguri (125km, 4 hours).

Mr Kesang Lachungpa

tel	+91 (0)3592 205 197
mobile	+91 (0)9434 137 409
fax	+91 (0)3592 205 197
email	enquiry@hiddenforestretreat.com
web	www.hiddenforestretreat.com

A

Map 6 Entry 5

Nor-Khill

Stadium Road, Gangtok, 737 101 Sikkim

The huge and beautifully decorated lobby was originally the King's ballroom when this was the royal guest house. The royal charm lives on, in the serenity and the designs and the fabulous food (nettle soup and bamboo shoots, perhaps, or chicken momo served with the local tipple, chang). As a hotel it is individual and luxurious in the nicest way, with fine wooden-floored bedrooms and some original pieces, and much satisying detail: old silver, engraved breakfast pepper and salt pots, hand-woven tray mats and chair covers, wooden floors and a general sense that the house has known good times. The King and his American wife, Hope Cook, had a hand in the decoration and he held his parties here. When Diamond Oberoi bought it he spruced it up but left it largely intact. There is a Sikkimese altar in the main corridor with two circular seating areas at each end covered with hand-woven material in bold colours. Expect wall-hangings, intricate painted designs, an old wood-burning stove, a stone floor and lots of red. If it was good enough for the Dalai Lama and Shirley McLean it may do you.

rooms	32: 28 doubles, 4 suites.
price	Full-board Rs4,800. Suites Rs6,500. Plus 10%. Peak season: March–June; September–December.
meals	Full-board only.
closed	Rarely.
directions	Just above the Palzor Stadium in Gangtok.

	Mr Basudev Sahoo	Hotel
tel	+91 (0)3592 220 064	
res. no	+91 (0)3322 269 878	
fax	+91 (0)3592 225 639	
email	newelgin@cal.vsnl.net.in	
web	www.elginhotels.com	

Map 6 Entry 6

Bamboo Resort
Sajong, Rumtek, 737 101 Sikkim

A lovely east-meets-west sort of place, with low double beds, Sikkimese cushions and rugs and all the vibrancy of Sikkimese culture. Although the building is of solid stone there is a big emphasis on bamboo; there's plenty of it around. The floors are of grey marble and the feng shui bedrooms, each a different colour to represent an element, are a main feature. Indeed, the whole building was built according to feng shui principles. Helen is Swiss and her passion for ecology is reflected in this serene and special place. She grows vegetables and herbs organically in the resort's garden and buys locally. Fern, wild yams, stinging nettle, fermented mustard leaves, even orchids are a selection of the fresh ingredients used – and there are pizzas from a pizza oven for those with less adventurous tastes. There's a beautiful meditation room, a library and a room for herbal regenerating baths. In three acres of ox-ploughed paddy fields with breathtaking mountain views, Bamboo Resort is no distance at all from bustling Gangtok. *Workshops include Mandala paintings, Tibetan medicine & cookery.*

Hotel

rooms	12 doubles.
price	Full-board Rs2,900-Rs3,750. Singles Rs2,000-Rs2,500. Peak season: March-May; September-November.
meals	Full-board only.
closed	Rarely.
directions	From Gangtok 19km along Rumtek road to Sajong village. Call to announce your arrival so staff can help with luggage.

	Helen Kaempf
tel	+91 (0)3592 28664
res. no	+91 (0)3592 252 516
email	info@sikkim.ch
web	www.bambooresort.com

B ✗ ◊ ⛍

Map 6 Entry 7

Yangsum Farm Homestay

Yangsum Farm, P.O. Rinchenpong, District Gyalsing, 737 111 West Sikkim

Near the small bazaar village of Rinchenpong, a delightful working family farm run by Thendup Tashi and his sister Pema Chuki – warm and gracious hosts. The place has a gentle, calming atmosphere. Come to write, draw or help out on the 44-acre farm that grows everything from cardamom and ginger to avocados, oranges, mangoes and tea. The simple, wooden-floored bedrooms are colourful with Sikkimese fabrics and family photographs; the bathrooms are spotless and some are shared. Check out the traditional Buddhist altar room where you can meditate should the mood take you. There's a communal sitting room indoors and a courtyard where you can enjoy the sunshine. The food is superb – try the local dishes that incorporate nettles, ferns and bamboo. (Other Indian food is served, too.) Thendup and Pema are likely to accompany you on some great walks, including those to a rhododendron forest, an aristocratic Lepcha house and a Buddhist monastery – quieter and more remote than any on the Sikkimese tourist route. And when the clouds clear, the views to Kanchenjunga are spectacular.

rooms	5: 3 doubles; 2 doubles, each with separate bath.
price	Full-board $75-$81. Peak season: January-June; September-November.
meals	Full-board only.
closed	Rarely.
directions	2km down from Rinchenpong. Airport: Bagdogra (4 hours). Train: New Jalpaiguri (125km, 4 hours).

Homestay

	Mr Thendup Tashi & Ms Pema Chuki Tsechutharpa
res. no	+91 (0)3595 245 322
mobile	+91 (0)9733 085 196
	or +91 (0)9434 179 029
email	yangsumfarm@yahoo.com
web	www.yangsumfarm.com

B

Map 6 Entry 8

Himalayan Hotel

Upper Cart Road, Kalimpong, 734 301 Kolkata and West Bengal

Still in the Macdonald family after all these years and going strong, with Himalayan oak ceilings, teak pillars, walnut and teak furniture, open fireplaces in most rooms and Tibetan memorabilia in the dining room. Tim's grandfather built it in 1920 and after a career in tea planting Tim and his wife Nilam are now firmly rooted here. No wonder – Kalimpong is within sight of Kinchinjunga and is a centre for birdwatching, hill-walking and anything to do with mountains. Indeed, hardly a famous mountaineer has failed to stay here – Hilary and Tenzing, Mallory and Irving – let alone any author writing about Tibet and the mountains. It is a fine old hotel, airier than one would imagine, with delightful staff, solidly dependable food, red carpets and Nepalese rugs, whitewashed walls and deep peace. Rooms in the cottages are fine, though less exceptional than those in the main building; but they do have king-size beds. "A commonplace name for an exceptional place" – as the British writer, James Cameron, wrote. The garden is superb. *Picnics by the river, barbecues in winter. Golf can be arranged.*

Hotel

rooms	16: 4 doubles, 12 twins.
price	Rs2,500. Plus 10% tax. Peak season: March–May; September–January.
meals	Breakfast Rs160. Lunch & dinner Rs320 each.
closed	Rarely.
directions	Up the hill from town centre, a 10-minute walk from 'Silver Oaks'.

	Mrs Nilam Macdonald	
tel	+91 (0)3552 255 248 or (0)3552 258 602	
fax	+91 (0)3552 255 122	
email	himalayanhotel@gmail.com	
web	www.himalayanhotel.com	

B 🗇 ⌀

Map 6 Entry 9

Samthar Farmhouse

c/o Gurudongma Tours, Hill Top, Kalimpong, 734 301 Kolkata and West Bengal

On the edge of a remote Lepcha village, framed by forests, terraced fields and snow ranges, this wood and stone farmhouse has an intimate feel and breathtaking views. What a place for a walking holiday! After a trek, enjoy a foot bath on the veranda while sipping your tea, a loll in the hammock or a swing in the lovely terraced garden with its rocky outcrops. Inisde are solar lights, a wood-fired Bhukhari to heat the house, and lamps to illuminate the living area at night. Relax on the hand-woven cushion seats and yak-skin rugs and peruse the Lepcha musical instruments, Buddhist thankas and Sikh daggers that line the walls. Pine-panelled bedrooms are furnished in simple comfort, the two in the main house the ones for the sunrise views. All have western-style toilets and baths with hot water on demand. And you get hot water bottles at night. Local people staff it all under the expert supervision of Catherine, a keen cook; food may be Indian, Nepali or Tibetan, but it will always taste good. Afterwards, enjoy a snifter of chang, the local tipple, or General Jimmy's brandy. *They run Gurudongma Tours & Treks.*

rooms	6: 2 doubles. Cottages: 4 doubles.
price	Full-board $82. Singles $40. Transport & activities included. Plus 10% tax. Peak season: Feb-April; Oct-Dec.
meals	Full-board only.
closed	Rarely.
directions	80km from Kalimpong in remote village; do not try to get here by yourself! Airport: Bagdogra (110km, 3.5 hours). Train: New Jalpaiguri (110km, 3.5 hours).

Guest house

	General Jimmy Singh
tel	+91 (0)3552 255 204
mobile	+91 (0)9434 047 372
fax	+91 (0)3552 255 201
email	gurutt@sancharnet.in
web	www.gurudongma.com

B 🌶 🍶

Map 6 Entry 10

Dekeling Resort at Hawk's Nest

2, A J C Bose Road, Darjeeling, 734 101 Kolkata and West Bengal

Waking to heart-thumping views of snow-capped Kanchenjunga makes up for the steep pull to this Raj summer retreat that hangs, semi-hidden, above the town. Retaining a distinct Britishness – Victorian tiled fireplaces, polished wooden floors – lounges have been softened with bright Tibetan touches. Norbu will greet you – all smiles and openness – and settle you in but his family live in the town. Bedrooms (suites, really) are vast yet low-key in style with sturdy, old-fashioned furnishings and the occasional elegant chair or wardrobe. The glowing wood panelling and working fires (two per suite, lit on cool nights) add a homely touch while Tibetan rugs and paintings give colour. It's so relaxed and unpretentious, you would be forgiven for thinking Norbu had invited you to stay in his home. Wonderful meals – Indian, Chinese, Tibetan, continental – are taken around a shared dining table where he occasionally joins you. After a day's trekking or sightseeing – colonial buildings, Tibetan monasteries, Himalayan culture – relax in the garden gazebo or the all-window lounge and soak up the views.

Guest house

rooms	4 suites.
price	Rs2,400. Plus 10% service charge. Peak season: mid-March–June; mid-Sept–mid-Jan.
meals	Breakfast Rs150. Lunch & dinner Rs250 each.
closed	Rarely.
directions	Taxi to Base Road; sign on left 200m up steep hill. Hawk's nest at top of path, past school. Airport: Bagdogra (90km, 3 hours). Train: Darjeeling Toy Train (2km, 20 mins).

	Mr Tshering Norbu Dekeva
tel	+91 (0)3542 253 092
fax	+91 (0)3542 253 298
email	dekeling@sify.com
web	www.dekeling.com

B 🏃 👮 ✕ 📷 👟

Map 6 Entry 11

The Elgin

18 H.D. Lama Road, Darjeeling, 734 101 Kolkata and West Bengal

Diamond Oberoi is indeed a member of the hotel family but this is his own creation in the old home of a maharaja's daughter. He went to school in town and loves it still; he has the quiet elegance of his own hotel and enjoys chatting to guests during the months he is here. The walls of the bar are hung with prints by the Anglo-Indian artist, Gordon Douglas, and elsewhere there are lithographs and paintings and old photos of Darjeeling. A piano player plays during dinner – for which you will probably want to dress up – and afterwards you can withdraw to one of the many cosy corners. Built as a home, the hotel still has some of the domesticity of the house. There are open fires and a long garden in which to relax – and take tea whenever you want it. A gazebo has enchanting white wooden tables and chairs. Diamond owns another heritage hotel, too, the Nor-Khill at Gangtok in Sikkim (entry 6). You are right in the centre of town yet secluded. Close to perfection.

rooms	25: 20 doubles, 5 suites.
price	Full-board Rs4,100. Suites Rs6,500. Plus 10% tax. Peak season: March-June; September-December.
meals	Full-board only.
closed	Rarely.
directions	5-minute walk from Chowrasta, the main square; 7-minute walk to the Chock Bazaar bus stand; 10-minute walk from station.

Hotel

	Mr Badal Majumder
tel	+91 (0)3542 254 114
res. no	+91 (0)3322 269 878
fax	+91 (0)3542 254 267
email	newelgin@cal.vsnl.net.in
web	www.elginhotels.com

Map 6 Entry 12

Windamere Hotel

Observatory Hill, Darjeeling, 734 101 Kolkata and West Bengal

This is pure, ureconstructed Raj — yet Jan Morris wrote of it as a latter-day paradise. The Windamere is a buoyant reminder of a more leisured age, one which treated travellers with ceremony. It still resists the concept of travel as an 'amusement' industry. No modern brashness, TV, slot machines or kiosks — just irresistibly personal service, a hot water bottle for each foot and a real fire for your bedroom. The brass sparkles, the silver gleams, the logs glow and all is wholesomely clean. The plumbing is old but superb, the bathrooms have enamelled Victorian tubs and power showers and the bedrooms are superb and old-fashioned. Dinner here was always an event in Darjeeling society, and still is: make the most of such delights as bread and butter pudding and steak and onion pie. It is all owned by one remarkable Tibetan family and though they are generally absent, they employ an excellent staff. The best way to arrive is, of course, by the very slow 'toy' railway, taking in views of the impossibly beautiful, five-peaked Kanchenjunga. A mellow, thoroughly Edwardian dream.

rooms	37: 35 doubles, 2 singles.
price	Full-board $130-$165. Singles $108. Plus 15% tax. Peak season: March-May; September-December.
meals	Full-board only.
closed	Rarely.
directions	Just above Chowrasta, the main square, on Observatory Hill. 500m from Darjeeling Toy Train.

Hotel

	Mr S Tenduf
tel	+91 (0)3542 254 041
fax	+91 (0)3542 254 043
email	reservations@windamerehotel.net
web	www.windamerehotel.com

Map 6 Entry 13

Glenburn Tea Estate
Darjeeling, 734 101 Kolkata and West Bengal

Husna-Tara is a woman of charm, vision and flair. With these qualities she has created something of a dream – effortlessly stylish, mercifully comfortable and wickedly indulgent. A Scottish tea company established the estate in 1860, no doubt enticed by the luxuriant hillsides and cool climes reminiscent of the glens of Scotland; the spartan side of the Scottish inheritance has been left behind. The suites are delightful – hand-printed fabrics from Delhi, matching cupboards delicately painted with Himalayan flowers, open fires, wicker chairs in bay windows. Every effort has been made to pamper: you start the day with 'bed' tea – one of India's finest institutions – and end with hot water bottles. Sumptuous picnics are laid out on linen next to a burbling river and beneath the gaze of the misty Kanchenjunga: lashings of homemade jam and honey are doled out with homemade brown bread, washed down with pots of the Glenburn tea. And there are great vegetarian options at dinner. I could go on… but see for yourself. An idyllic spot, and readers are full of praise. *Fishing, tea tours, trekking.*

rooms	4 suites.
price	Full-board $275. Singles $180. Activities & transfers included.
meals	Full-board only.
closed	Never.
directions	Airport: Bagdogra (2.5 hours). Train: New Jalpaiguri (2.5 hours). Pick-up from either. Or call for directions.

	Mrs Husna-Tara Prakash
tel	+91 (0)3322 885 630
res. no	+91 (0)9832 024 030
mobile	+91 (0)9830 070 213
email	info@glenburnteaestate.com
web	www.glenburnteaestate.com

Homestay

Map 6 Entry 14

The Park

17 Park Street, Kolkata, 700 016 Kolkata and West Bengal

Forget old world charm – this is new age glamour. And it is as much a place to go to be seen as it is a place to lay your head – 'cutting edge' India, where, from the moment you enter, you feel all senses gratified. Yet there's no pomposity – that's what's so nice about the place. You can dress as you please. The Park, one of a small chain, opened in the Sixties but each level has been recently redesigned to create a different mood and bedrooms are in the process of being updated. We advise you to go for a 'luxury' room not a 'de-luxe'; they may not be huge, but they are lavish, minimalist, colourful and shiny, and flaunt rain showers as well as baths. Glass sinks too, and marble benches and floors, and lush toiletries. The coffee shop has a 24-hour vibe, the 'Tantra' is for pubbers and clubbers, the 'Saffron' restaurant specialises in Indian cuisine, the 'Zen' in Thai and the 'Roxy' does cocktails. No garden, no views, but a health club and an outdoor pool (and pool parties at weekends). None of it's cheap but you are in the heart of fabulous, friendly Calcutta, in one of its hippest hotels.

Hotel

rooms	149: 132 doubles, 17 suites.
price	$225-$300. Suites $350-$375.
meals	Two restaurants, coffee shop & bar.
closed	Rarely.
directions	Airport/train: Kolkata (20km, 1 hour). Take taxi to hotel.

	Mr Garcha (Manager)
tel	+91 (0)3322 499 000
fax	+91 (0)3322 494 000
email	resv.cal@theparkhotels.com
web	www.theparkhotels.com

E 人 ⩰

Map 6 Entry 15

Fairlawn Hotel

13/A Sudder Street, Kolkata, 700 016 Kolkata and West Bengal

Heinz ketchup on the tables, posters advertising Somerset and Assam tea, old furniture (some of it painted), heavy brown floral curtains, bric-a-brac – it is an oasis in the frenzy of Calcutta, utterly devoted to the past and determined to hang on. You can see why it is so popular, though: the rooms are big and airy, you are served banana custard for lunch, the devoted staff who have been there for ever wear white gloves and cummerbunds at dinner, there are several lounges, a large, green and pleasant garden and you are made to feel immensely at home. Avoid, if you can, the three window-less rooms and if you are single (it's a fine place for singles) ask for No 9. There's a rooftop garden on the annexe, chairs and tables on the main roof and space to be yourself. It is all rather wonderful, a place to be calm, to create, to paint or write a novel. The atmosphere is welcoming and 'family' and people come back year after year. The bar is a watering place for expatriates of every hue and for locals intent on a gossip. They probably find it.

rooms	20: 13 doubles, 5 triples, 2 singles.
price	$60. Triples $90. Singles $50. Plus 16% tax. Full-board option. Peak season: October–March.
meals	Lunch & dinner from Rs250 each.
closed	Rarely.
directions	Next to the Indian Museum, opposite the Salvation Army. Airport: Kolkata (20km, 1 hour). Train: Howrah (5km, 30 mins).

	Mrs Violet Smith
tel	+91 (0)3322 521 510
fax	+91 (0)3322 521 835
email	fairlawn@cal.vsnl.net.in
web	www.fairlawnhotel.com

Guest house

B 💳 🛁 🧍

Map 6 Entry 16

Himachal Pradesh, Ladakh, Punjab

The 'Abode of Snow', Himachal Pradesh borders Ladakh, the Punjab and Tibet. Its mountain landscape is thick with oak, deodar and pine at lower altitudes, alpine meadows higher up. Manali hill station, in the idyllic Kullu Valley, is a good place to start treks; the Kangra valley is filled with apple orchards and is the seat of the Tibetan government in exile in Dharamasala. In the remote Lahaul and Spiti valleys, great monasteries cling to high cliffs where eagles roam.

Ladakh is the north-eastern part of Jammu and Kashmir and is a high-altitude desert. Its capital, Leh, was once the central trading port between the Punjab and central Asia, Kashmir and Tibet. Leh is a stunning place – Sengge Namgyal, a Ladakh king, built its nine-storey Palace. Mountains of every shade of brown, and barley fields that turn from green to gold with the seasons, surround the town. Further north, the Nubra Valley has willow, poplars, sand dunes, hot springs, remote monasteries and double-humped camels; a permit is needed to visit this area. Flights to Leh are available but you need 24 hours to acclimatise before trekking.

The vast, dry plains of the Punjab were transformed by the 'Green Revolution' of the 1960s. With the help of modern farming techniques, this area now produces much of India's wheat, rice and dairy products. Punjabi culture has its own language, religion, cuisine and music. Revel in the beauty of the awesome Golden Temple – the very heart of Sikh religion – at Amritsar. At the rural sports festival in Kila Raipur you can watch men ride astride two galloping horses, tent pegging, bullock-cart racing and strongmen competitions. Be modernised by Le Corbusier's visionary designs of utopia in the capital Chandigarh, with its functional concrete buildings, quirky rock garden and tree-lined avenues.

Best time to visit
Himachal Pradesh: mid May-mid-Oct; late Dec to March
Ladakh: May-Oct
Punjab: Oct-March.

Photo top Indian Tourist Board
Photo bottom Callum Chiverton

Fort Nalagarh

Nalagarh, District Solan, 174 101 Himachal Pradesh

Character, and stacks of it! Hidden turrets, deer on the dewy morning lawn, oleander and bougainvillea. Aspects of the past are nurtured but Nalagarh Fort has cast aside regal stuffiness: the constant battle to keep things in order leaves no time for grand pretence. Built in 1421 as the capital of the Hindur Kingdom, the Fort marks the point where the oceans of hot summer plains lap against the first folds of the Himalayan foothills. For many Indians and their families, it is an escape from the Delhi chaos. For travellers it is a wonderfully unstuffy, comfortable break in the journey between Delhi and the Himalayas (so there's a good mix of Indian and Western visitors). The beds are comfortable and the rooms delightful in their pistachio tones and cotton throws, their large, cool spaces giving blessed relief from the heat. The hotel's popularity makes sure that the atmosphere never deadens and the dust never settles – the staff are on always on their toes and unfailingly warm and attentive. A memorable stopover.

rooms	22: 18 doubles, 3 suites, 1 family suite.	
price	Rs2,200–Rs2,500. Suites Rs2,990. Family suite Rs5,900. Plus 10% tax. Peak season: November-February.	
meals	Breakfast Rs175. Lunch Rs275. Dinner Rs300.	
closed	Rarely.	
directions	60km from Chandigarh. At Nalagarh centre, turn right through narrow streets & up out of town towards the fort.	

	Mr Tikka Jayatendra Singh	Hotel
tel	+91 (0)1795 223 179	
res. no	+91 (0)1124 634 139	
fax	+91 (0)1795 223 021	
email	fortresort@satyam.net.in	
web	www.caravantraveltalk.com/nalagarh-fort.htm	

B

Map 2 Entry 17

Chapslee

Elysium Hill, Shimla, 171 001 Himachal Pradesh

If you have pottered up the mountainside in that splendid little train, filled with expectations of Shimla, you may have been underwhelmed by the town. For its glorious past and parochial present are at odds. But to find yourself in Chapslee is a treat. One of the oldest houses in Shimla (1835), it was the summer residence of the late Raja Charanjit Singh of Kapurthala and the present owner is his grandson. There are some marvellous rooms and furniture and an hour in the library will convince you that you are back in Scotland. Bedrooms are immensely comfortable: good reading lights, framed paintings or prints, white-painted Georgian-style doors, writing desks, perhaps a Victorian pitcher and bowl... sparkling white paint and fine bathrooms, too. The sitting room is in hunting-lodge style. It is all very old-fashioned and the British will feel vaguely at home; others will be bemused. (Note that the web site places the house, unnaturally, against a mountain backdrop, and there is a school, albeit a quiet one, in the old grounds.) Mr Singh will tell you all the history. *Lawn tennis & croquet.*

rooms	6: 4 doubles, 1 single, 1 suite.
price	Full-board Rs8,750-Rs10,000. Single Rs11,000. Suite Rs11,000.
meals	Full-board only.
closed	January-February.
directions	Next to Aukland House Senior School, between Lakkar Bazaar & Longwood.

Homestay

C ♪ ♀ ▣ ▯ ♿ ♞ 👞

	Mr Kanwar Ratanjit Singh
tel	+91 (0)1772 802 542
fax	+91 (0)1772 658 663
email	chapslee@vsnl.com or chapslee@sancharnet.in
web	www.chapslee.com

Map 2 Entry 18

Hotel Madan Kunj
The Mall, Shimla, 171 004 Himachal Pradesh

Step into an English fairytale – *Goldilocks & the Three Bears* perhaps. This is olde-worldy, fantastically unexpected and delightfully off the beaten track. The 19th-century cottage, now a heritage hotel, is in the leafy end of town, a half-hour walk – downhill – from Shimla. Up above the road, sheltered behind trees (not easy to find), Madan Kunj may not look all that promising from outside but, once inside, it's a gem. Bedrooms, a little twee but full of homely English charm, have rug-dotted parquet floors, trinkets, pictures and comfortable beds (circular in one room!). The family suite, our favourite, has its own little balcony; bathrooms are simple affairs, some with tubs. Mod cons extend to western loos and TVs, and friendly, relaxed staff are on hand when needed. No sitting room, but a dining room with an extension planned, serving meals that are simple and good value. If you're not expecting to be pampered, this is a charming couples' retreat, but note that the hotel welcomes children too, with slides and a wooden frame in the grassy garden.

rooms	7: 6 twins/doubles, 1 family suite.
price	Rs1,200-Rs2,800. Plus 10% tax.
meals	Lunch Rs100. Dinner Rs150.
closed	Rarely.
directions	Taxi from Shimla or ask hotel to arrange one. From Shimla head downhill towards Viceroy Gardens.

	Mr Mohinder Seth
tel	+91 (0)1772 657 444
fax	+91 (0)1772 654 854
email	rajeevmadan@yahoo.com

Hotel

B

Map 2 Entry 19

The Chalets Naldehra

Naldehera, Shimla, Himachal Pradesh

While the monsoon rains pound on the roof – or the sun pours in – what bliss to take a dip in the glass-and-timber pool. You could be swimming with the cedars. Lord Curzon, Viceroy of India, used to abandon the splendours of his viceregal lodge and camp in the beautiful woods of Naldehra; his legacy is the golf course (1905) that laps at your feet. As for the chalets (built in 2002), they bring a touch of Mégève to Himachal Pradesh. The interiors may lack rugs and cosy touches but they are so finely crafted from Finnish timbers that the lumberjack walls and polished parquet floors exude a warm feel. The chalets have log fires for winter, the apartments have kitchenettes and the white-and-wood bathrooms are perfect. Colour schemes are bright, tasteful and extend to well-groomed gardens overlooked by the restaurant – simple, appealing and serving three cuisines: Indian, Chinese and continental. Well-heeled Naldehra may not bounce with bonhomie but families are well catered for, with play areas outside and an activity centre within. And, of course, that gorgeous pool.

rooms	12 + 5: 2 doubles, 2 family suites, 8 chalets for 2-4. 5 self-catering apartments for 2.
price	Rs4,000. Chalets Rs7,000-Rs9,500. Apartments Rs5,000.
meals	Lunch & dinner from Rs150 each.
closed	Rarely.
directions	45-minute taxi ride from Shimla.

Resort

Mr Yatish C. Sud

tel	+91 (0)1772 747 715
mobile	+91 (0)9418 062 003
fax	+91 (0)1772 747 562
email	contact@chaletsnaldehra.com
web	www.chaletsnaldehra.com

B

Map 2 Entry 20

Banjara Camps & Retreats
Batseri Village, Sangla Valley, Kinnaur, Himachal Pradesh

Nearly 3,000 metres up, and a short drive from Chitkul, the last village on the old Hindustan-Tibet trade route, is a remote and remarkable encampment. Reached by roads liable to landslides (come by jeep), surrounded by towering mountains, crouched among apple orchards on the banks of a surging Baspa river, its 'tents' are cosier than you could imagine. Step through a flap from a wicker-furnished porch to a most comfortable and comforting space. Rajasthani fabrics enclose you, rugs lie underfoot, dressing tables, cosily clad beds, heaters and hot water bottles – this is no typical tent. A second flap opens to your own bathroom with tiled floor, stone sink, western loo and hot-water bucket shower, while 'public rooms' extend from bamboo-thatched dining tent to picnic tables for barbecues to hammocks by the fire. Batseri village and temple are a 15-minute walk away, jeep safaris can take you further. The Sangla Valley is reputed to be the most beautiful in the Indian Himalaya – and how often can you combine such natural splendour with such comfort and service? *Bring your own alcohol.*

rooms	18 tents for 2.
price	Full-board Rs3,900. Peak season: April–June.
meals	Full-board only.
closed	November–March.
directions	Airport/train: Shimla (232km, 8 hours). Taxi from Shimla approx. Rs4,000.

Under canvas

	Rajesh Ojha & Ajay Sud
tel	+91 (0)1126 861 397
mobile	+91 (0)9810 040 397
fax	+91 (0)1126 855 152
email	info@banjaracamps.com or banjara@vsnl.com
web	www.banjaracamps.com

B 🚶 🐟

Map 2 Entry 21

Country Cottage

Chandpur Tea Estate, Palampur, 176 061 Himachal Pradesh

Hemmed in by pine giants 5,000 feet up in the western Himalayas, just shy of the summer snow line and above an army cantonment, the Sarin family's huddle of blue mountain stone and knotted-pine cottages is a marvellous base for exploration of the Himachal interior. The first person to establish trekking proper in Himachal, Mr Sarin Snr, is a fount of perambulatory know-how and, with his son Navin, runs his own trekking company. Their passion for honest simplicity is evident in the basic but considered design of the huts and cottages that have all you need, and no more. All stone walls and wooden cladding, sisal flooring and slate roofing, these snug abodes sit among citrus and pine trees through which you can snatch tantalising glimpses of the mountains and the sprawling tea gardens. The more basic Forest and Eucalyptus huts are just that — a step up from camping, with a hot water bottle thrown in for chilly winter nights. The food is fresh, deliciously spiced and entirely local — you get what's available and the concoctions are old family recipes. *Trekking, camping, birdwatching & fishing.*

Guest house

rooms	5 cottages for 2.
price	Cottages Rs 1,800-Rs2,500. Plus 10% tax..
meals	Breakfast Rs165. Lunch Rs300. Dinner Rs320.
closed	Rarely.
directions	1km from Palampur on road to Kulu; left through large cantonment gate; follow road to Chandpur; left just below helipad, then right. Country Cottage 800m down road.

Mr Karan Sarin

tel	+91 (0)1894 230 647
mobile	+91 (0)9816 030 647
fax	+91 (0)1894 230 417
email	ksarin@sancharnet.in
web	www.countrycottageindia.com

A 🚜

Map 2 Entry 22

Negi's Hotel Mayflower

Old Manali Road, Manali, District Kullu, 175 131 Himachal Pradesh

Handsome, unpretentious and comfortable – and a great place to escape to in poor weather. There are log fires in your room and chairs to draw up and settle into. There is even cold-weather 'comfort' food, such as grilled trout and jam and sponge pudding! Hot water – in bathfuls – and an open fire in the dining room too, where you are surrounded by a wood-lined rustic simplicity reminiscent of the Alps. The smell of pine is redolent and the veranda is wide, comfortable and attractive. The backdrop is of tall pines and you may glimpse the snowy peaks. The little garden is on the other side and full of blossom in the spring. (You can hear the road and its miscellaneous noises in the day, but not at night.) Wood-cosseted bedrooms are simple but amply comfortable, with good lighting, rough cotton-weave curtains and slightly elderly bathrooms that are immaculately clean. (A few rugs are UK-pub-style – but spotless.) The staff are delightful and the food is excellent and cooked to order. The owner runs Himalayan Adventures; if you wish to go trekking, you are in good hands.

rooms	20: 18 doubles, 1 single, 1 suite.
price	Rs1,800. Single Rs500. Suite Rs2,000. Plus 10% tax. Peak season: May-mid September.
meals	Breakfast Rs175. Lunch & dinner Rs550 each.
closed	Rarely.
directions	From Manali Town, straight up towards old Manali village for 1km.

	Mr Prem Negi
tel	+91 (0)1902 252 104
res. no	+91 (0)1902 250 256
mobile	+91 (0)9816 341 914
email	negismayflower@sancharnet.in
web	www.negismayflower.com

Hotel

Map 2 Entry 23

Johnson Hotel, Johnson Lodge & Jimmy Johnson Lodge

Circuit House Road, The Mall (top of Mall Road), Manali, Himachal Pradesh

You're close to Manali but away from the rush. The peaceful wooded Nehru Park is opposite, the Dhungri Temple is up the hill and as you enter the well-kept gardens you feel you're entering the grounds of a private club. Special care has gone into the bedrooms of the hotel. Bright, fresh and warm, the best are on the first floor with mountain views and the smallest are at the top (avoid in summer!). Bathrooms have posies of garden flowers, walls display local art. The three self-catering cottages (Jimmy Johnson Lodge) are older but equally good, in an English farmhouse-cosy way. The café/restaurant specialises in trout dishes and Italian cuisine — something of a rarity round these parts — and has become *the* place in Manali to eat. Across the gardens is Johnson's Lodge — run by Piya's brother — with 15 pleasingly simple rooms, a large hotelly bar with TV, a restaurant specialising in Kullu dishes and a cyber café. Johnson's may be too sociable to be classified as a 'hideaway' but it's tranquil and famously laid-back, thanks to the people who run it — professional and full of good humour.

Hotel

rooms	12 doubles. Johnson Lodge: 15 doubles. Jimmy Johnson Lodge: 3 self-catering cottages for 4.
price	Rs1,500-Rs2,000. Cottages Rs4,000-Rs4,500.
meals	Lunch & dinner from Rs350 each.
closed	Never.
directions	Turn left at Nehru Park; sign for Johnson's Restaurant. Go to Johnson Lodge Reception.

Piya & Mehul Johnson

tel	+91 (0)1902 253 023
mobile	+91 (0)3816 279 223
fax	+91 (0)1902 245 123
email	jayajc@hotmail.com or johnsonshotel@gmail.com

B ⓑ

Map 2 Entry 24

Pema Thang Guest House

Hotel Bhagsu Road, McLeod Ganj, Dharamsala, 176 219 Himachal Pradesh

Reserve your rooms early – both guest house and village are enchanting. The guest house was built in 1999, the *darcho* – Tibetan flag pole – stands proudly outside and prayer flags flutter in the breeze. The restaurant has a friendly feel and the food is probably the best in the village – vegetarian and delicious, a mix of Italian and Tibetan. No living room, but balconies with seating and stupendous views. Bedrooms – cream walls, wooden floors, Tibetan beds with futon-like mattresses – are as spotless and as simple as you'd expect, those on the top floor with the views. Each has a kitchenette, with a modest rental charge for pots and pans: useful for families. The owners are two sisters – both singers who also work closely with the Tibetan Welfare Office. Staff are humble and professional and keen to help you enjoy your stay. The Dalai Lama lives in peaceful McLeod Ganj where people stop each other on the street and conversations flow. 'Little Lhasa', as the area is called, is a special place awash with temples and shrines, and walks to the waterfall and around the hills are wonderful. *Vegetarian food; no alcohol.*

rooms	15 twins.
price	Rs660-Rs990.
meals	Breakfast Rs90. Lunch & dinner Rs130 each. Self-catering option.
closed	Rarely.
directions	Minutes from Chinar Lodge. Building has long red and green strips along the eaves.

Guest house

	Mr Tenzin Geche Tethong
tel	+91 (0)1892 221 871
mobile	+91 (0)9418 247 728
email	pemathanghouse@yahoo.com
web	www.pemathang.net

A 👟

Map 2 Entry 25

Chonor House

Near Thekchen Choling Temple, McLeod Ganj, Dharamsala, 176 219 Himachal Pradesh

Tibetan culture will never be lost while places like this continue to inspire and nourish visitors. Everything matters – from the way you are received to the tiniest detail. Tibetan wall-paintings on the bedroom walls, hand-embroidered cushions, attractive lightshades and brightly coloured exterior... everything is respectful. Each bedroom depicts some aspect of Tibetan life in bold murals around which each room is individually furnished and named. The aesthetic voyeur in you will demand you enter each room; the artistry comes from the Norbulingka Institute. The bathrooms are dark but functional, with stone tiling and western-style loos. There's a library and cosy sitting room too, a delightful restaurant serving Tibetan food and great pastries and a sun-dappled courtyard with marble-topped tables and wrought-iron chairs set among bushes and trees. One last, unexpected, bonus: an internet café called Cyber Yak. Your money goes to the charity that owns Chonor, Norling Guesthouse (entry 27) and the Norbulingka Institute, and it's wise to book early.

Guest house

rooms	11: 10 doubles, 1 suite.
price	Rs1,900–Rs2,400. Suite Rs2,800. Plus 10% tax.
meals	Breakfast Rs150. Lunch & dinner Rs300 each.
closed	Rarely.
directions	Walking from Temple Road, take hairpin left–turn up Thardoeling Road.

	Mr Dechen Namgyal Maja (Manager)
tel	+91 (0)1892 221 006/468
mobile	+91 (0)9418 031 468
fax	+91 (0)1892 220 815
email	chonorhs@norbulingka.org
web	www.norbulingka.org

B ✉

Map 2 Entry 26

Norling Guesthouse

PO Sidhpur, Dist Kangra, Dharamsala, 176 057 Himachal Pradesh

An oasis of peace and Tibetan culture and a very special place. The Institute to which the guest house is attached is built in traditional Tibetan style following a ground plan based on the proportions of Avalokiteshvara — the Bodhisattva of Compassion. It rises up the hillside from the entrance gate to the temple, through terraced gardens, pools, waterfalls, past offices, workshops, museum and shop. It is a fascinating place and its backdrop is the Himalayas; here just 12 years, it feels deeply rooted. The guest house has a similar charm, and there's a 'refectory' feel to the cool upstairs corridor with its potted plants and cane easy chairs. All is simple, colourful, thoughtful, restful — truly Tibetan. The bedrooms with high ceilings and a sense of air and space are perfect canvases for furniture, paintings, wall-hangings and bedcovers made by craftsmen at the Institute. Food is served in the café where you can eat on the rooftop — with mountain views — or in the garden. The Kangra valley — all clear streams, old-style farming and green fields — is a lovely foreground.

rooms	10: 8 doubles, 2 suites.
price	Rs1,150. Suites Rs1,800. Plus 10% tax. Peak season: March-June; September-November.
meals	Breakfast Rs120. Lunch & dinner Rs190 each.
closed	Rarely.
directions	In valley 6km below Dharamsala.

Guest house

	Norbulingka Institute
tel	+91 (0)1892 246 405/406
mobile	+91 (0)9816 120 110
fax	+91 (0)1892 246 404
email	guesthouse@norbulingka.org
web	www.norbulingka.org

A ✗

Map 2 Entry 27

The Judge's Court

Heritage Village, Pragpur, Kangra Valley District, 177 107 Himachal Pradesh

Pragpur is very beautiful, 1,800 feet up in the Kangra Valley and with views of the snow-tipped Himalayas. The village has cobbled streets, mud-plastered and slate-roofed houses and a very fine ornamental 'tank'. There is a strong whiff of aristocracy here, or ancestry. Vijai is proud of having had the village designated as 'heritage'. Justice Sir Jai Lal was educated in England and the house was built for him by a proud father. Vijai is his grandson and has returned to his roots with a passionate commitment to rebuilding the house. It is eclectic and surprising: butler service with pyrex dishes, touches of post-war affluence, cocktails before dinner, musicians from the village. All the staff are villagers and are learning the ropes. The bedrooms are comfortable, even elegant, and have a mix of antique and more modern furniture. If you are lucky enough to find Vijai and Rani living at home you will find a house full of bonhomie. It is all delightfully quiet, genteel almost, and there is much to do in this lovely countryside so fecund and fruitful – Pragpur means 'country of pollen'.

rooms	10: 6 doubles, 3 suites, 1 serviced apartment.
price	Rs2,800. Suites Rs3,500. Apartment Rs2,800. Plus 10% tax.
meals	Breakfast Rs150. Lunch Rs250. Dinner Rs350.
closed	Rarely.
directions	Train to Una (overnight), then 60km by road. Good directions on web site.

Guest house

	Mr Vijai Lal
tel	+91 (0)1970 245 035/335
res. no	+91 (0)1124 114 135
fax	+91 (0)1970 245 823
email	info@judgescourt.com
web	www.judgescourt.com

B

Map 2 Entry 28

Hotel Shambha-La
Skarra Road, Leh, 194 101 Ladakh

A discreet entrance leads you into a green, tranquil garden. Hammocks swing gently under soaring poplars, white chairs and tables are grouped invitingly on the grass and prayer flags flutter. The owners are Pintoo and Tsering Narboo. He's Ladakhi and knowledgeable about the area (no surprise – he was a minister for tourism); she is Tibetan. They're relaxed, immensely kind and are usually here all summer. Bedrooms are cosy and unpretentious with modern furniture; bathrooms are functional and balconies overlook the garden with views to the mountains. But perhaps the best place from which to drink in those tantalising snowy peaks is the terrace. Ringed by more prayer flags, it is wonderful to sit out by moonlight, gazing across the valley and listening to the stream below. The garden brims over with organic vegetables and herbs and the meals, mostly Indian or Chinese, are good, wholesome and smilingly served. It's all wonderfully peaceful, one of the advantages of being just out of Leh – a five-minute taxi ride or a 25-minute walk. Shambha-La, in Buddhist philosophy, means 'heaven on earth'. This is close.

rooms	24 doubles/twins.
price	Full-board Rs3,000. Singles Rs2,500.
meals	Full-board only.
closed	November-April.
directions	5-minute taxi ride from Leh centre, or call hotel for pick-up.

Guest house

	Mr & Mrs Narboo
tel	+91 (0)1982 251 100
mobile	+91 (0)9419 177 900 or (0)9868 888 876
fax	+91 (0)1982 252 607
email	ladakh@hotelshambhala.com
web	www.hotelshambhala.com

A ✕ 📖 ♂

Map 2 Entry 29

Himalayan Homestays

Snow Leopard Conservancy, IBEX Hotel Complex, Rinchen Wangchuk, Leh, 194 101 Ladakh

As authentic a place as you'll find. Domestic yak graze the banks of the mountain streams while farmers tend their fields. The unbroken views of the endless mountain scenery are worth the trip alone, but at 5,000m the altitude as well as the scenery will take your breath away (only the healthy and properly acclimatised should consider the journey). The homestays take in guests on a rotational basis so that income is shared around, and the rooms could not be more basic (that's the charm): you sleep on a thin mattress on the floor and toilets are 'long drops'. Meals are taken in the kitchen with the family – delicious curries made with local ingredients. Herders tell of their encounters with snow leopards and while the chance of seeing one of these magnificent creatures is remote, it is possible you'll come across their scats and scrapes on the walks around the village... it all adds to the enchantment. The warmth and generosity of your hosts provide a privileged insight into Ladakhi culture and will make you feel closely connected to the ecotourism ideal. Remarkable. *Snow leopard trekking.*

Homestay

rooms	1 room for 4-5, sharing bath & wcs.
price	Half-board US$10 p.p.
meals	Half-board only.
closed	Never.
directions	The Himalayan Homestay Office arranges car transfer from Leh (6 hours) to the nearest village & directs guests for the final 1km walk up track.

	Rinchen Wangchuk
tel	+91 (0)1982 250 953
fax	+91 (0) 1982 252 735
email	slcindia@sancharnet.in or overland@sancharnet.in
web	www.himalayan-homestays.com

A 🏃 🚜

Map 2 Entry 30

Silver Cloud Guest House

P.O. Box - 128, Dumbang, Sankar, Leh, 194 101 Ladakh

Share the life of a Ladakhi family; you can even lend a hand picking veg if you wish. This is a guest house run by humble, hospitable, hard-working people who live a simple, good life. Sonam and Padma occupy the ground floor with their young daughter and grandmother; guests have the rest. The family prides itself on how much wood they have used in their new home, and it all feels warm and comfortable in a wonderfully uncomplicated way. The double-glazed, sun-flooded suites are especially lovely because of their sweeping wooden floors and rafters; the other rooms are backpacker style. Bathrooms and shower rooms are a pleasant surprise. There is a dining room – somewhat plain – but do ask to eat with the family at least once; in Ladakhi custom, you will sit on colourful cushions beautifully arranged on the floor. There's no sitting room but an outdoor porch, and, in summer, a meditation centre on the rooftop. It is a 15-minute, green valley walk into Leh, with its palace and bazaaar, and two minutes from the Sankar Monastery. Rise early and catch morning *puja*.

rooms	4 suites.
price	Rs1,500-Rs3,000.
meals	Breakfast Rs125. Dinner Rs150.
closed	November-February.
directions	Pre-paid taxi from airport, approx. Rs150. Near Sankar Monastery.

Guest house

Mr Sonam Dumbang

tel	+91 (0)1982 253 128
email	silvercloudstd@rediffmail.com
	or silvercloudpsd@hotmail.com
	or scsladakh@yahoo.com
web	www.reachladakh.com/silver_cloud.htm

B

Map 2 Entry 31

Padma Guest House and Hotel
Fort Road, Leh, 194 101 Ladakh

The approach is enchanting, the garden deeply fragrant. Leave the jostling main road and wander down tiny, poplar-lined paths edged with irrigation channels: in just two minutes you find yourself in an astonishingly rural setting. Padma comes in two parts – the older, traditional guest house and the newer hotel next door. Both are efficiently run by the same warm, helpful family, smilingly used to the vagaries of westerners. If you want simplicity, choose the guest house (buckets of hot water must be requested from reception – bring your own towels and loo paper); for a touch more luxury, opt for the hotel (though hot water is still limited). The rooms are bright and functional – but avoid no.109 which is a little noisy. The family are aware of Ladakh's fragile eco system and use solar water heating and grow organic fruit and veg. Buffet dinners, served on the open-air terrace, are mostly Indian/Tibetan. This is a busy, sociable place packed with every nationality in high season, but sitting on a balcony with a book and a view is a blissful antidote to the bustle of town. *Library & Buddhist meditation room.*

Guest house

rooms	23 twins/doubles.
price	Rs1,050–Rs2,100.
	Half- and full-board optional.
meals	Lunch & dinner Rs50–Rs200 each.
closed	Rarely.
directions	10 minutes from centre of Leh. Signed off Fort Road; turn left and continue down small path lined with poplar trees. Follow signs; 2 minutes from main road.

B ⬧

Map 2 Entry 32

	Tsewang Yangjor
tel	+91 (0)1982 252 630
	or (0)1982 252 514
fax	+91 (0)1982 255 876
email	padma22@sancharnet.in
web	www.padmaladakh.com

Lha-Ri-Mo Retreat
Gyamthsa Valley, Leh, 194 101 Ladakh

You can walk here – two hours direct from Leh (five if you're seduced into visiting Gompas and the monasteries en route). Or take a bumpy half-hour ride in a taxi. Either way, this place is entrancing. The retreat rests at the end of a secret valley, and if you hadn't been told, you wouldn't believe there was anything other than streams, tumbling hillsides and snowy peaks. Everything is clean, simple and harmonious. It is run by Wangdu Kalon, a fascinating man with passionate views on sustainable tourism. He and his wife have ensured the least possible impact has been made on the land. Both the lobby/restaurant building and the cottage have been constructed of hand-crafted local materials and the tents are in small enclosures in a wooded area, with well-equipped shower rooms close by. If you prefer solid walls, ask for a room in the cottage. Meals are equally flexible – use the restaurant or cook your own (there's a barbecue, too). This is a working farm: watch, or participate in, the sand-roasting of barley, and learn how to make chang, the local spirit. Though you may forget how after a glass or two.

rooms	8 + 1: 8 tents, 4 with wc only, sharing showers. 1 cottage for 4.
price	Full-board Rs2,700. Singles Rs2,2000.
meals	Full-board only. Self-catering option in cottage.
closed	November-April.
directions	30-minute taxi drive from Leh.

Under canvas

	Mrs Kalon
tel	+91 (0)1982 252 101/177
mobile	+91 (0)9419 178 233
fax	+91 (0)1982 253 345

Map 2 Entry 33

Mrs. Bhandari's Guest House

10, The Cantonment, Amritsar, 143 001 Punjab

Definitely not for sybarites but, for those happy to rough it a bit, this place is fun. It owes its merry, relaxed atmosphere to the warmth of Mrs Bhandari Junior and her family. (The original Mrs B is 99 and has handed on the baton.) The house is 1950s and unassuming, in a quiet area on the outskirts of town, not far from the magical Golden Temple. Plain, basically furnished bedrooms vary in size and colour and each has an open fire. The bed linen is spotless and the no-frills bathrooms are clean. A cupboard full of books in the sitting room ensures that you don't run short of reading material. Mrs Bhandari serves excellent Punjabi food – she's quite likely to ask what you fancy for your three-course dinner – and you're welcome to go into the big kitchen and watch meals being prepared. The family's green credentials are impeccable, the mango pickle is superb, and everything is organic and home-grown. Large, pleasant gardens – and a family of buffalo for milk and butter – surround the house; there's a pool, and a small lawned area for a tent or two. Many of your fellow guests will be backpackers.

Guest house

rooms	12: 5 doubles, 4 triples, 1 quadruple, 2 singles.
price	Rs1,400-Rs1,700. Singles Rs1,100-Rs1,400.
meals	Lunch & dinner £7 each.
closed	Rarely.
directions	Airport: Amritsar (8km, 30 mins). Train: Amritsar (2.4km, 10 mins).

	Mrs Ratan Bhandari
tel	+91 (0)1832 228 509
fax	+91 (0)1832 222 390
email	bgha10@gmail.com
web	bhandari_guesthouse.tripod.com

A 🏃 🍴 💳 🧘 🏊

Map 1 Entry 34

Ranjit's Svaasa
47-A The Mall, Amritsar, 143 001 Punjab

Seven generations of the family have owned this charming, vivid place and you sense that each in turn has loved it dearly. A display of photos on the gallery shows them all – and a good-looking bunch they are! The house is delightful, 250 years old and constructed in the colonial style. Once a rather grand British guest house, it is now a small hotel, well restored, decorated in bright, clear, classic colours and filled with pretty Victorian furniture. (There must have been many devoted trips to antique shops to find the right pieces.) The family's three sons act as managers, adding a personal touch; smiling staff welcome you with cool towels, herbal tea or fresh juice. The meals, served in the wood-panelled restaurant, are irresistible. Each bedroom has its own colour scheme, some with jolly fabrics, others more demure. Bathrooms in the new wing are immaculate; others are more old-fashioned. There's also a superb spa with a host of treatments to try. Or, bask in the sun in a comfy wicker chair on a veranda. This is a quiet residential area, two miles from the golden domes of that most sacred of Sikh shrines.

rooms	17: 4 doubles, 14 suites.
price	Rs2,750-Rs3,100. Suites Rs3,650-Rs5,000. Singles Rs2,750-Rs3,650.
meals	Lunch & dinner Rs300-R350 each.
closed	Rarely.
directions	Airport: Amritsar (12km, 25mins). Train: Amritsar (2km, 5 mins).

The Mehra Family

tel	+91 (0)1832 566 618
fax	+91 (0)1835 003 728
email	spa@svaasa.com
web	www.svaasa.com

Hotel

Map 1 Entry 35

Uttar Pradesh, Uttaranchal

The magical, turquoise Ganges River rises in an ice cave in Gangotri and flows 2,525km through the mountain of Uttaranchal, the plains of Uttar Pradesh, Bihar and Bengal to enter the sea at the Bay of Bengal. In 2000, the hill areas of Uttar Pradesh became Uttaranchal. The hills are thickly forested, the snowy peaks reach 6,000 metres, and the rivers, glaciers and waterfalls bathe the area in water. In Haridwar you can watch the flickering candles float down the Ganges and be mesmerised by the chanting at sunset. The Corbett National Park is the place to spot tigers. There are the popular hill stations of Mussoorie and Nainital, river rafting and yoga in Rishikesh and superb treks in the Kumaon and Garhwal mountains – the Valley of the Flowers explodes with a rich and rare carpet of blooms, especially in early September. (Trekking: Feb & May; Sep & Nov).

Uttar Pradesh is not only the cultural heartland of Islam famous for the soul-stirring Taj Mahal and other great Islamic monuments, but also the spiritual heartland of Hinduism – the holy and vibrant city of Varanasi lies on the sacred Ganges River. Hindus believe that those who bathe in its waters are absolved of all sins and immersing ashes in the river guarantees salvation of the soul. The Ganges River flows through Uttar Pradesh and plays an important role in the economy, culture and religion of those who live in the Gangetic plains. This predominantly Hindu state is home to the sprawling plains of central India and is the most populous – and one of the most dominant political states in the country. Take time to wander barefoot around Akbar's abandoned red-sandstone palace at Fatepur Sikri at sunset and marvel at the Buddhist shrine at Sarnath. Holi Festival, where people play with colourful powders, is celebrated with abandon here in February and March.

Best time to visit
Uttar Pradesh and Uttaranchal: October to March
Photos Laura Kinch

Ganges View

B 1/163 Assi Ghat, Varanasi, 221 005 Uttar Pradesh

The roof terrace overlooks the great Mother Ganga and all those bustling rituals of washers, bathers, buffalo herders and marigold sellers – a fantastic setting. This is a family-run guest house with a colonial feel, converted by owner Shashank some 20 years ago – dark, cool rooms, marble floors, planters, portraits. Trompe l'oeil walls add an exotic touch and the rooftop rooms are the most inspiring (and the hottest in summer). Your host could not be kinder or more charming. Instead of television he provides a lobby full of books and an array of cultural events: traditional Indian music, talks from Buddhist scholars. This is a special retreat away from the Shiva energy of Varanasi that can be overwhelming – especially during festival time. You are on Assi Ghat, the southernmost ghat to which pilgrims flock for ritual bathing, and near the leafy area of the Benares Hindu University, popular with travellers and students of music and philosophy. The area teems with *chai* shops, round the corner is a good bookshop and, a few blocks away, the funeral pyres – life and death on the doorstep.

rooms	12 doubles.
price	Rs1,200-Rs2,500. Plus 10% tax. Peak season: October-March.
meals	Breakfast & lunch Rs150 each. Dinner Rs250.
closed	Rarely.
directions	Rickshaw ride from station approx. Rs70. Airport: Varanasi (26km). Train: Varanasi (7km).

Guest house

	Mr Prakash Kumar
tel	+91 (0)5422 313 218
mobile	+91 (0)9415 225 350
fax	+91 (0)5422 369 695
email	hotelgangesview@yahoo.com

B

Map 5 Entry 36

Shiva Ganges View

B-14/24 Mansarovar Ghat, Near Andhra Ashram, Varanasi, 221 001 Uttar Pradesh

Step through the door to this British-built four-storey family home and you'll instantly feel calm after the busy streets of Varanasi's old town. It has space aplenty but only eight rooms; best to book well ahead. All are painted cream and green, have high ceilings, cool stone floors and sitting areas; white-tiled bathrooms are basic but clean. Tandonjee and Ratna are your kind and peaceful hosts who will do their utmost to make you feel welcome in this enchanting city. Enjoy an Indian classical music recital in their inner courtyard, or one of Ratna's delicious vegetarian *thalis*, arranged in advance. Breakfast is extra, and can be taken in your room. There's a rooftop for yoga – or just to sit out on with an evening drink and people-watch; if you need a day off, stay up there. It's difficult to find such serenity and cleanliness in Varanasi unless you're in a five-star hotel – and better still, all of the rooms have balconies with fantastic views of life on the River Ganges. It's the tall red building on Monsarowar Ghat; don't let your rickshaw driver take you anywhere else! Ask about long term stays.

Guest house

rooms	8: 7 doubles, 1 family room.
price	Rs1,500-Rs2,400. Family room Rs.3,500. Peak season: August–April.
meals	Breakfast Rs125. Lunch & dinner Rs150 each.
closed	Rarely.
directions	Right on the famous Kedar Ghat, near the Andhra Ashram. Airport: Varanasi (25km, 1.5 hours). Train: Varanasi Cant (4km, 30 mins).

	Mr Surendra Tandon
tel	+91 (0)5422 450 063
res. no	+91 (0)5423 296 926
mobile	+91 (0)9935 307 700
email	saurabhrv2000@yahoo.com
web	www.varanasiguesthouse.com

B 👤 ⚲ 💳 ⚘ 👟

Map 5 Entry 37

Jain Paying Guest House
SN 14/3 A, Baraipur, Sarnath, 221 007 Uttar Pradesh

The Jain Paying Guest House, as it proudly announces itself, is run by Dr Jain and his wife who have, over time, converted more and more areas of their family home into rooms for guests… and introduced more and more guests to their delightful family. The food, which appears endlessly from the gently industrious kitchen, must be the most delicious in Sarnath, and the most suitable for delicate Western stomachs. (Being Jains, they serve kosher Hindu fare and exclude eggs.) It is a well-loved rest house for passing pilgrims to Sarnath, ancient cradle of Buddhism, and meal times are invariably stimulating with an eclectic gathering of people. The seven rooms are clean and modest; four have bathrooms, Indian-style – hot water is provided by the bucket. Prices reflect the simplicity. The roof has one of the best panoramas in Sarnath: views swoop over the deer park and the ancient *stupa* that marks the spot where the newly enlightened Buddha gave his first sermon, aptly symbolised as the Wheel of the Dharma.

rooms	7: 5 doubles, 2 singles (3 sharing showers).
price	Rs300. Singles Rs250. Peak season: November–March.
meals	Breakfast Rs40. Lunch & dinner Rs50 each.
closed	April–September.
directions	Near the Main Temple of Sarnath. Train: Varanasi (10km).

Guest house

	Dr Abhaya Kumar Jain
tel	+91 (0)5422 595 621
email	jpgh@rediffmail.com

A

Map 5 Entry 38

Carlton's Plaisance

Near the L.B.S.N.A Academy, Happy Valley Road, Mussoorie, 248 179 Uttaranchal

In five acres of orchards and gardens where salvias and fuchsias bloom, this 'place of peace' on the Mussoorie hillside sits dwarfed by towering pines. The whole area once belonged to the British East India Company, one of whose officials built the house after falling in love with a French-Indian woman who persuaded him to stay. Anu and Ajit, an affable pair, have left much of the Victorian architecture and period furniture intact; the stables under the house, shoe-scrapers and bear rugs are small signs of an existence that has been all but lost. Famous feet have walked these corridors (read Sir Edmund Hilary's comments in the guest book) and aspiring writers, artists and thinkers still come to stay. The area is stuffed with places to visit and things to do – temples, churches, birdwatching and great walks – about which Anu and Ajit are well versed. A comfortable place to stay, with snow-clad mountain views. And possibly the only place in northern India where you can find French sausages and Mississippi Honey Chicken.
Overnight trekking to elephant sanctuary.

Guest house

rooms	8: 4 doubles, 4 suites.
price	Rs1,800. Suites Rs3,500. Plus 5% tax. Peak season: May–June.
meals	Breakfast Rs120. Lunch & dinner Rs150–Rs300 each.
closed	Rarely.
directions	From Library Bazaar (Gandhi Chowk) take road to Happy Valley. On right, down signed driveway. Airport: Dehra Dun (55km, 1.5 hours).

	Mrs Ajit & Anu Singh
tel	+91 (0)1352 632 800
mobile	+91 (0)9358 120 911
email	carltonhotels@gmail.com or carltons@rediffmail.com
web	www.geocities.com/carltonhotels_india

A 🚶 👕 📖 🚲 👟

Map 2 Entry 39

Kasmanda Palace

The Mall Road, Mussoorie, 248 179 Uttaranchal

The only Mussoorie property still owned by royalty, Kasmanda was bought in 1915 as a summer retreat from the hot plains of Lucknow. Yet the Anglo-French house has had many reincarnations. Built in 1836 as part of the Christ Church complex, it became a sanitorium for British forces, a school, a private house and finally flung open its doors as a heritage hotel in 1992. Today territorial geese keep watch over its three acres of pine forest, terraced gardens and lawns up on one of Mussoorie's highest points – the hotel jeep now takes the strain out of the climb back from town. The colourful Rajkumar Sahib and his wife still live upstairs and bless you with their regal company over dinner – upon request – and the bedrooms are the staging ground for a silent battle between the antique and the modern. Tiger skins speak of the past; today the thrills come from sports offered here. Towering log fires fend off the winter chill and thick, whitewashed stone walls keep the summer heat at bay, and the gardens are lovely. *Whitewater rafting, trekking, paragliding & birdwatching.*

rooms	18: 12 doubles, 6 suites.
price	Rs2,500–Rs2,800. Suites Rs3,500. Plus 5% tax. Peak season: March–August.
meals	Breakfast Rs100. Lunch & dinner Rs250 each.
closed	Rarely.
directions	From main road on past Padmini Niwas; 1st left up hill; pass church on left. Kasmanda signed at top. Airport: Dehra Dun (55km, 2 hours); Train: Dehra Dun (35km, 1 hour).

	Mr Dinraj Pratap Singh
tel	+91 (0)1352 632 424 or +91 (0)1352 633 949
fax	+91 (0)1352 630 007
email	kasmanda@vsnl.com
web	www.welcomheritagehotels.com

Hotel

Map 2 Entry 40

Padmini Niwas

Library, The Mall, Mussoorie, 248 179 Uttaranchal

Blessed with views over the Doon Valley to the Ganga (on a clear day) and in an enviable spot to catch the winter sun, Padmini Niwas is a half-eco, half-regal 1860s bungalow. Built during the British Raj, passed down from the Maharaja of Rajpipla, the guesthouse was built in the British colonial style. Mrs Worah, a warm and generous host with a regal touch of her own, passionately recycles and has put in solar panels to catch a little of the Himalayan sun. She runs a nursery here with more than 400 varieties of plants, many of which adorn the flowery verandas and balconies, lily gardens and rose bowers – the perfect spots to laze with books and tea, drinking in the scents and colours, perhaps with large, hairy Meru the dozing Himalayan Bhutia dog for company. Mrs Worah and family are deeply involved in the local scene; daughter, Sejal, whizzes between India and Africa for the WWF, weaving in local eco-tourism projects with wider work on environmental sustainability. The trekking here is wonderful. *Indian cookery classes (small groups only).*

Guest house

rooms	26: 24 doubles, 2 singles.
price	Rs1,700–2,800. Singles Rs1,000. Plus 5%. Peak season: 15 May-end-August; festival time.
meals	Breakfast Rs75. Lunch & dinner Rs130 each.
closed	Rarely.
directions	Halfway between Library bus/taxi stand and the ropeway, a 5-minute walk from the Library. Airport: Dehra Dun (55km, 1.5hours).

	Mrs Harshada Worah
tel	+91 (0)1352 631 093
fax	+91 (0)1352 632 793
email	harshada@vsnl.com
web	www.hotelpadmininivas.com

B

Map 2 Entry 41

The Glasshouse on the Ganges

P.O. & Village Gular-Dogi, Rishikesh, District Tehri Garwal, 249 303 Uttaranchal

It is a fine thing to dip one's feet into the 'Ganga' at sunset – even finer to meditate on a rock by the water's edge. All this only a few metres from the Glasshouse, where luxury and good taste face the raw tumbling vitality of the river as it flows through green hills towards Rishikesh. The main building, like a large modern cottage, still has – strangely – some ceilings of raw concrete, but the glass provides floor-to-ceiling river views through lush greenery, scented frangipani trees, butterflies and birds. Bedrooms are either in cottages or in the main building. Huge and handsome rooms are, on the whole, pretty, even if the odd detail is amiss. A path leads to the cottages, whose bedspreads and curtains throw colour onto the white walls; one has a solid marble sink fed by the hotel's spring water and a giant bed. The dining area and veranda have comfortable cane furniture and cloth-covered tables. The ayurvedic centre has wonderfully relaxing healing treatments – do indulge. The buffets are good, the management low-key and the setting unforgettable. *Whitewater rafting. Own sand beach. Free yoga classes.*

rooms	15: 5 doubles, 4 twins, 2 triples, 4 suites.
price	Rs2,500-Rs7,000. Plus 5% tax. Peak season: September–March.
meals	Breakfast Rs150. Lunch Rs250. Dinner Rs300. Plus 8% tax.
closed	Rarely.
directions	23km from Rishikesh on the road to Badrinath.

Resort

	Mr Neeraj Jain
tel	+91 (0)1378 269 224
res. no	+91 (0)1124 356 145
fax	+91 (0)1124 351 112
email	sales@neemranahotels.com
web	www.neemranahotels.com

C

Map 2 Entry 42

Corbett Call of the Wild

Katami Gajar, Betalghat, District Nainital, Uttaranchal

Arrive in the evening and Ludley the elephant may take you for a sunset ride along deserted jungle tracks beside the Kosi river. This place is as close to nature as you can get without sleeping beneath canvas. (Though that is an option.) In dense forest, stone steps lead down to the lodge house and a clutch of cottages dotted amongst lawns, lemon trees, secret sitting areas and flowerbeds. Wisely, rooms don't try to compete with nature. Large, airy, with high wooden ceilings, the style is rustic and spare in natural beige and brown tones while bathrooms are surprisingly large. (Running hot water in peak season; in low season, it comes in a bucket.) The lodge's rooms share a central veranda while the cottages have open porches. The dining room may be crisp with white linen but the style is informal. After a good buffet dinner, sit around a campfire and swap stories of the animals you've spied – tiger, leopard, wild boar, perhaps – or the fish you've caught. Imagine sunrise and sunset safaris, nature treks, riverside picnics – and lounging on your porch as parakeets and bulbul chatter in the trees. Magical.

rooms	15: 9 doubles, 2 twins, 4 cottages for 2. Tents available.
price	Full-board Rs4,500. Treks included.
meals	Full-board only.
closed	Rarely.
directions	60km from Nainital. Train: Ramnagar (2 hours).

Safari lodge

tel	+91 (0)5942 235 972
fax	+91 (0)5942 235 493
email	wildcall@mickyonline.com
web	www.corbettscallofthewild.com

B

Map 2 Entry 43

Kalmatia Sangam Himalaya Resort

Kalimat Estate (near Kasar Devi), Post Bag 002, Almora, 263 601 Uttaranchal

The scattered houses in the valley below are slate-roofed and whitewashed with brightly painted doors and windows. The terraces produce wheat and vegetables, buffalos graze with goats, the women wear startling colours. It is not at all remote, for Almora is close – with a good market (woollens and jewellery), and the area feels prosperous. Geeta inherited this hilltop estate and after living in Germany she and Dieter took a deep plunge to create an Indo-European hotel. Dieter's style is German, Geeta bubbles with enthusiasm, the staff are impeccable, the manager is English, the furniture is imaginative (modern, wrought-iron, Scandinavian, dhurries on the floor), the food delicious – a fusion of Indian and European. You can light a fire in your bedroom and sleep in a cottage of your own; they are scattered among the pine trees, each with views and space galore, big beds and duvets, stone walls, good bathrooms. Practice yoga, have reflexology or meditate on a special terrace. The Reebs have a strong eco-policy: take a walk among the trees they have planted and collect herbs and mushrooms in season.

rooms	9 cottages: 7 for 2, 2 for 1-2.
price	$84-$163. Singles $60.50-$111.50. Plus 5% tax. Peak season: October-December; March-June.
meals	Breakfast $6.75. Lunch $11.25. Dinner $13.50.
closed	Never.
directions	Upper Binsar road towards Kasar Devi temple. Resort 1km before temple, on right. Airport: Delhi (380km). Train: Kathagodam (2.5 hours). Pick-up possible.

Resort

	Dieter & Geeta Reeb
tel	+91 (0)5962 233 625
fax	+91 (0)5962 231 572
email	geeta1@nde.vsnl.net.in
web	www.kalmatia-sangam.com

Map 2 Entry 44

Deodars

Papparselli, Almora, 263 601 Uttaranchal

The warmth and easy-going nature of your hosts make this solid, modest guest house hard to leave. The owners will regale you with tales of guests who have become family friends; perhaps you, too, will be lucky enough to return. The old house has been in the family for years; *deodars*, or cedars, surround it and the crisp mountain air is redolent with the scent of conifers. There's a wonderful stone veranda for alfresco meals – English breakfasts, Indian lunches, continental dinners – and a swing seat from which you can gaze on a clear day on the snow-covered heights of Nanda Devi and Trisul. More spots for contemplation in the lovely garden, and a small shrubbery with gnomes. Big bedrooms have high ceilings and fireplaces, stripes and flowery chintz; one has a private porch, another a bathroom with a big tub. The old-fashioned mood continues with knick-knacks and plastic flowers, tiger skins in the hall, books and games to keep children happy; the sitting room is super-cosy at night. Almora is a short drive or a long walk. *Guided forest walks & sight-seeing can be arranged.*

Homestay

rooms	3 doubles.
price	Full-board Rs4,000. Singles Rs3,000.
meals	Full-board only.
closed	Rarely.
directions	2.5 hours from Kathagodam. 40-minute walk from Almora or 10 minutes in car. Airport: Kathagodam (2.5 hours).

	Richard and Elizabeth Wheeler
tel	+91 (0)5962 233 025
mobile	+91 (0)9412 344 706
email	rwheeler@rediffmail.com

B 🏊

Map 2 Entry 45

Ramgarh Bungalows

Ramgarh (Malla), Kumaon Hills, District Nainital, 263 137 Uttaranchal

The valley drops away, your eyes skim the fruit trees to the tree-covered slopes on the other side. At night only a few distant lights breach the darkness. Below some of the cottages is a little school that awakes you with its chant and chatter. The rooms are simple yet pretty, one with blue curtains and white walls and a modern bathroom. The veranda drops to a greenish patch of grass, wicker chairs and table and a row of irises, daisies and petunias. A brick path leads up to the dining room, a long, white-washed building set about with flowers, yellow curtains, paved floor, prints and plain colours. Indian music and scents mingle with the French mood to make a delightful space for delicious meals. Breakfast is European, with homemade local jams. The Old Bungalow, higher up, has a fine, pillared veranda and more pretty rooms. There are handsome chestnuts (and an avenue of them outside the gate) but less 'view'. Much is ill-kempt but the aesthetic is appealing overall. It is a place to spend several days in order to enjoy the magic, sit, write, walk, eat and read – far from the non-stop bustle of India.

rooms	9: 3 doubles, 6 suites.
price	Rs1,200–Rs2,500. Suites Rs1,500–Rs5,000. Plus 5% tax. Peak season: April–10 July.
meals	Breakfast Rs150. Lunch Rs200. Dinner Rs250.
closed	Rarely.
directions	15km from Bhawali town. Take train from Delhi to Kathagodam, then 2-hour taxi ride.

Guest house

	Mr K S Mehra
tel	+91 (0)5942 281 156 or (0)5942 280 037
res. no	+91 (0)1124 356 145
fax	+91 (0)1124 351 112
email	sales@neemranahotels.com
web	www.neemranahotels.com

B

Map 2 Entry 46

Himalayan Village Sonapani

Village Satoli, close to Satkhol ashram, Nathukhan, District Nainital, 263 138 Uttaranchal

Ashish Arora has two passions – to serve his local community and to preserve the environment. Sonapani is his creation and his vision. Follow the path to this glorious 20-acre smallholding, with its scattering of holiday cottages and unbroken views. It is named Sonapani – 'gold water' – after a healing spring close by. Two thousand metres up in the Himalayas, surrounded by wild rhododendrons, oaks and pines, the cottages are connected by pathways and divided by organic vegetable plots, orchards of apple, apricot and plum, flower gardens and herbs. The well-insulated cottages are constructed of compressed blocks of earth, with mud-plaster interiors and tin roofs. Touches of comfort come from new mattresses on pine beds, bright bed linen and hot-water 'en suite' showers. Your music is the trilling of birds, your entertainment the view. Be a hermit by day, a socialite by night – there are campfires and communal eating and a lovely friendly feel. The dining room is similarly rustic, the buffet meals varied and wholesome. *Guided walks to villages & jungle treks. Bring your own alcohol.*

rooms	12 cottages: 10 for 2, 2 family.
price	Full-board Rs2,800–Rs3,200. Peak season: March–June; September–November.
meals	Full-board. Extra meals available at Rs150.
closed	Rarely.
directions	69km from Kathagodam; pick-up can be arranged. A 25-minute walk along sandy path from dropping off point.

Resort

SPECIAL GREEN ENTRY
see page 18

B 👤 🚜 👟

Map 2 Entry 47

	Mr Ashish Arora
tel	+91 (0)9719 005 900 or (0)9810 633 350
mobile	+91 (0)9810 881 491
email	ashish@himalayanvillage.com
web	www.himalayanvillage.com

Sitla Estate
P.O.Mukteshwar, Mukteshwar, District Nainital, 263 138 Uttaranchal

Snuggle up with a hot water bottle at the end of the day. Vikram Maira runs his father's estate and this guest house in a hospitable and confident manner; indeed, he lends a helping hand at mealtimes and enjoys accompanying guests on village excursions. As you take afternoon tea beneath the ancient plum tree and gaze on the mountains and forests, a sense of oneness with the world will envelop you... only disturbed by the wagging of the German Shepherd dogs' tails. The main part of the guest house is a hundred years old, and later extensions have been built in a sympathetic style. Simple bedrooms have splashes of colour from traditional wall hangings, curtains and throws, and glorious views of the Himalayas. Ceilings are beamed, brick walls are white, mattresses are comfortable, and you find fluffy towels and toiletries in the bathrooms – a rare treat. Good food, served at one sociable table, can be as Indian or as European as you like. For winter cosiness there are sofas around the open log fire. It's hands-on, homely and tranquil.

rooms	7: 6 doubles, 1 suite.
price	Full-board Rs3,000-Rs4,500.
meals	Full-board only.
closed	Rarely.
directions	2 hours from Kathagodam, 8 hours from Delhi. Can arrange pick-up.

Guest house

	Mr Vikram Maira
tel	+91 (0)5942 286 330/030
email	maira_40@yahoo.co.uk
web	www.sitlaestate.com

B 🐾

Map 2 Entry 48

Delhi & Haryana

India's crazy capital, Delhi, is the transport hub of northern India and home to over 14 million people; it's a fascinating and challenging place that teems with paradoxes. Modern cars, buses, lorries, taxis, cycle rickshaws and the odd elephant pack out the roads; booming business has brought three-piece suits and glitzy restaurants with fabulous food; designer bars and shopping malls rub shoulders with souk-like bazaars; ragged beggars and shoeless Saddhus offer a street blessing. Ancient temples, ugly tower blocks, smart neighbourhoods with colonial mansions sit alongside desperate slums. Migrants come from all over India, especially Punjabis who came post Partition. Pollution can be fierce, particularly when temperatures soar to over 40 degrees. Delhi is known as the 'Seven Cities' – where seven rulers built seven fortress settlements. In Old Delhi are 16th and 17th-century Mughal-built monuments and bustling old bazaars; New Delhi mixes 1930s British, colonial mansions with modern shopping malls, government and diplomatic buildings and wide avenues. It is a great experience to visit this eye-popping, jaw-dropping city. Explore around the Red Fort, breathe easy in Lodi Gardens, visit Jumayan's Tomb and save some time for shopping.

The flat and fertile river plains of Haryana and neighbouring Punjab are known as the 'granary of India' producing more than half of the rice, millet and wheat grown in the country. The majority of people who live in Haryana are Hindus. The capital, Chandigarh, governs Haryana (and the Punjab) and was newly built in the 1950s by Le Corbusier. His Open Hand monument stands for 'post-colonial harmony and peace'. There is an excellent art gallery and museum here and the rock garden is a quirky, fairytale fantasy. The song-filled Sultanpur Bird Sanctuary just outside Delhi is home to hundreds of species of birds, including the Saras crane.

Best time to visit
Delhi: mid October-mid-March.
Haryana: October-March.

Photo top Toby Sawday
Photo bottom Laura Kinch

Delhi Bed & Breakfast

Friends Colony East, Delhi, 110 065 Delhi

One night at this guest house gets you closer to the real India than a month at Delhi's finest hotel. Pervez and Lubna gather you into their family (two young children and grandma) with a passion. A quiet retreat this is not! Pervez (an estate agent but from a hotelier family) is raconteur, entertainer, information guide wrapped in a bundle of joviality. Lubna is a dream cook who will take you to market and share her kitchen secrets. The three-storey house, in a smart suburb of south Delhi, is comfortable and colourful, overflowing with batik wall hangings and patterned rugs, bright cushions and carved sofas, knick-knacks and Bollywood DVDs. Spotlessly clean bedrooms and bathrooms have all you need but you're more likely to linger with your book on one of the plant-filled terraces or in one of the two lounges... and you will scarcely get a page read before Pervez charms you with the latest Delhi gossip. He will happily take you to the city's sites, some of which – Humayun's tomb, Red Fort, Lodhi Gardens – are only 20 minutes away. Warm and fun family living, Indian style.

rooms	3: 2 doubles, 1 twin. Extra beds.
price	Rs2,300. Single Rs2,100. Plus 12.5% tax. Peak season: September–April.
meals	Lunch & dinner Rs350 each.
closed	Rarely.
directions	Find Aashram Crossing, then State Bank of India, behind petrol pump. In lane adjacent. Airport: Delhi (20km, 40 mins). Train: Nizamuddin Rey (2km, 10 mins).

	Lubna Pervez (Manager)
mobile	+91 (0)9811 057 103
fax	+91 (0)1126 913 201
email	delhibedandbreakfast@gmail.com
web	www.delhibedandbreakfast.com

Homestay

Map 2 Entry 49

Ahuja Residency

193 Golf Links, New Delhi, 110 003 Delhi

A peaceful oasis in the effervescent, sometimes overwhelming, capital. Delhi Golf Club is next door, and Khan Market – the city's High Street Ken – a powerful putt away. Marble staircases with wrought-iron railings twist through the six floors of this 50s giant, which you'll come to recognise by its rather bizarre white trestle frontage. Rooms vary in size and view; some have private balconies bursting with potted plants. Furniture is modern – mostly pine; floors are tiled and walls white. There's nothing over-patterned or mismatching here, just fresh blue stripes or orange checks. Outside, carpets of creepers cling to the brickwork of the spectacular high-walled garden – ensconce yourself in the greenery of it all. There's a homely feel yet the place is run with an assured professionalism. Rashmi is an impressive and highly educated woman who knows her stuff and has been taking in guests since the Asian Games in 1982. The family live on the ground floor but join you for breakfast. Of the owner's various properties, this is the one we recommend.

rooms	12 doubles.
price	Rs2,200. Plus 12.5% tax.
meals	Breakfast Rs75. Lunch & dinner Rs180 each.
closed	Never.
directions	In a small colony close to Khan Market. Call when you arrive in Delhi to organise pick-up. Airport: Delhi (20km, 40 minutes). Train: Nizamuddin Rey (2km, 10 minutes).

Guest house

	Mrs Rashmi Ahuja
tel	+91 (0)1124 611 027
fax	+91 (0)1124 649 008
email	info@ahujaresidency.com
web	www.ahujaresidency.com

B

Map 2 Entry 50

The Imperial
Janpath, New Delhi, 110 001 Delhi

Lutyens conceived the Imperial as the most luxurious hotel in his New Delhi, a blend of Victorian, colonial and informal Art Deco. It still works – an impeccable place, with an attention to detail that conquers the sceptical. Delhi has several fine hotels but this one stands out for its elegance and grace. Italian marble, Burmese teak, the plushest plumbing – all is understated luxury. Have just a cup of tea in the Atrium and be made to feel like a Rajah. Dine in the Coffee Shop overlooking the gardens – or in one of innumerable restaurants – and be astonished by the furniture, the décor and the watchful, regimented waiters. Prints of India's history add a country-house touch – and note that the Imperial has a huge collection of lithographs. The pool is a refuge from the heat and maniacal activity of Delhi. Although the bedrooms vary, many are big and luxurious with every need considered; the Deco suites are stunning. Spend languid hours downstairs people-watching, admiring the rare collection of 18th- and 19th-century art, and the flights of fancy all around in the décor.

rooms	234: 162 doubles, 27 twins, 45 suites.
price	$280-$340. Suites $400-$1,100. Plus 12.5% tax. Peak season: mid-Sept-mid-April.
meals	Breakfast from Rs400. Lunch from Rs515. Dinner from Rs675.
closed	Rarely.
directions	In the city centre, near Connaught Place.

Hotel

	Mr Pierre Jochim
tel	+91 (0)1123 341 234
fax	+91 (0)1123 342 255
email	luxury@theimperialindia.com or adhir@theimperialindia.com
web	www.theimperialindia.com

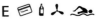

Map 2 Entry 51

Master Paying Guest Accommodation

R-500 New Rajinder Nagar, New Delhi, 110 060 Delhi

The luxury of having somewhere so small is that you can lavish attention on every corner. Avnish and Ushi's guest house is an expression of their principles and especially of their spiritual leanings – all encased in an unremarkable building in suburban north Delhi. Each room – choose from Mughal, Krishna, Ganesh or Lucky – has been decorated with spiritual calm in mind, the placing of every object carefully measured according to principles of balance and harmony. Ushi is a reiki master (her treatment room is on the roof garden) and Avnish is a genial, hospitable man who spent years working for Taj Hotels. He now runs his own radio show offering hot business tips. The two rooms on the roof open onto a shaded, plant-scattered terrace where creepers climb the bamboo fence and spring evenings are easily lost to good conversation and books. The family live downstairs and occasionally eat with guests – Avnish and Ushi talk fondly of past travellers who have become friends. Welcome relief from the mayhem of central Delhi, 20 minutes away by rickshaw. *Owners run Offbeat Tours in & around Delhi.*

Guest house

rooms	4 doubles.
price	Rs900-Rs1,000. Plus 12.5% tax. Peak season: July-April.
meals	Breakfast, lunch & dinner Rs150 each.
closed	Rarely.
directions	Near the crossing of Shankar Road & Ganga Ram Hospital. 4km from Connaught Place. Entrance at back of house.

	Avnish & Ushi Puri
tel	+91 (0)1128 741 089
email	urvashi@del2.vsnl.net.in
web	www.master-guesthouse.com

A ⅄

Map 2 Entry 52

Pataudi Palace

Village Pataudi, District Gurgaon, Haryana

Cricket, Bollywood and British colonial – it's an interesting mix for a grand white palace. Built in 1935 by Nawab Ibrahim Ali Khan, the house echoes on an even grander scale the residences of imperial Delhi. More recently, it was the home of legendary cricketer Nawab Mansur Ali Khan (there's a pitch alongside) and his film star wife. It's tranquil, beautiful and remote, and all around, stretching to infinity, are pomegranate orchards and farmland. Drive past posing peacocks and gardens reminiscent of England to the palace itself, where smiling staff will take you on a tour of the delightful rooms, courtyards, galleries, terraces. The main house bedrooms are vast, luxurious and a touch old-fashioned. Many have four-poster beds, sandalwood wardrobes, fantastic art and silk rugs; beds are comfy, pillows soft. Interconnecting rooms in the garden annexe are smaller and floors are mosaic or black and white check. The food, served buffet style in any one of three dining rooms, or outside, is fresh and delicious, and there's an old-fashioned billiards room where you can play and sip beer all night long.

rooms	16: 3 doubles, 7 suites, 1 single. Annexe: 3 doubles, 2 suites.
price	Rs3,000-Rs6,000. Suites Rs5,000-Rs7,000. Single Rs2,000.
meals	Breakfast Rs150. Lunch Rs300. Dinner Rs400.
closed	Never.
directions	From Bilaspur, 9km on NH8 Delhi–Jaipur. Airport: Delhi (60km, 1.25 hours). Train: Helimandi (4km, 15 mins).

Hotel

	Nawab Mansur Ali Khan
tel	+91 (0)1242 672 976
	or (0)1242 672 244
fax	+91 (0)1242 672 976
email	sales@neemranahotels.com
web	www.neemranahotels.com

Map 2 Entry 53

Tikli Bottom

Manender Farm, Gairatpur Bas, P.O. Tikli, Gurgaon, 122 001 Haryana

The perfect soft landing into India. Martin and Annie are true Delhi-ites, having been here for 20 years. Both have a profound knowledge of India and its machinations, and are immensely affable and generous hosts. Finished in 2000, their Lutyens-style farmhouse, an hour outside the craziness of Delhi, displays impeccable taste. It is at once English and Indian – in winter a roaring fire blazes in the study; in summer, relax in the cosy living room where only the dormant fan above is a reminder of one's whereabouts. In summer you can sleep on the rope-strung beds (*charpois*) in either garden, or in one of the elegant bedrooms, each of which opens onto the veranda'd courtyard. The gardens, encircled by the only real hills around the capital, have been a labour of love – tiered lawns and flowerbeds bursting with colour, a discreet sunken pool hewn from rural mustard fields. Martin will walk you round his organic farmstead, where citrus fruits flourish and kitchen vegetables grow in neat rows. They keep pigs and buffalos (for milk) too. Peace, good conversation, beautiful food and the warmest of welcomes.

Homestay

rooms	4: 2 doubles, 2 twins.
price	Full-board £115. Singles £75.
meals	Full-board only.
closed	20 April-30 June.
directions	Airport: Delhi (33km, 45 mins). Train: Delhi (50km, 1.25 hours). They will pick you up from Delhi station or airport.

Martin & Annie Howard

tel	+91 (0)1242 766 556
mobile	+91 (0)9899 459 123
email	honiwala@vsnl.com
web	www.tiklibottom.com

Map 2 Entry 54

Rajasthan

Known by the British as 'Rajputana', 'Land of Kings', glorious Rajasthan is one of India's most popular tourist destinations. Before Independence in 1947, there were 18 feudal kingdoms ; many rulers from the Hindu Rajputs to their Muslim overlords, the Moghuls, made their fortune from taxing traders passing from Pakistan to India across the Thar Desert and poured this into building vast forts, carved Temples and bejewelled palaces. Eighty per cent of the population live in rural communities, working the land and herding animals. Local festivals bring excitement to an otherwise routine rural life with puppet shows, camel racing, trading, socialising and feasting. The caste system in Rajasthan is particularly rigid, with strict codes of honour, but things are starting to change: the Rajputs continue to dominate politics, land and the economy (many have turned their homes into 'heritage' or 'palace' hotels) but recently the government has introduced university places and jobs for lower castes. Literacy rates are as low as 40% but are improving. Rural development schemes are bringing schools, water and hospitals to remote areas.

It has to be one of the most colourful states in India and incredible images abound: men in red, yellow and orange turbans with coiffed moustaches, women in dazzling mirrored saris, children with bells on their ankles, ambling camels, beggars, haunting music, thick white arm bangles and colour everywhere. Even the towns are different colours. In the 'Golden City', the desert fortress town of Jaisalmer are incredible carved balconies, mirror mosaics, elephantine entrance gates, latticed screened havelis. From a rooftop in the 'Pink City', Jaipur, gorge on Indian sweets and watch the fireworks during 'Diwali' Festival. In the 'Blue City', Jodhpur, square houses are painted blue – visit the coloured-glass fort. Pushkar town is a pilgrimage site with 400 temples and a holy lake; make a beeline for the camel fair in November for one of the most colourful spectacles on earth. Find the sloth bear in Ranthambhore National Park or see a myriad of bird species and snakes at Bharatpur Bird Sanctuary.

Best time to visit mid-October-mid March.

Photos Laura Kinch

Neemrana Fort-Palace

Neemrana Village, District Alwar, 301 705 Rajasthan

If the marauding hordes descending on this maze of a palace got as lost I did, the inhabitants might never have been defeated. The warren spreads over ten layers, the ramparts and colonnaded walkways leading to open courtyards are as confusing as an Escher sketch. A sensitive, modest yet beautiful restoration of near ruins, this 'non-hotel' is a powerful example of the triumph of good taste and moderation over standardised luxury. Built over ten years, the rooms have slowly taken shape, reflecting the mindfulness of history that runs through. Some have their own *jharokha* balconies facing out onto plains peppered with plots of bright mustard; others have bathrooms open to the skies. You can sleep in the old royal court, or in a tent on the top of the highest turret. All are simply furnished with colonial and Indian antiques in an eclectic style. The place embodies holiday calm; there's fabulous food (French and Indian), ayurvedic massage and afternoon tea in the gardens. No TVs or phones in the rooms, just endless corners, courtyards and turrets in which to lose yourself. Heaven. *Yoga & meditation.*

Hotel

rooms	46: 20 doubles, 1 family room for 4, 4 singles, 21 suites.
price	Rs2,500-Rs6,000. Family room Rs15,000. Singles Rs1,500-Rs2.500. Suites Rs3,500-Rs8,000. Plus 10% tax. Peak season: September-March.
meals	Breakfast Rs200. Lunch & dinner Rs400 each.
closed	Rarely.
directions	2 hours south-west of Delhi along NH8 to Jaipur. Turn right at signs in Neemrana Village.

	Mr Ramesh Dhabhai
tel	+91 (0)1494 246 006
res. no	+91 (0)1124 356 145
fax	+91 (0)1124 351 112
email	sales@neemranahotels.com
web	www.neemranahotels.com

C ✉ ❖ ⚘ 🌊

Map 2 Entry 55

The Hill Fort Kesroli

Village Kesroli, via M.I.A., Alwar, 301 030 Rajasthan

The architectural equivalent of a security blanket, the massive walls of this delightful 14th-century fort enclose pretty, flowered courtyards to create a retreat from the harsher world outside. Perched imposingly 200 feet above the plain, inside it has the feel of an intimate – and impeccably restored – castle made for two. Each of the rooms is distinct. From the blue-and-white ceiling of the Hindola Mahal bedroom swings a large seat facing a window that frames the sunrise at dawn; the Mubarak Mahal suite is tucked away in one of seven turrets. Rooms are reached by steep, narrow, stone steps leading to private terraces that overlook an agrarian landscape of mustard fields. In winter, the fort looks like a ship afloat in a yellow sea. There is a sense of total privacy and seclusion. Take tea on your arched veranda among the swooping parakeets, or dine among the ramparts in the glow of the setting sun – the sound of distant voices is the only reminder of the toil of village life below. *Visits to Sariska Tiger Sanctuary & boating on Siliserh Lake.*

rooms	21: 14 doubles, 7 suites.
price	Rs2,000–Rs3,500. Suites Rs2,500–Rs5,000. Plus 10% tax. Peak season: September–March.
meals	Breakfast Rs150. Lunch Rs300. Dinner Rs350.
closed	May–July.
directions	12km from Alwar train station. Airport: Delhi (3 hours).

	Mr Pramod Bist
tel	+91 (0)1468 289 352
res. no	+91 (0)1124 356 145
fax	+91 (0)1124 351 112
email	sales@neemranahotels.com
web	www.neemranahotels.com

Hotel

Map 4 Entry 56

Laxmi Vilas Palace

Kakaji Ki Kothi, Bharatpur, 321 001 Rajasthan

Set around a wicker-chaired courtyard — cosy even in winter — this beautiful
small palace was built in 1887 for the brother of the Maharaja of Bharatpur.
It had the reputation for being one of the most impressive shoots in India — up to
90 guns would be lined up and guests would perform until the viceroy got bored.
There are photos to prove it. These days guests are encouraged to stalk with
binoculars not guns — rent a rickshaw or bike and spin off to Keoladeo, one of the
most fascinating bird-feeding and -breeding grounds in the world. The rambling
Laxmi Vilas perfectly combines Mughal and Rajput architectural styles, and its
rooms are furnished with a mixture of traditional and colonial pieces. Fabulous
Rajasthani murals adorn the walls and georgous fabrics the beds. Bedrooms are
comfortable — the suites the biggest — with decorative floor tiles and carved or
brass beds. Buffet-style meals are home-grown and good, the family is charming
yet unobtrusive, the lovely landscaped grounds hold a Jacuzzi and fine pool, and
there's badminton and croquet. We love this place. *Evening puppet shows.*

rooms	25: 12 doubles, 13 suites.
price	Rs2,450. Suite Rs3,300. Plus 10% tax. Peak season: October–March.
meals	Breakfast Rs175. Lunch & dinner Rs300 each.
closed	Rarely.
directions	Near the Bharatpur bird sanctuary. 5km from Bharatpur train station & bus stand.

Hotel

	Mr Prem Prakash
tel	+91 (0)5644 231 199
fax	+91 (0)5644 225 259
email	reservations@laxmivilas.com
web	www.laxmivilas.com

Map 4 Entry 57

The Bagh

Agra–Achnera Road, Pakka Bagh Village, Bharatpur, 321 001 Rajasthan

Set in 200-year-old walled pleasure gardens, this place oozes calm and serenity. Rooms are spread across three white sandstone buildings, some as old as the garden – tranquil spaces of Moghul arches, verandas and inlaid marble floors. Every window, it seems, overlooks the garden. Bedrooms are elegant and cool with hand-crafted furniture, luxurious silk bedcovers and five-star marbled bathrooms. There are quiet patios to retire to, and ten acres of flowering plants and fruit trees to get lost in. You can even bird-watch from your veranda. Serious bird-lovers will head for neighbouring Keoladeo National Park, one of the world's foremost bird sanctuaries, bristling with 350 different species; the Singh brothers are bird experts as well as engaging hosts and will help you plan a visit. Locally-sourced food is very fresh and simple while the dining room, tucked in the garden, is like an elaborate summer house. Ask the kitchen to prepare a picnic and it comes wrapped in a white linen cloth. A luxury chill-out irresistibly close to nature with ecological leanings. *Groups can rent their own wing.*

rooms	22: 4 doubles, 16 twins, 1 single.
price	$120-$135. Plus 9% tax. Peak season: October–March.
meals	Breakfast $8. Lunch $12. Dinner $15.
closed	Never.
directions	3km from Keoladeo National Park in Bharatpur. Airport: Agra (55km, 1.5 hrs). Train: Bharatpur (5km, 15 mins).

Hotel

	R N Mathur (Manager)
tel	+91 (0)5644 228 333 or (0)5644 225 415
fax	+91 (0)5644 225 191
email	thebagh@hotmail.com
web	www.thebagh.com

Map 4 Entry 58

Dera Rawatsar

D-194/C, Vijay Path, Bani Park, Jaipur, 302 016 Rajasthan

Come face-to-face with history. Grandma Laxmi Chandawat rules the roost, she was the first woman in Rajasthan to break with purdah and the fire still burns unabated. Set around neat lawns, Dera Rawatsar is a stylish, unfussy place, soothingly white and crowned by a hint of Rajput balcony. The quiet comes as a surprise given this residential area is a stone's throw from the main bus station. The ladies of the house run things here, so you would expect the rooms to have an understated elegance, light in feel and uncluttered. A gauze veil curtains off the bed area, which is vast and silkily comfortable. Each bathroom has its own cute animal mat to step out onto after a hot shower. Husband and wife, Veena and Mandvi, have a charmingly relaxed manner and are helpful when it comes to Jaipur orientation. The family can trace its origins back to the Rawatsar clan, pre-eminent in the Bikaner region, and claim to offer an authentic Rajput experience: huge servings of food don't disappoint and you'll be taking grandma's biography to bed.

Hotel

rooms	15: 12 doubles, 3 suites.
price	Rs1,500-Rs2,500. Plus 8% tax. Peak season: October-March.
meals	Breakfast Rs150. Lunch & dinner Rs250 each. Plus 9% tax.
closed	Rarely.
directions	Airport: Jaipur (11km, 25 mins). Train: Jaipur (3km, 5 mins).

Veena Chauhan & Mandvi Ranawat

tel	+91 (0)1412 360 717
mobile	+91 (0)9314 506 391
fax	+91 (0)1412 362 556
email	service@derarawatsar.com
web	www.derarawatsar.com

B ⚒ 👤 📧 🧍 ⚙ 👟

Map 4 Entry 59

Jaipur Inn
B-17 Shiv Marg, Bani Park, Jaipur, 302 016 Rajasthan

Once across the cattle grid, past the office block and through the Jaipur Inn arch, everything changes. It all began as a campsite for backpackers in the 1970s and it still welcomes them; there's an open-hearted mood here, and the ineffably generous Pushpendra offers a free room to anyone who has a gift or a talent to bring. The wooden extension on the first floor is Dutch-designed and very appealing. Basic bedrooms are cheered by splashes of colourful Anokhi fabrics, bright blankets and bold paintwork. In some rooms there is free-standing Babul wooden furniture; in others, storage is built-in. It's all a touch spartan but perfectly fine, while practical, marble-floored bathrooms offer flip-flops and towels. The higher rooms have fine views over Jaipur; climb further and you find the Amber Nectar roof café for sociable nights. There's a simple but good value buffet supper often served on the roof, overseen by Pushpendra. (Join in the cooking if you wish!). Cheap, cheerful, generous, surprising. *Bikes for hire. Six-day pottery courses nearby.*

rooms	16 doubles.
price	Rs500–Rs600. Peak season: 15 October–15 March.
meals	Breakfast Rs80. Lunch Rs100. Dinner Rs200.
closed	Rarely.
directions	2km from train station on Shiv Circus, at crossroads between Shiv Marg & Todarmal Road.

Guest house

	Mr Pushpendra Bhargava
tel	+91 (0)1412 201 121
fax	+91 (0)1412 200 140
email	jaipurin@sancharnet.in
web	www.jaipurinn.com

Map 4 Entry 60

Hotel Madhuban

D-237 Behari Marg, Bani Park, Jaipur, 302 016 Rajasthan

A prancing elephant fresco, and probably one of their three dogs or two children, greet guests to the Singhs' home. As they say, "Madhuban is not luxury. It is a comfortable way of life". You're about a kilometre from the old town, in a pretty, quiet, leafy residential area; there's a swimming pool in the sheltered garden and the occasional partridge or peacock strutting between the tables and chairs dotted about the lawn – a good place to write and read. Digvijay, 'Dicky', is thoroughly at home with westerners, and understands their preoccupation with cleanliness and their desire for cornflakes and milder meals from time to time; his wife Kavita is welcoming though more reserved. The style here is quite sedate and proper: the sitting and dining rooms are formal, bedrooms come with traditional wooden furniture, heavy brocade drapes, curtains and bed covers, rugged, marble-chip floors and spotless bathrooms. Some rooms give on to a pleasant rooftop area with potted plants and easy chairs in the shade. A thoroughly reliable place – with free basic yoga sessions, from sunrise, in the next door ashram.

Hotel

rooms	18: 15 doubles, 3 suites.
price	Rs1,400–Rs1,800.
	Suites Rs2,000–Rs2,700.
	Singles from Rs1,300.
	10% tax on rooms over Rs1,000.
	Peak season: October–March.
meals	Breakfast Rs175.
	Lunch & dinner from Rs250 each.
closed	Rarely.
directions	2km from train station & bus stand.

Mr Dicky Singh Patan

tel	+91 (0)1412 200 033
fax	+91 (0)1412 202 344
email	madhuban@usa.net
web	www.madhuban.net

Map 4 Entry 61

Hotel Meghniwas

C-9 Sawai Jai Singh Highway, Bani Park, Jaipur, 302 016 Rajasthan

The old Colonel is a genial soul with a twinkle in his eye and a bear-like handshake – a man happy with his lot. Having spent many years with the Indian army, he has returned to the roost to do what he loves most. The building is Forties-modern, not fancy, and sits gleaming white in green gardens that are neat but not fussy. Established 20 years ago as a functional, friendly place from which to explore Jaipur and the surrounds, the hotel is just this. Bedrooms are smartly, sedately furnished and come with all mod cons (including good lighting – a treat in India); some rooms have very fine views. It is, however, the Colonel and his gentle wife, Indu, who make 'the house of the clouds' special – they love meeting new people and helping visitors uncover the hidden corners of Jaipur. The gardens are green, floral, walled and private. Croquet balls skim across the neat front lawn; a deckchair-lined pool is sunk into the grass at the back of which the Colonel's cosy travel bureau lies. No fuss, no pretence; the Meghniwas is run with all the trimmings of a western hotel yet has a family feel.

rooms	22: 21 doubles, 1 suite.
price	Rs1,600-Rs1,900. Suite Rs2,600. Singles Rs1,400-2,400. Plus 8% tax. Peak season: October-March.
meals	Breakfast Rs175. Lunch & dinner Rs275 each.
closed	Rarely.
directions	Half-way down Jai Singh highway, opp. ATM booth. 15-min auto-rickshaw ride from Jaipur station. Airport: Jaipur (12km, 30 mins).

Hotel

	Colonel & Mrs Indu Singh
tel	+91 (0)1412 202 034/5/6
mobile	+91 (0)9829 010 104
fax	+91 (0)1412 202 953
email	email@meghniwas.com
web	www.meghniwas.com

Map 4 Entry 62

Hotel Shahpura House

D-257 Devi Marg, Bani Park, Jaipur, 302 016 Rajasthan

One sighs with relief in India when sinking into a bed that is not like a marble plinth. Shahpura House has memorably soft beds. The seat of the head of the Shekhawat clan of Rajputs, the building stands in a residential enclave surrounded by high walls. It is relatively modern but has managed to avoid the worst of Fifties' Indian architecture by strictly following old architectural practices. Mixing Mughal and Indian styles, the facade with its domes lends a stately but not overbearing air. The Shekhawat influence is in the shape of hand-painted walls, stained-glass doors and skylights, and blown-glass-lamps – all set against pristine white walls and swathes of delicately inlaid marble. The place is immaculate and uncluttered, the bathrooms spotless, and the atmosphere inviting. Some of the old retainers of the royal household are still around, serving guests with gracious hospitality. People settle in for days, though the atmosphere is more hotel than guest house. And the candlelit dinners, sometimes accompanied by musicians, are delicious. *Horse-drawn carriages available for sightseeing.*

Hotel

rooms	34: 20 doubles, 14 suites.
price	Rs2,000. Suites Rs2,750 – Rs3,400. Plus 9% tax. Peak season: October-March; August.
meals	Breakfast Rs170. Lunch Rs325. Dinner Rs325.
closed	Rarely.
directions	In residential area of Bani Park, to west of Chandpol Gate. Airport: Jaipur (24km, 45 mins).

	Mr Surendra Shekhawat
tel	+91 (0)1412 202 293
res. no	+91 (0)1412 203 392
fax	+91 (0)1412 201 494
email	shahpurahous@usa.net
web	www.shahpurahouse.com

B

Map 4 Entry 63

Umaid Bhawan

D1-2A, Behind Collectorate, Behari Marg via Bank Road, Bani Park, Jaipur, 302 016 Rajasthan

Krishna dances through the halls and rooms of Umaid Bhawan, playfully delighting milk maids, decently of course. Equally heartening is that you'll find pennies remaining in your pockets after a stay here, a good-value choice of base for discovery of Jaipur. Serious looking, purple-backed furniture in rooms is lightened by glass ceilings and sweet *jharokha* balconies that look out onto the pool area, hemmed in by murals of rural Rajasthan. The sandstone pink-red building was first renovated in 1956 before becoming a hotel in 1993, yet three generations of the Rathore warrior clan have lived here since the turn of the last century. Military photographs line the walls but the current owner is far from ferocious and will happily give you the low-down of all that's worth seeing in the city. The hotel is in a quiet residential neighbourhood – although not quite the deer park it once was – and the old city is a short ride away. Surmounting the building are antique guard posts softened by cushions and low tables; lazy spots to enjoy a city sunset, or dinner served by friendly Nepalese waiters.

rooms	33: 28 doubles, 5 suites.
price	Rs1,600-Rs2,000.
	Suite Rs2,400-Rs2,800.
	Singles Rs1,500-Rs1,750.
	Peak season: October-March.
meals	Lunch & dinner Rs300 each.
closed	Rarely.
directions	Airport: Jaipur (21km, 20 mins).
	Train: Jaipur (0.8km, 5 mins).

Hotel

	Mr Karan Rathore
tel	+91 (0)1412 206 426
mobile	+91 (0)9314 503 423
fax	+91 (0)1412 207 445
email	email@umaidbhawan.com
web	www.umaidbhawan.com

Map 4 Entry 64

Alsisar Haveli
Sansar Chandra Road, Jaipur, 302 001 Rajasthan

Rajput interiors have a tendency to be unwelcoming: high ceilings, heavy furniture, grave ancestral portraits and an almost tangible stuffiness. This place is a little different. Though not entirely free of dark wood, the rooms are hugely varied and show a more considered design approach. The block-printed covers and curtains match the newly painted arches, and the old inlay and stained glass has been scrubbed and polished to keep its original sparkle. However, it is the unstuffiness of the atmosphere that makes Alsisar stand out. The few common areas are inviting and comfortable and where there are antiques, they are uncluttered and attractive. The original 1892 building and its more recent additions (there may be some building noise) stand in cosy grounds with great old neem trees and an inviting pool surrounded by high walls — a haven of peace. Stone elephants flank the steps up to the paved terrace where open fires flicker throughout the evening and turbaned waiters serve Rajasthani hotel food. Many people go out to eat, though the restaurant is adequate. *Daily Bhopa dance shows.*

Hotel

rooms	48: 20 doubles, 21 singles, 7 suites.
price	Rs3,000. Singles Rs2,400. Suites Rs3,650. Plus 10% tax. Peak season: October-mid-April.
meals	Breakfast Rs225. Lunch Rs350. Dinner Rs350.
closed	Rarely.
directions	Archway off Sansar Chandra Road, opposite Madawa Haveli. 10-minute rickshaw ride from station.

B 🖾 ⅄ ⌇

Map 4 Entry 65

	Mr Gaj Singh
tel	+91 (0)1413 268 290
res. no	+91 (0)1415 107 157/167
fax	+91 (0)1412 364 652
email	alsisar@satyam.net.in
web	www.alsisar.com

Arya Niwas

Behind Amber Towers, Sansar Chandra Road, Jaipur, 302 001 Rajasthan

Arya Niwas is unusual among Rajasthani hotels and is prized by the wandering hoardes of small-time international jewellery traders who settle in here for weeks on end. The hotel is efficient, friendly and great value. Tucked away down a side street, it's a retreat after the Jaipur mayhem – and its green lawn and trails of potted plants are a rare sight in a dusty town. On the long veranda, weary wanderers sink into low wicker chairs to drink sweet tea, wipe the dust from their brows, and muse. The atmosphere is convivial and the guests mostly mature and involved – it would be hard to be lonely here. You can totally relax without fear of being 'touted' or 'hawked', eat cheap and cheerful food, and buy from a 'fixed price' craft shop. Plain and functional, the building is frill-free and the simple bedrooms (some have no outside window though many have TV) are always clean – crisp white linen, polished tiled bathrooms, a separate bolt for your own padlock. The appeal lies in the rare feeling that you're getting just what you paid for. *Morning yoga.*

rooms	90: 60 doubles, 30 singles.
price	Rs600–Rs1,000.
	Singles Rs500–Rs700.
	Peak season: August–April.
meals	Breakfast Rs90.
	Lunch & dinner Rs120 each.
closed	Rarely.
directions	Behind Amber towers, off Sansar Chandra Road.
	Airport: Jaipur (20km, 30 mins).
	Train: Jaipur (2km, 10 mins).

Hotel

	Mr Tarun Bansal (Manager)
tel	+91 (0)1412 372 456
fax	+91 (0)1412 361 871
email	info@aryaniwas.com
	or aryahotel@sancharnet.in
web	www.aryaniwas.com

Map 4 Entry 66

Hari Mahal Palace

Jacob Road, Civil Lines, Jaipur, 302 006 Rajasthan

Those familiar with the term 'splendid isolation' will recognise the appeal of Hari Mahal Palace. Built by the descendants of Maharaja Prithvi Raj, balconies, windows and porticoes all bear Rajput influences, but the simple grandeur of this 1930s mansion, occupying its own (large) corner of a foreign field, is decidedly colonial. A huge lawn unfolds, in true British propriety – past wrought-iron garden furniture, umbrellas and drums of stacked firewood – towards tree-lined fringes interspersed by ordered flower beds. Marbled and expansive, rooms are traditionally decorated with gilt furniture, copper antiques and other original pieces still intact. Perhaps the tallest ceilings in Jaipur can be found in the bathrooms, reached through dressing rooms, that dwarf good-sized tubs. Breakfast can be enjoyed among the mini-palms of the charming inner courtyard, while gala dinners and mock weddings are among the more unusual services on offer. Some of the staff may have the air of retired curators... but this is a good place to escape the city, live in style and feel private.

Hotel

rooms	14: 11 doubles, 3 apartments.
price	Rs2,800–Rs3,500. Apartment Rs4,500. Plus 8% tax.
meals	Breakfast Rs150. Lunch Rs250. Dinner Rs300.
closed	Rarely.
directions	Airport: Jaipur (25 minutes). Train: Jaipur (10 minutes).

	Dr B P Singh
tel	+91 (0)1412 226 920 or (0)1412 221 399
fax	+91 (0)1412 226 920
email	info@harimahalpalace.com
web	www.harimahalpalace.com

B 🖂 🍶 👤 ➢ 👞

Map 4 Entry 67

Bissau Palace

Outside Chandpole Gate, Jaipur, 302 016 Rajasthan

Faded photos of past and present British royals take pride of place in the comfortable, wooden-floored sitting room where old weapons and vast portraits of steely-gazed ancestors remind you that peaceable Jaipur has seen more unruly days. The family were forced to build outside the Pink City walls because of their refusal to pander to the Mughal tormentors with whom the Maharaja of Jaipur had created a cosy alliance. The palace is therefore tucked away down an inconspicuous backstreet, off which you find the large driveway leading up to this austere edifice. Slightly scuffed around the edges, Bissau has an appealing informality – you can sit quaffing a cold beer in the living room without fear of upsetting etiquette, and feel unusually free of the old-world stuffiness that is synonymous with some heritage hotels. Juno, the present maharaja, is an affable, lively chap whose relaxed take on regal life infuses the hotel. The rooms have plain walls, delicately painted archways, heavy wooden beds and clean modern bathrooms. The suites are large and marvellous value. *Lawn tennis. Travel agency at hotel.*

rooms	45: 27 doubles, 18 suites.
price	Rs1,500-Rs1,800. Suites Rs2,100-Rs2,700. Plus 10% tax.
meals	Breakfast Rs150. Lunch & dinner Rs240 each.
closed	Rarely.
directions	Out of Chandpol Road & turn right. Keep right; hotel set back on left.

Hotel

Mr Sanjai Singh of Bissau

tel	+91 (0)1412 304 371
fax	+91 (0)1412 304 628
email	bissau@sancharnet.in
web	www.bissaupalace.com

Map 4 Entry 68

Diggi Palace

SMS Hospital Road, Jaipur, 302 004 Rajasthan

Perhaps the tranquil garden – mature trees fringing the big lawn, hundreds of potted plants, flowers and birds – draws people more than anything else and holds them for extra nights of rest from the hustle and bustle of the town. (It's just a rickshaw ride to the main sights and shops.) But what the vivacious Diggi family also manage so successfully is to show guests a way of Indian life that is privileged and traditional yet neither pompous nor narrow-minded. Everyone who works here is either family or from one of the villages near their country property. The hotel, open since 1990, is part of the original haveli of the Thakkurs of Diggi. You can choose from a wide number of rooms, from the simply functional to the fairly swish with their own bathrooms, sitting rooms and air conditioning. All rooms have TVs and hot showers. There's choice, too, about where to sit and what to eat. Breakfasts are relaxed affairs, with newspapers. Simple meals, with some home-grown vegetables are taken in the restaurant or on the veranda. Backpackers love it, some stay for months at a time. *Golf can be arranged.*

Hotel

rooms	43 doubles.
price	Rs900-Rs2,000. Peak season: October-March.
meals	Breakfast Rs125. Lunch & dinner from Rs150 each.
closed	Rarely.
directions	Take Sawai Ram Singh Road, turning right into Shivaji Marg, just after Maharani College, coming from Ajmeri Gate.

Mr Ram Pratap Singh

tel	+91 (0)1412 373 091
res. no	+91 (0)1412 366 120
fax	+91 (0)1412 370 359
email	reservations@hoteldiggipalace.com
web	www.hoteldiggipalace.com

B 人

Map 4 Entry 69

Castle Pachar

Pachar, District Sikar, 332 729 Rajasthan

Not the easiest place to find but you arrive to a courteous, old-fashioned welcome from members of the same family to whom the Maharaja of Jaipur gave the village of Pachar as a reward for bravery in battle. Staying here may remind you of visits to affable but formal relatives. The grandeur is faded but the central *rang mahal* is impressive: a giant carpet on the decorated stone floor, sink-in sofas and chairs with brightly coloured patchwork throws, and a massive chandelier. Some of the best bedrooms, with painted pillars and garden or village views, lead off the first-floor gallery. They have a smattering of family photos and books, and genuine old furniture with the odd modern touch. Bathrooms were state-of-the-art — a few decades ago. There's a pleasant dining room with more family-abilia, and the food is good, local and simply cooked — it's nice to see the papadums drying in the open air. Relax around the tree-shaded swimming pool or gaze out across the flat, open Rajasthani countryside from the rooftop terrace, and observe an Indian way of life. *Bullock cart rides can be arranged.*

rooms	15 doubles.
price	Rs1,800. Plus 10% tax. Peak season: October–March.
meals	Breakfast Rs125. Lunch Rs225. Dinner Rs275.
closed	Rarely.
directions	Take Bikaner road north out of Jaipur to Chomu, then left to Renwal Station & Kishangarh. Pachar is 9km north of Kishangarh. Not easy to find; phone ahead.

	Mr Hanuman Singh	
tel	+91 (0)1576 264 611	
res. no	+91 (0)1412 382 955	
fax	+91 (0)1412 373 671	
email	info@castlepachar.com	
web	www.castlepachar.com	

Hotel

Map 4 Entry 70

Roopangarh Fort

Roopangarh, Ajmer District, 305 814 Rajasthan

We can't promise all the delights of a 17th-century court but we can promise the luxury of space. Most bedrooms are bigger than those of your wildest fantasies, furnished with a rare individuality and an antidote to the magazine design culture. This was the abode of kings, a centre of culture and fine living and there is a lot to live up to – and somehow it happens. Where to begin? The sheer splendour of the scale, of course, but it is the sense of being somewhere very special that demands attention. Courtyards, decorated columns, green swards and courtyards, bougainvillea, cane chairs poised to receive you in marbled corners, a rooftop tennis court (why not?), bright red tables under decorated arches, a mad miscellany of marble in a bathroom. Then, lovely old mahogany desks against white walls, a chain mail suit on the wall above dining tables, polo sticks above the bed, an exquisite double/treble bed floating on a sea of white marble – on it goes. Yet this is not western luxury. Above it all looms the massively impressive fort, a comforting symbol of stability. *Complimentary camel rides.*

Hotel

rooms	19: 18 doubles, 1 suite.
price	Rs2,300-Rs3,000. Suite Rs2,500. Plus 8% tax. Peak season: October-February.
meals	Breakfast Rs200. Lunch Rs300. Dinner Rs350. Plus tax 9%.
closed	Rarely.
directions	Turn off Jaipur-Ajmer highway at Kishangarh; north for 22km along NH 8. Into Roopangarh; fort entrance at far end of main street.

	H H Maharaja Brajraj Singh
tel	+91 (0)1497 220 444
mobile	+91 (0)0982 917 510
fax	+91 (0)1463 242 001
email	roopangarhfort@yahoo.co.uk
web	www.royalkishangarh.com

B ♿ 🏃 ⊟ 人 🐦 👟

Map 4 Entry 71

Phool Mahal Palace
Kishangarh, 305 802 Rajasthan

By the old city gates and beneath its fort, this lakeside palace feels like a grand and quirky family home. It appears in paintings of the Kishangarh Miniature School and is home to India's version of the *Mona Lisa*, a beguiling 18th-century painting of sharp-profiled Radha. The Mararani is as passionate about her hotel venture as she is about local arts and culture; small study groups come to paint, draw or take part in jewellery workshops, and work with local artists. The bedrooms are individual, with all the essentials plus strong colours, ornate fabrics and some early furniture. All have murals reflecting the family's history, and local plant and birdlife (this is a great place for birdwatching once the lake has filled, post-monsoon). The deluxe rooms have the best watery views, but you can also gaze upon the lake from an armchair in the marble-tiled sitting room. Kishangarh is off the standard tourist trail, and a wander around the old buildings and the jostling market, where silversmiths and sweet-makers rub shoulders, is quite something.

rooms	17 doubles.
price	Rs1,800–Rs2,500. Plus 10% tax. Peak season: September–March.
meals	Breakfast Rs150. Lunch Rs250. Dinner Rs350.
closed	Rarely.
directions	On the lakeside by the gates into the old city beneath the fort.

	Mr D D Purohit	Hotel
tel	+91 (0)1463 247 405/505	
fax	+91 (0)1463 42001	
email	phoolmahalpalace@yahoo.com	
web	www.royalkishangarh.com	

B

Map 4 Entry 72

Bhanwar Vilas Palace
Karauli, 322 241 Rajasthan

The tiger stands facing the door, stuffed and splendid like so many of the ancestral figures that prowl the corridors of this house. Yet it was built in the 1930s because the maharaja's City Palace was getting beyond repair; much of the furniture came across to Bhanwar Vilas and looks magnificent here. There's a lot of mahogany, some modern striped sofas under the portraits of ancestors, some beautiful spaces and gentle plain colours on the walls. The suites are somewhat colonial and elderly, while the other rooms are being brightened with colourful fabrics and white walls. The cottage rooms are more basic. Bathrooms are excellent, without being state-of-the-art. It's a place of wide verandas and cool places to sit – a family mansion with a strong whiff of splendour; the Maharajah and his wife are often here and are delightfully welcoming. They are also deeply committed to their area and people and have a lot of projects on the go. Karauli is very alive and not at all touristy – so no touts. This is a lovely corner of Rajasthan and these interesting, unpompous people can bring it alive for you.

Hotel

rooms	37: 30 doubles, 7 suites.
price	Rs2,300-Rs2,750. Suites Rs3,000. Plus 8% tax. Peak season: October-April.
meals	Breakfast Rs180. Lunch Rs330. Dinner Rs350.
closed	Rarely.
directions	Karauli 60km off Jaipur-Agra highway; hotel not in Old City Palace. Airport: Jaipur-Agra (180km, 4.5 hours). Train: Gangapur (31km, 45 mins).

	H H Krishna Chandra Pal
tel	+91 (0)9414 054 257
res. no	+91 (0)1412 290 763
mobile	+91 (0)9414 059 257
email	karauli@sancharnet.in
web	www.karauli.com

B 🖂 🚜 🧎 🏊

Map 4 Entry 73

Dev Vilas

Village Khilchipur, Ranthambhore Road, Sawai Madhopur, 322 011 Rajasthan

To breakfast outside, overlooking the pool and the distant hills, is a joy. And on winter nights there are candles, braziers and a great fire to keep you warm... an enticing spot for swapping safari stories with fellow guests, both Indian and European. The comforts are considerable at this lavish new hotel, where everything is done with grace and good humour, including the early wake-up safari call. This you cannot miss – the Ranthambhore National Park, the most famous tiger reserve in India, is minutes away. (October to April is the time to visit.) Your entertaining host Mr Singh is passionate about nature and conservation, which adds to the fascination of the place. Expect tiger paintings and luxurious sofas in the bar, silk rugs, comfy chairs and perfect beds in the rooms, big white baths and fluffy white towels, pugmark-stone soap dishes with jars to match, and ayurvedic massage. Outside are vegetable gardens, a small formal garden, a giant metal sculpture of deer and, in the far corner, the family pet – an elderly elephant who will give you rides. Come to be thoroughly spoiled!

rooms	21: 15 doubles, 4 twins, 2 suites.
price	$225-$250. Full-board option. Peak season: October-March.
meals	Lunch & dinner Rs450 each.
closed	July-September.
directions	Fork left shortly before Khilchipur village; hotel on left, within sight. Airport: Jaipur (180km, 3.5 hours). Train: Sawai Madhopur (7km, 15 mins).

Hotel

	Balendu Singh
tel	+91 (0)7462 252 168
fax	+91 (0)7462 252 195
email	devvilas@datainfosys.net
web	www.devvilas.com

D 🖃 🛢 🏌 🏊

Map 4 Entry 74

Ranthambhore Bagh

Ranthambhore Road, Sawai Madhopur, 322 001 Rajasthan

Whatever this place may lack in comforts is compensated for by Aditya and Poonam. They are a vibrant, cheerful, hardworking couple, with natural smiles and endless energy. He's an amateur wildlife photographer and she a sculptress, so there is an artistic, eco-friendly mood. This is a great place for exploring the National Park; the railway station is nearby and there are bikes for hire. The building, on the outskirts of town, is around two small, unexciting courtyards of concrete and stone, enlivened by plants and amusing 'ethnic' decorations. The atmosphere is fun and friendly, the maps of the park are superb, the wildlife information excellent, and the game 'drives' are the main topic of conversation. Jeep safaris head out before breakfast or you can take a larger vehicle and book a day or two ahead. Bedrooms are basic but have crisp white linen, white-painted walls and traditional plaster. The luxurious tents have solid stone bases, beds and good linen and a 'bathroom' at the back. (Sound travels well through canvas!). It is charming – and a great place to unwind.

Safari lodge

rooms	23: 10 doubles, 1 family room, 12 tents.
price	$40. Tents $50. Peak season: October–April.
meals	Breakfast Rs150. Lunch Rs250. Dinner Rs300. Plus 12.5% tax.
closed	July–September.
directions	From Sawai Madhopur station take Ranthambhore Road towards National Park; 4km. Airport: Jaipur (175km, 3 hours).

Aditya & Poonam Singh

tel	+91 (0)7462 221 728
res. no	+91 (0)1126 914 417
mobile	+91 (0)9414 031 221
email	tiger@ranthambhorebagh.com
web	www.ranthambhorebagh.com

A 🦅 📖 🍶 🧘 ⛷ 👟

Map 4 Entry 75

Sher Bagh
Sherpur-Khiljipur, Sawai Madhopur, District Sawai Madhopur, 322 001 Rajasthan

This is Jaisal's brainchild. He has known the Ranthambhore National Park since his infancy, is deeply drawn by its magic and has created its first luxurious tented site. Tents, inspired by those of maharaja hunters, sit on plinths, have specially designed beds, verandas with rattan chairs, stunning shower rooms, huge soft pillows, lashings of hot water, heaters and fans. The bar/café has sofas and books, the camp fire is fun, you are surrounded by wildlife and there's a hillock from which to gaze on the ancient Aravalli hills. You are also closer to the park entrance than others in the area, so, no long morning drives in the back of the jeep. This is one of the finest places in the world for spotting wild tigers, and you have the keen eyes and the sharp ears of some experienced trackers at your disposal. Hunting was banned in 1971, Project Tiger was launched, and Jaisal, passionate about promoting constructive, sustainable tourism, is making his mark. Outdoor lunches are continental, dinners are Rajasthani, produce is fresh, local and organic. It is a joy to be here, and Usha and her staff are all smiles. *Safaris extra charge.*

rooms	12 tents for 2.
price	Full-board $300. Singles $270. Plus 10% tax. Peak season: November-March.
meals	Full-board only.
closed	15 April-September.
directions	7km from Sawai Madhopur along the Ranthambhore Road. Signed from National Park. Airport: Jaipur (170km, 4 hours). Train: Sawai Madhopur (15km, 25 minutes).

Safari lodge

	Mr Jaisal Singh
tel	+91 (0)7462 252 120/119
res. no	+91 (0)1123 743 194
fax	+91 (0)1123 312 118
email	sherbagh@vsnl.com
web	www.sherbagh.com

D 💳 🛁

Map 4 Entry 76

Brijraj Bhawan Palace

Civil Lines, Kota, 324 001 Rajasthan

A gorgeous palace, perched on the banks of the Chambal, built as the British Residency in 1830. Today it belongs to the Maharaja of Kota and is run as a small hotel; the royal family live on the uppermost floor, the guests below. Ijyaraj used to be a banker in Delhi and has brought a youthful zip to the place; the family are charming, the style 'hands-on'. Meet fellow guests – perhaps hosts – over dinner, held in the regal dining room or on a terrace overlooking the luminous river. Vegetables and herbs come from the kitchen garden, milk from the dairy and the menu should please all tastes: Indian, Rajasthani, continental, Chinese. Whatever you choose, it'll be good. Retreat to the as-splendid drawing room, or your reassuringly traditional bedroom, big enough to lounge in; some have dressing rooms and river views. The furniture dates to the Raj and hunting photographs and trophies abound. You are on the edge of Kota but this is a truly tranquil spot… beautiful gardens lead down to the river, birds trill in the shrubs and trees, shuttlecocks swoop. Such value, too. *Excursions to prehistoric etchings at Alinia.*

Hotel

rooms	7: 4 doubles, 1 single, 2 suites.
price	Rs2,350. Single Rs1,700. Suite Rs2,900. Plus 8% tax. Peak season: October–March.
meals	Breakfast Rs240. Lunch Rs375. Dinner Rs410. Plus 9% tax.
closed	Rarely.
directions	Near to the Collectorate Circle, right next to the PWD office on the river Chambal. Aiport: Jaipur (240km). Train: Kota (3km, 15 mins).

	Maharaja Brijraj Singh of Kota
tel	+91 (0)7442 450 529
fax	+91 (0)7442 450 057
email	brijraj@datainfosys.net
web	www.indianheritagehotels.com

B 🚶 🗁 🧎 ♨

Map 4 Entry 77

Shahpura Bagh
Shahpura, District Bhilwara, 311 404 Rajasthan

Shahpura Bagh would look very different if Rajadhiraj Nahar Singh had not mortgaged the family jewels – a century ago – to build earth dams and bring water to his people. There would be no pastures, mustard crops or evergreens and the 19th-century family home, a neat right-angle of limestone, would not be surrounded by lushness. Columns rise to staggered levels of vast flagstone terraces, great for yoga, and to an unusual purdah viewing gallery. At the top of the house, large and cool bedrooms are well served by light and by bathrooms with old claw-foot tubs, warmed by solar power. Eat together, and well, in the dining room as you feel for the secret switch under the table. The family will entertain you with hilarious anecdotes of Rajasthan's most "colourful characters" and royal life pre-Independence. Something of the past remains here: Shah Jehan's handprint for one, but most of all Uncle Indrajit, who continues a tradition of care as a homeopath. Something of yourself stays in this unhurried, beautiful place; you will return. *Great lakeside walks. Boat trips. Festival of Ram Dwara (March).*

rooms	8: 3 doubles, 5 suites.
price	Rs5,400. Suites Rs7,000. Plus 10% tax. Peak season: October–March.
meals	Lunch Rs350. Dinner Rs450.
closed	Rarely.
directions	220km between Jaipur & Udaipur on NH79. Airport: Jaipur (220km, 3.5 hours). Train: Bijainagar (50km, 1 hour).

Hotel

	Mr Jai Singh & Mr Sat Singh
tel	+91 (0)1484 222 077
mobile	+91 (0)9828 122 012/013
email	res@shahpurabagh.com
web	www.shahpurabagh.com

Map 4 Entry 78

Deogarh Mahal

Deogarh-Madaria, District Rajsamand, 313 331 Rajasthan

Built in 1670, huge, yellow-and-white and rambling, Deogarh Mahal has an aristocratic and eccentric spirit. It is also the most fairy-tale palace in Rajasthan. Step into the courtyard (replete with WWII jeep used for safaris) and you feel the scale and the warmth of the place. Staff are friendly and kind, the head cook is full of smiles and the princely brothers have energy and charm. Cauldrons of burning wood at night help keep winter chills at bay as you recline on the courtyard's wicker chairs. In summer, there's a bursting lotus-shaped pool – where the elephants once stood. Lose yourself in the bustling streets of the little town, join a camel and bullock-cart procession to the family's hunting lodge in the rugged, rocky hills, return to spacious and elegant bedrooms, one with a polished antique swing, another with a luxurious divan, all fabulous. Everything shimmers, from stained-glass windows to intricate bedspreads. This is a luxurious place – with unforgettable views.

Hotel

rooms	60: 34 doubles, 26 suites.
price	Rs5,390. Singles Rs4,455. Suites Rs7,040-Rs12,100. Plus 10% tax. Peak season: October-February.
meals	Breakfast Rs225. Lunch Rs350. Dinner Rs450. Plus 9% tax.
closed	Rarely.
directions	Airport: Udaipur (135 km, 2 hours), Train: Deogarh (0.5 km, 5 minutes).

	Mr Veerbhavra Singh
tel	+91 (0)2904 252 777
res. no	+91 (0)2904 253 333
mobile	+91 (0)9314 420 016
email	info@deogarhmahal.com
web	www.deogarhmahal.com

C & 🍴 📧 ◊ 人 ⟶ ♨

Map 4 Entry 79

Castle Bijaipur
Bijaipur, District Chittorgarh, 312 001 Rajasthan

In a stunningly remote spot in southern Rajasthan, this 16th-century castle once defended the Mewar empire from the Mughals and Marathas. The multi-layered, icing-white building, still in the family, has recently opened its doors to guests… yet little has changed! Furniture and linen are basic, hot water and electricity can be erratic, and the choice of menu is limited. Yet the views are breathtaking, your host, the Thakur, and his family are charming, and the bedrooms, although sparse, look over the colourful inner garden (suites have sitting areas and large carved beds). Tasty meals are served in the half-open dining room – or by the pool – and cooked by the family's retainers. Afterwards, recline with an evening drink and watch tribal folk dances in the garden. It feels utterly remote here, amid the serene Vindhyachal ranges, and yet Chittorgarh, former capital of the state of Mewar, is really not too far. Consider a horse or camel safari into the neighbouring state, and don't miss the fascinating towns of Begun and Menal. A simple, hospitable place. *Horse safaris (1-7 days) & trekking.*

rooms	22: 12 doubles, 10 suites.
price	Rs1,855. Suites Rs2,170. Peak season: October-March.
meals	Breakfast Rs150. Lunch Rs250. Dinner Rs350.
closed	Rarely.
directions	Airport: Udaipur (130km, 2 hrs). Train: Chittorgarh (40km).

Hotel

	Mr Rao Narendra Singh
tel	+91 (0)1472 240 099
fax	+91 (0)1472 240 099 or (0)1472 243 563
email	hpratapp@hotmail.com
web	www.castlebijaipur.com

Map 4 Entry 80

Devi Garh

Village Delwara, Tehsil Nathdwara, District Rajsamand, Rajasthan

Heading along the narrow track, you catch a sudden, thrilling glimpse of battlements, turrets and towers… then a small army of guards salutes your arrival. Enter one of India's finest heritage hotels, where cool design and neutral colours are offset by amber silk and flashes of gold and silver. The 18th-century palace-fort is a modern take on Rajput design, and the Indian industralist family who saved it have achieved something rare and special. Immerse yourself in your luxuriously minimalist suite, whose walls are traced with animals and trees and whose views sweep over village dwellings to hills beyond. Dine on sophisticated food in a courtyard filled with banana trees and spider lilies, or head downstairs to sample delicious combinations of 'street food' from a sumptuous divan. Themed candlelit dinners may be held in unusual places, including a magical turret. Treat yourself to an ayurvedic massage after a camel trek to the hunting lodge of maharajas; bask in the loveliness of verdant walled gardens and marble rooftop pool. *Star gazing, kite flying & bicycling.*

rooms	39 suites.
price	Suites $400-$1,300. Plus 8% tax. Peak season: October-March.
meals	Breakfast $15. Lunch $30. Dinner $35. Plus 12.5% tax.
closed	Rarely.
directions	North-east of Udaipur on NH 8. Airport: Udaipur (27km). Train: Udaipur (30km).

Hotel

	Mr B Venkatesh
tel	+91 (0)2953 289 211/220
res. no	+91 (0)1123 354 554
mobile	+91 (0)9414 170 211
email	reservations@deviresorts.com
web	www.deviresorts.com

G 🛏 ▤ 🍷 🧘 🏊 🚲 👟

Map 4 Entry 81

Udai Bilas Palace
Dungarpur, 314 001 Rajasthan

Escape the hubbub of daily life and wind down in 'antique India'. Lying on the banks of the Gaibsagar Lake – a paradise for birds – the hilltop palace, still a royal residence, has a supremely serene setting and a deliciously faded grandeur. Greenery intermingles with the history; sweep away the palms to find a swimming pool with a sunken bar and water-pouring elephants. The palace bursts with arches, vaulted windows and tiles and frescos among the finest examples of their kind. No less exquisite are the suites, each with its own character, from traditional and floral to Art Deco, all with balconies, plump pillows, sumptuous divans. Big marble bathrooms have handmade soaps and luxurious towels. Guests come together for buffet dinner at the huge table in a dining room lined with stags and crowned by crystal chandeliers; spot more exotic hunting trophies as you lounge in the Africa Room. Both rooms have a 1930s Scottish lodge feel and staff are attentive – supremely so. There's boating on the lake and the family's 13th-century palace Juna Mahal awaits discovery. *Performances of music & dance.*

rooms	22: 3 doubles, 3 singles, 16 suites.
price	Rs3,850. Singles Rs3,025. Suites Rs4,600-Rs5,750. Plus 8% tax. Peak season: October-March.
meals	Breakfast Rs250. Lunch Rs400. Dinner Rs450. Plus 9% tax.
closed	Never.
directions	120km from Udaipur; 175km from Ahmedabad. Airport: Udaipur (130km, 2 hours).

	Mr M. K. Harshvadhan Singh
tel	+91 (0)2964 230 808
res. no	+91 (0)1245 068 852
fax	+91 (0)2964 231 008
email	contact@udaibilaspalace.com
web	www.udaibilaspalace.com

Hotel

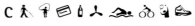

Map 3 Entry 82

Karni Fort, Bambora

Bambora Village, Tehsil Girva, Udaipur, Rajasthan

The terraced gardens of the 300-year-old fort slope down to one of the most romantic swimming pools in India. Peacocks strut, birds trill, frogs serenade and sunsets can be arranged from every window. The 1710 Sisodia outpost has been restored from a ruinous state, the comforts are princely and the cheerful young staff cannot do enough for you. Towels are laid out by the pool, massages with aromatic oils are yours for the asking. High up above Bambora, with views to the rolling Aravalli hills, this is a deeply rural spot. Picnic by the reservoir, joyous with tree-pies and bee-eaters, kingfishers, swallows and kites; cool off in the marble pool, complete with island. Inside, gold furniture and glittering silks abound. The bar, with fake gas lamps, is regal, and the bedrooms are lush and large, with arches, cornices and bay windows for views. Meals are buffet style or you dine on your balcony; many rooms have one. When the pampering palls, there's the village bazaar to browse and local tribes to visit: book a horse safari. Udaipur, dominated by the labyrinthine City Palace, is 50 kilometres away.

Hotel

rooms	30: 19 doubles, 11 suites.
price	Rs3,450. Suites Rs3,750. Singles Rs2,450. Plus 10% tax. Peak season: October–March.
meals	Breakfast Rs150. Lunch Rs275. Dinner Rs375. Plus 9% tax.
closed	Never.
directions	Airport/train: Udaipur (50km, 1.5 hours).

	Mr Kanwar Vikramaditya Singh Sodawas
tel	+91 (0)2942 398 283/4
res. no	+91 (0)2912 512 101/2/3/4
fax	+91 (0)2912 512 105
email	karnihotels@satyam.net.in
web	www.karnihotels.com

B

Map 3 Entry 83

Amet Haveli
Outside Chandpole, Udaipur, 313 001 Rajasthan

First came the restaurant, dominating the terrace that juts out into the water. It has become an institution in its own right, with fabulous, unfussy food and views that rival those from any lakeside in the world. A huge mango tree casts its shade over the wrought-iron chairs and marble-topped tables – more Provençale than Mewari, though certainly with a touch of India. The old handlebar-moustachioed owner saw that his spot was the envy of Udaipur, and renovated a few of his collapsed rooms. The result is ten bedrooms done with admirable restraint and taste. They have a low-ceilinged, airy, almost Mediterranean mood, with bare white interiors that can only work in a hot country. Any heritage touches are subtle: where there are coloured lines they accentuate the curves of the arches, and where patterns are used they are modest. Neither hotel nor homestay, this is one of Udaipur's most intriguing places to stay – the luxury lies not in opulent furnishings or obsequious staff, but in that feeling that you have found somewhere genuinely special. Come to eat if you cannot stay.

rooms	10: 3 doubles, 7 suites.
price	Rs1,250. Suites Rs3,000. Plus 10% tax. Peak season: November-February.
meals	Breakfast Rs200. Lunch Rs350. Dinner Rs400. Plus 10% tax.
closed	Mid-March, during Holi Festival.
directions	Outside Chandpole on Hanuman Ghat, 2km from main town. Opposite City Palace.

Guest house

Mr P P Singh

tel	+91 (0)2942 431 085
mobile	+91 (0)9414 163 085
fax	+91 (0)2942 431 085 or +91 (0)2942 522 447
email	regiudr@datainfosys.net

A 🖃 ₫

Map 3 Entry 84

Fateh Prakash Palace

City Palace, Udaipur, 313 001 Rajasthan

Ask for a room with a view. The lakeside sunsets are exquisite. Rooms in the old palace are aging gracefully and are full of character; those in the new Dovecote wing have black-and-white chequered marble floors, *jharokha* balconies and marble bathrooms. Heavy wool rugs and oil paintings of majestic Mewar ancestors line these winding corridors, and fabrics are dark and rich. Yet the atmosphere verges on the cosy, unusually so in a region where architects have created open, cool spaces to combat the challenges of Rajasthani summers. The spaces are smaller, too — more European castle than Indian palace. Walking along the tapestried gallery that looks down into the mighty Durbar Hall to find your suite feels a bit like sneaking about behind the scenes in a museum — you really do feel you're staying in a maharaja's palace and a working, living one at that. The present Maharaja's vision is to create a pragmatic and sustainable living heritage in the city palace that is relevant to the society of today.

Hotel

rooms	31: 21 doubles, 10 suites.
price	$275-$350. Suites $350. Plus tax. Peak season: October–March.
meals	Breakfast $10-$15. Lunch & dinner $15-$20 each. Plus tax.
closed	Rarely.
directions	In centre of City Palace complex.

	Mr A Singh (Manager)
tel	+91 (0)2942 528 016
fax	+91 (0)2942 528 006
email	crs@udaipur.hrhindia.com
web	www.hrhindia.com

E ▨ ⬦ 人

Map 3 Entry 85

Shiv Niwas Palace
City Palace, Udaipur, 313 001 Rajasthan

The old royal guest house, a crescent-shaped building wrapped exquisitely around an 1880s marble swimming pool and half-moon courtyard, has an almost European air and most rooms are free from the fussy mirror-work and spindly furniture used in other palaces in Rajasthan. The best rooms lie around the pool, raised on a wide marble terrace that runs round the courtyard, and some with truly regal views across Lake Pichola. Yet it is not the bedrooms you come for (in spite of silver bowed beds and trickling bedroom fountains in the suites) but the knowledge that you are sleeping within the walls of a living, working palace – the main focus of the most romantic city in India. Entered through huge, two-storey wooden doors and with a ceiling that reaches heavenwards, the bar's stately palace interior suggests – wrongly – the ties between imperial Britain and Udaipur's royal family. Though the counter is padded leather, the footrail polished brass and the chandeliers of European fluted crystal, the walls are hand-painted and inlaid in traditional Mewari style. A vibrant, fascinating place. *Solar-powered boats available.*

rooms	36: 19 doubles, 17 suites.
price	$275. Suites $350-$1,000. Ask for low season rates. Plus tax. Peak season: October-March.
meals	Breakfast $10-$15. Lunch & dinner $15-$20 each. Plus 12% tax.
closed	Rarely.
directions	In centre of City Palace complex.

Hotel

	Mr H A Subramanium (Manager)
tel	+91 (0)2942 528 016
fax	+91 (0)2942 528 006
email	crs@udaipur.hrhindia.com
web	www.hrhindia.com

Map 3 Entry 86

Lake Palace Hotel

PO Box No 5, Lake Pichola, Udaipur, 313 001 Rajasthan

Stay here and you're part of the views. Like a glittering white liner, Udaipur's classic heritage hotel rests in, not on, Lake Pichola. When the lake is full, there's no finer setting. Built as a summer palace in 1746, set among fairy-tale gardens, it was restored to its original glitzy glory in 2000. Prepare to be seduced by scalloped archways, blue glassware, cream sofas, intimate courtyards, flute music from the roof… and the knowledge that *Octopussy* was filmed here. Regal splendour is matched by old-world charm and it's hard to say where the public rooms end and the gardens begin. No outdoor dining, sadly, but the glassware is crystal, the cutlery silver and the service first-class. Note: the restaurant is open to non-hotel guests, so can be busy. Bedrooms, from small to vast, display a multitude of princely detail: marble pillars, carved screens, intricate paintings, mosaic'd floors and a scattering of silk rugs and cushions that royal wallets can afford. There are snowy white towels in marble bathrooms, coconut milk massages in the spa and the rooftop or pontoon for the best outdoor views.

Hotel

rooms	83: 52 doubles, 31 twins.
price	$370. Suites $550-2,500. Plus 8% tax.
meals	Breakfast $17. Lunch $35. Dinner $45. Plus 12% tax.
closed	Rarely.
directions	In the middle of Lake Pichola. You pick up the hotel launch from beneath the City Palace.

Ashrafi Matcheswala (Manager)

tel	+91 (0)2942 528 800
fax	+91 (0)2942 528 700
email	lakepalace.udaipur@tajhotels.com
web	www.tajhotels.com

F 太 🖻 🛈 人 🏊

Map 3 Entry 87

Jagat Niwas Palace Hotel
23-25 Lal Ghat, Udaipur, 313 001 Rajasthan

You know you're onto something good when you see local families eating in the restaurant. The food here is wonderful: simple, generous, and enjoyed with views through the *jharokha* arches to the Aravalli hills beyond. Rarely do you see people sitting in *jharokhas* – they serve more to decorate than to entice – yet here, clutches of folk recline in the overhanging balconies three storeys above the lake. Jagat Niwas is more like a hotel than its next door neighbour, Kankarwa Haveli (entry 89) – there are shops, an internet café and a travel desk – but this more formal set-up doesn't dampen the easy atmosphere. It's fine to lounge about. The building is large and ramshackle, dominated by the central split courtyard around which run the wide, marbled verandas dotted with pot plants and the odd antique. The rooms are less cluttered than most, with the usual dark wooden beds and miniatures in alcoves and Rajasthani bedspreads to add colour. A perfect place in which to organise yourself, and if you don't stay here, at least come to eat.
Camel trips & boating on lake.

rooms	29: 25 doubles, 4 suites.
price	Rs1,250-Rs1,895. Suites Rs3,000-Rs3,999. Plus 10% tax. Peak season: October-March.
meals	Breakfast Rs185. Lunch Rs350. Dinner Rs400.
closed	Rarely.
directions	Right on the Lal Ghat. Enter through a covered alley on right of entrance to Kankarwa Haveli. Airport: Dabok (25km, 40 mins). Train: Udaipur (3km, 10 mins).

Hotel

	Mr Vimal Sahu
tel	+91 (0)2942 420 133
fax	+91 (0)2942 418 512
email	mail@jagatniwaspalace.com
web	www.jagatniwaspalace.com

Map 3 Entry 88

Kankarwa Haveli
26 Lal Ghat, Udaipur, 313 001 Rajasthan

This is heritage as it should be. There is nothing extra here, no tat, no plastic, no hassle; it is a romantic, laid-back, lakeside guest house run by delightful people. Indeed, the rooms are 'to die for', intelligently renovated to show the simple majesty of the architecture. Cushioned *jharokhas* hang over the Lal Ghat steps, delicately stitched lace-work curtains stretch across the arched windows and Rajasthani block-printed bedspreads provide the only real dose of colour. The interiors, although sparse, are immaculately maintained; the old building is a handsome structure in which it would have been sacrilege to go for fuss. There is a refreshing absence of mirror-work, glass inlay or coloured walls that can go so 'wrong'; simplicity is the hallmark and the essence. Your host is an intelligent man, relaxed and extremely helpful. His weakness is magazines: there's an unexpectedly huge collection of glossies! Those who return each year — having happened upon a place so close to ideal — often add to the pile. Wonderful value. *Vegetarian meals, apart from breakfast, served on roof terrace.*

Guesthouse

rooms	15 doubles.
price	Rs750-Rs1,850. Plus 8% tax. Peak season: July-April.
meals	Breakfast Rs200. Lunch Rs150-Rs250. Dinner Rs150-Rs250.
closed	Rarely.
directions	Right in the Lal Ghat. You can't miss it. Airport: Dabok (25km, 30 mins). Train: Udaipur (10 mins).

	Mr Janardan Singh
tel	+91 (0)2942 411 457
fax	+91 (0)2942 521 403
email	kankarwahaveli@hotmail.com or khaveli@yahoo.com
web	www.indianheritagehotels.com

A Ѫ ₸ ▤ ⅄ 👞

Map 3 Entry 89

Udai Kothi
Hanuman Ghat, Udaipur, 313 001 Rajasthan

There's a refreshingly new gloss about Udai Kothi and its precarious layers of white that might just shake its illustrious neighbours out of their complacent opulence. Balconies, arches and exterior art rise, like a fantastic wedding cake, towards what is arguably the best roof-top terrace in town. It's a great vantage point with a pool and romantic jacuzzi, but the best time is evening and dinner, served from a silver buffet, when the whole of Udaipur lights up below you. Sitting comfortably within modern surrounds, four-posters and antique pieces lend stateliness to bedroom scenes, cushioned alcoves overlook the precipitous frontage and marble stretches all the way into solid bathrooms. Bhuwneshwari has an eye for beautiful things to spoil her "baby" and the hotel is filled with collectables from her travels. There are surprising touches in the garden too, including a house shrine and musicians' performance area. An almost-politician turned entrepreneur, it was husband V V Singh who built Udai Kothi from scratch six years ago. Even with a scrambled grandeur, no wobbling white elephant this.

rooms	25: 16 doubles, 9 suites.
price	Rs3,300–Rs3,800. Suites Rs4,300. Plus 10% tax.
meals	Breakfast Rs275. Lunch Rs300. Dinner Rs400.
closed	Rarely.
directions	Airport: Udaipur (24km). Train: Udaipur (3km).

Hotel

	Mr Vishwa Vijay Singh
tel	+91 (0)2942 432 810/812
fax	+91 (0)2942 430 412
email	udaikothi@yahoo.com
web	www.udaikothi.com

Map 3 Entry 90

Rangniwas Palace Hotel

Lake Palace Road, Udaipur, 313 001 Rajasthan

It's rare to find a Rajasthani heritage hotel with such an informal atmosphere. There are no turbaned doormen, no hushed attendants, no rules and no fusty managers. You can splash in the pool and lounge in the grass courtyard – people 'hang out' here. Run by the affable Vikram, whose regal past is all but hidden by liberal charm, the hotel is an odd mix of 'backpacker' and 'heritage'. There's a dark austerity that comes from heavy rosewood furniture and low lighting. One suite has a massive bathroom with two loos, wooden screens, an Oxford bath and swathes of marble. Its adjoining bedroom is cool and dark, with double doors that swing open to the marbled balcony over the courtyard. It is grand, a feeling created by dark, colonial wooden furniture and high ceilings, though the delicate glass inlay and handpainted lotus flowers soften the mood. The main rooms are charming: those upstairs have cosy *jharokha* balconies and plenty of space, the downstairs ones are geared more towards younger travellers. Slightly Victorian in design, Rangniwas is easy, perfectly comfortable and unpretentious.

Hotel

rooms	24: 18 doubles, 6 suites.
price	Rs660-Rs1,100. Suites Rs1,800-Rs,2,500. Plus 10% tax.
meals	Breakfast Rs175. Lunch Rs300. Dinner Rs350.
closed	Rarely.
directions	On the Lake Palace Road. Well-signed.

	Mr I C Shrimali
tel	+91 (0)2942 523 890
fax	+91 (0)2942 527 264
email	rangniwas75@hotmail.com
web	www.rangniwaspalace.com

A 人 ≈

Map 3 Entry 91

Devra

Sisarma-Burja Road, Kalarohi, Udaipur, Rajasthan

Wraparound verandas and a sweeping roof terrace give endless views of the
Udaipur countryside yet that ancient city is beguilingly close. Across Lake Pichola
the City Palace glints while on a nearby hill stands the Monsoon Palace. Inspired
by her family home, Jyoti has designed a modern building and tucked in a garden
strewn with statuary, capturing the warmth and intimacy of a private house and
adding a swish of class. Lounges – more than strictly necessary – are scattered
with over-size wicker armchairs, low tables and earthy-toned cushions. Plenty of
space to be alone or share sightseeing stories with fellow guests. Family photos
and fresh flowers give an informal feel which continues in the bedrooms –
uncluttered spaces of classically styled furniture, some four-posters, rich fabrics
and mosaic floors, and bed linen as crisply white as the bathrooms. Meals –
outside if possible – are from the organic garden or Jyoti's family farm. Chill out
(no TVs, no phones) and let Jyoti suggest tomorrow's trip, arrange a yoga lesson
or fix a cool drink. Warm, professional and cultured, your hostess spoils you.

rooms	4 doubles.
price	Rs2,800.
	Peak season: October-March.
meals	Breakfast Rs150. Lunch Rs250.
	Dinner Rs350.
closed	May-June.
directions	Airport: Udaipur (32km, 40 mins).
	Train: Udaipur City (13km, 20 mins).

Guest house

	Jyoti Jasol (Manager)
tel	+91 (0)2942 431 049
mobile	+91 (0)9828 163 311
fax	+91 (0)2942 431 049
email	devra2004@india.com
web	www.devraudaipur.com

Map 3 Entry 92

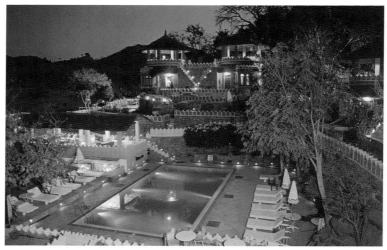

The Aodhi Hotel
Kumbhalgarh, Kelwara, 313 325 Rajasthan

It's one of the smartest hotels in Rajasthan, yet you are wrapped in nature. The excitement starts on the journey here: carts crowd the roads and buffalo move for no-one. The Aodhi is a new hotel that exudes an old-world charm. And it's an outdoorsy place that blends beautifully with the landscape – hard to see where the stone and thatch ends and the mountains begin. At its heart lies a crystal-blue pool and coffee bar with views of the dense hills, and beyond, the private suites and mini hunting lodges for two – linked by walkways and gardens and a stream that appears during the monsoon. Bedrooms are themed, bathrooms white. His Highness Shriji Arvind Singh Mewar devotes most of his time to various projects and lets his young staff get on with the job – and how! Dressed in burgundy suits and white turbans, they are fabulously professional yet full of smiles. No buffet meals here, just first-class service in a restaurant with a huge fire under a copper hood to keep chills at bay. A mile away at Kumbhalgarh is one of the few panther reserves in India – and an impressive ancient fort.

rooms	26: 23 doubles, 3 suites.
price	Rs5,000-Rs6,500. Plus tax. Peak season: Oct-March.
meals	Breakfast Rs225-Rs275. Lunch & dinner Rs300-Rs375.
closed	Rarely.
directions	Airport: Udaipur (105km, 2.5 hours). Train: Udaipur (90km, 2 hours).

Hotel

	Mr Chavhan (Manager)
tel	+91 (0)2954 242 341 to 46
res. no	+91 (0)294 528 008
fax	+91 (0)294 242 8008
email	crs@udaipur.hrhindia.com
web	www.hrhindia.com

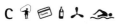

Map 3 Entry 93

Rawla Narlai
Village Narlai, Pali District, Rajasthan

Anyone looking for the Heritage Experience on a small scale should come here. The regal 17th-century hunting lodge is tucked into the tiny, holy village of Narlai – alongside some 300 temples – and is exceptionally peaceful. Rajput arches, porticoes and balconies rise on two levels, their once-white brilliance tempered to a faded grandeur. Expect to be warmly greeted by Mr Ajay Pal, led into a bourganvillea'd courtyard-lawn for tea and served by a tremendously turbaned staff. Later you will bed down in a white, luxury, carpeted tent – or a small but cosy bedroom in the Palace where elegant quilts adorn good beds, morning sunshine filters through cool blue drapes and embossed doors add authenticity. The covered lounge area is sumptuous with rich oranges and reds and a host of royal portraits (the lodge is still owned by the family), while the upstairs terrace is surprisingly bohemian; recline on faded yet colourful mattresses and cushions and soak up views of village and hills. Best of all are the weekly processions by ox-cart to extravagantly candlelit dinners in the old stepwell – sublime.

rooms	30: 21 doubles, 4 suites, 5 tents.
price	Rs4,500. Suites Rs5,000. Luxury tents Rs5,500. Plus 10% tax. Peak season: September–March.
meals	Lunch Rs400. Dinner Rs550. Thali Rs650. Plus 8% tax.
closed	Rarely.
directions	Midway between Jodphur & Udaipur, 25km from Ranakpur temples.

Hotel

	Mr Ajay Pal
tel	+91 (0)2934 260 443/425
fax	+91 (0)2934 260 596
email	reservations@ajitbhawan.com
web	www.ajitbhawan.com

Map 3 Entry 94

Chhatra Sagar
Nimaj, Pali District, 306 303 Rajasthan

A chance to star in your own Indian epic. The savannah unfolds from across the banks of a 100-year-old family-built reservoir, overlooked by your white Shikar tent and home to over 250 species of migratory birds. All this makes for a wonderful view from atop the nearby hill, well worth the sharp climb if only for the reward of a "summit sundowner" courtesy of Harsh, the Stetson-wearing owner. Alternatively, relax in your own sit-out and witness the birds give their daily fly-by performances. Smartly contained within a rigging of white canvas and furnished in elegant Rajput style, bedrooms cause you to teeter on the edge of tent-reality, while marble and slate 'bathrooms' transport you to another – indoor – dimension completely; there's hot water too. A (second?) honeymoon can easily be imagined here as you are warmed by camp fires and dine in style by candlelight. All is exemplary, from lessons on village lore to surely the freshest (and helpfully explained) food in the region. Head to bed by torchlight and snuggle in with a hot water bottle.

Under canvas

rooms	11 tents.
price	Full-board Rs12,000. Singles Rs10,000. Includes jeep & birdwatching tour.
meals	Full-board only.
closed	April-September.
directions	2 hours from Jodhpur on Ajmer-Jodhpur highway.

	Nandi & Harsh Vardhan
mobile	+91 (0)9414 123 118
email	harsh@chhatrasagar.com
web	www.chhatrasagar.com

Map 4 Entry 95

Rohet Garh
Village P.O., Rohet, District Pali, Rajasthan

An established heritage hotel, but a family affair; the Singhs speak excellent English and are welcoming and delightful. Keen riders, too, and breeders of the beautiful Marwari horse, they can take guests out on Bishnois village 'safaris'. The fortified desert home of the Rathores' descendants, on the banks of a birdlife-rich lake, has been beautifully restored in traditional style, and every room and space skilfully painted with traditional Indian scenes. Semi-circular verandas are furnished with wicker seating and red and gold cushions; bedrooms, some large, some less so, are bright, airy and charmingly designed by Mrs Singh. Expect matching soft furnishings, spotless linen and views over garden or lake. Peacocks perch under finely carved archways and delicious buffets are brought outdoors where you dine next to a lovely pool – illuminated at night, surrounded by flowers, serenaded by musicians. After a trip into the desert (courtesy of camel, bike, horse or jeep), take a massage, lounge on the rooftop terrace, soak up the views. An engaging stopover on the road south from Jodhpur to Udaipur.

rooms	34: 29 doubles, 2 singles, 3 suites.
price	Rs3,500-Rs4,000. Singles Rs2,750. Suites Rs5,000. Plus 10% tax. Peak season: October-March.
meals	Breakfast Rs250. Lunch Rs400. Dinner Rs500.
closed	Rarely.
directions	Airport/train: Jodhpur (40km, 45 minutes).

Hotel

	Mr Sidharth Singh
tel	+91 (0)2936 268 231/531
res. no	+91 (0)2912 431 161
mobile	+91 (0)9314 711 016
email	rohethouse@dataone.in
web	www.rohetgarh.com

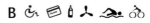

Map 3 Entry 96

Fort Chanwa

VPO Luni, Dist. Jodhpur, Luni, 342 802 Rajasthan

The impressive, slightly austere fortress, carved out of the famous red sandstone of Jodhpur, is a fine example of the architecture of 18th-century Rajasthan. Discover ornately carved lattice work friezes, intricate *jharokhas*, courtyards, towers, little passages, unexpected stairways and secret pavilions that lead to rooftops with shimmering views over the village to the desert beyond. Owned by the son of one of the uncles of the current Maharaja of Jodhpur, Fort Chanwa was close to ruin before its reincarnation as a luxury hotel – now the tour groups descend. Bedrooms are cool, high-ceilinged, beautiful: here an exquisite arch, there a splash of coloured glass, a decorative wall hanging, an antique bed. The bar and bazaar lend bustle and magic to the evenings, the staff are delightful, the food is tasty, there's a serene pool, an ayurveda spa and croquet in the wonderful oasis-like gardens. The village of Luni is interesting and unspoilt, though the honking of the nearby trains can be a distraction – hail a horse, camel or jeep and escape into the desert.

rooms	47 twins/doubles.
price	Rs3,000–Rs6,000. Plus 10% tax.
meals	Breakfast Rs175. Lunch Rs300. Dinner Rs375.
closed	Rarely.
directions	Airport/train: Jodhpur (35km, 45 minutes).

Hotel

	Mr Veer Vikram Singh
tel	+91 (0)2931 284 216
res. no	+91 (0)1141 646 287
fax	+91 (0)1146 252 85
email	info@fortchanwa.com
web	www.fortchanwa.com

C 🏃 📧 🍾 🧘 🏊

Map 3 Entry 97

Ajit Bhawan Palace

Near Circuit House, Jodhpur, 342 002 Rajasthan

Close to the heart of the lovely Blue City, yet peaceful and surrounded by trees, the palace is still home to the Maharaja. Behind the lobby is a public room lined with portraits and golden beige sofas but the nicest places to relax are outside – in secluded spots near the curvaceous pool and its wonderful, cascading water wheel. Bedrooms, suites and two tent 'villages' are linked by walkways through coconut palms and mature trees creating a sense of intimacy – hard to believe this is a 100-bed hotel! Staff are young, friendly and eager to please. Bedrooms are individually and traditionally designed, their solid beds beautified with Rajastani covers, crisp sheets and feather pillows. Bathrooms – even those in the tents – are lovely, new and 'eco', their used water channelled to the gardens. From the baby elephant frolicking by the entrance to the bird cages illuminated at night, every detail will charm you. And as you rest in the shade of an oak, sated on sweet pastries, eggs and fresh fruits, serenaded by chipmunks and birds, you'll vow to return. *Horse safaris can be arranged. Vintage cars for hire.*

rooms	55: 50 doubles, 5 suites. 10 tents for 2-3.
price	Rs2,400-Rs3,000. Suites Rs3,500. Plus 10% tax. Peak season: October–March.
meals	Breakfast included. Lunch Rs450. Dinner Rs600.
closed	Never.
directions	Right in the centre of Jodhpur, 2km from the train station.

	Mr Chetan
tel	+91 (0)2912 510 410
fax	+91 (0)1126 221 419
email	reservations@ajitbhawan.com
web	www.ajitbhawan.com

Hotel

Map 3 Entry 98

Pal Haveli

Gulub Sagar, Jodhpur, 342 001 Rajasthan

Dine on the roof terrace, the bewitching panorama of the Blue City rolled out beneath you – unforgettable. The haveli was built by the Thakur of Pal in 1847 and has been lived in by his descendants ever since. Its golden walls rise directly from the street, and enfold a series of central courtyards. Though recently turned into a hotel (and continuously being improved), this is still a family home with an intimate feel. If you're lucky, you'll be invited to join the charming owners for cocktails in their treasure-filled sitting room. The bedrooms are gorgeous, each in an individual way, their cream walls and cool floors contrasting with reds, oranges and golds of the Rajasthani fabrics. Unexpected touches – antique coloured glass squares in doors and windows, hand-painted pillars and archways – add delight. There are also a beautiful, chandeliered restaurant (rarely used as guests find the roof terrace irresistible) and a fine, formal sitting area, open to a courtyard. The place is run by the young son of the current Thakur, passionate about his heritage and eager to share it. A swimming pool is planned.

rooms	20 doubles.
price	Rs1,500-Rs1,800.
meals	Lunch Rs250.
	Dinner Rs300.
closed	Rarely.
directions	A 10-minute walk from the clocktower towards the Fort.

Guesthouse

	Mr Mahesh Karan Singh Rathore
tel	+91 (0)2913 093 328
	or (0)2912 638 344
email	palhaveli@yahoo.co.in
web	www.palhaveli.com

A

Map 3 Entry 99

Indrashan Guest House

593 High Court Colony, Jodhpur, 342 001 Rajasthan

A lush, flower-filled garden surrounds this neat, pretty house in one of Jodhpur's quietest neighbourhoods – you might walk by and wonder enviously who lives here. Your hosts are keen to emphasise this is a homestay, not a hotel; they take all meals with their guests and often join them on sightseeing expeditions. Bedrooms, a decent size, are spotless; much of the furniture belonged to Chandrashekhar's grandfather. Three of the rooms, one with its own entrance from the garden, would be ideal for families. Food is fresh and home-cooked to order by Bhavna, who wins the gong of 'Best Meal Eaten in India' from satisfied guests. But you're also encouraged to help yourself in the kitchen – and from a generously stocked bar in the living room. The Singhs' tour company, Rajputana Discovery, does something few others do, sending you on week-long tours through Rajasthan, staying with aristocratic relations of the family and being drawn into the heart of Indian households. The guest book bears testament to the magic of the trips. Genteel Indian hospitality at its finest – don't rush it.

rooms	8 doubles.
price	Rs1,100. Singles Rs900. Peak season: October–April.
meals	Breakfast Rs125. Lunch Rs250. Dinner Rs275.
closed	Rarely.
directions	Airport/train: Jodhpur (3km, 15 minutes). Note: no English sign or number on house.

	Mr Bhavna & Chandrashekhar Singh	Homestay
tel	+91 (0)2912 440 665	
fax	+91 (0)2912 438 593	
email	rajdisk@satyam.net.in	
web	www.rajputanadiscovery.com	

Map 3 Entry 100

Shahi Guest House

City Police Gandhi Street, Opposite Narsingh Temple, Jodhpur, 342 001 Rajasthan

Small, original, atmospherically ramshackle and lovingly restored, Shahi Guest House attracts those seeking character and authenticity. It sits down a fascinating, cobblestoned alley in the heart of Jodhpur's Blue City, and its roof terrace has some of the finest views of the city and the mighty Fort towering above. Your hosts are delightful people for whom nothing is too much trouble; interesting and fun, they have learnt to speak English from their guests. Bedrooms are great value, bathrooms are basic. In one suite, where the women of the house used to meet in purdah, are a sweeping mosaic floor, a golden arch, a sleeping gallery for children. The honeymoon suite has an antique bed with magnificent views, the balconied Jharokha room has 16 windows. Shelves are filled with family curios, rose oil sprinkled on curtains keeps rooms smelling sweet, and you feast off platters of Anu's home-cooked *thali* on that glorious rooftop. A favourite with backpackers, this is a happy household and a charming place to stay. *Palm reading, yoga, meditation & classes on Hindu traditions.*

Guest house

rooms	4: 3 suites, 1 family suite.
price	Rs600–Rs1,200. Peak season: October–March.
meals	Breakfast Rs95. Lunch & dinner from Rs150 each.
closed	Rarely.
directions	In city centre, 2km from train station, 2.5km from bus station. Airport: Jodhpur (5km, 20 minutes).

	Anu & Vishal Jasmatiya
tel	+91 (0)2912 623 802
mobile	+91 (0)9828 252 120
email	shahigh@rediffmail.com

A ⚘

Map 3 Entry 101

Ratan Vilas

Loco Shed Road, Ratanada, Jodhpur, 342 001 Rajasthan

Brijraj Singh's great-grandfather built this dignified red sandstone villa; a hundred years of family memories – including four generations of championship polo teams – line the walls of the cosy drawing room. Brijraj, his wife Namrata and his spry parents are immensely kind, sharing hosts. Rooms are big and pleasingly simple: mosaic stone floors, crisp Indian print bedcovers, spotless bathrooms. The Singhs' hobby is buying and restoring antiques and each piece of furniture has its own story. Ask for a delectable buffet dinner; everything will be chosen from a local market on the day. The family cow provides fresh milk, yogurt and cottage cheese and when the rains are sufficient, the Singhs grow vegetables. A cheerful courtyard in the middle of the house is filled with red and white hibiscus – Brijraj's favourite flower – and the heady scent of jasmine. A swing seat and deckchairs in the sun, armchairs under a shaded patio, a fire in winter and plenty of books; this is a tremendously hospitable and environmentally-friendly homestay. *Jeep safaris.*

rooms	15: 14 doubles, 1 single.
price	Rs800-Rs1,800. Plus 10% tax on rooms over Rs900. Peak season: October-March.
meals	Breakfast Rs150. Lunch & dinner from Rs200 each.
closed	Rarely.
directions	Train: Jodhpur (2.5km). Airport: Jodhpur (4km, 10-15 minutes).

Homestay

	Mr Brijraj Singh
tel	+91 (0)2912 613 011
mobile	+91 (0)9829 127 877
fax	+91 (0)2912 614 418
email	ratanvilas_jod@rediffmail.com

A ⅄

Map 3 Entry 102

Chandelaogarh
Chandelao, Jodhpur, Rajasthan

History has seeped into the dusky pink walls of this fort built in 1744 for the local thakur – a reward for serving the maharaja; it is still lived in by his descendants. In ornate Rajasthani style, it overlooks peaceful Chandelao village where women still gather at the wells. Beyond, the deserts of Rajasthan. Less hotel, more living museum, its walls are covered with ancestral portraits, ancient wicker armchairs beckon in the garden, tiger skins cover the floors and, in the lounge, sofas ask to be sunk into and photograph albums of grand tours of 1902 to be browsed. Bedrooms are a comfortable mix of family furniture, Indian antiques and the odd newer piece. Locally printed fabrics in rich colours cover cushions and beds, bathrooms are shining temples of tile and marble. Pradhuman and his mother – warm and enthusiastic, both – mix with guests and share meals and stories about the village and their community projects (volunteer if you wish). This is tourist-free India: Pradhuman can arrange a camel cart safari, and dining under the stars atop the fort's gateway in the light of flaming torches is pure fantasy.

rooms	14: 8 doubles, 6 twins.
price	£25. Singles £21. Peak season: October–March.
meals	Lunch Rs250. Dinner Rs250.
closed	Rarely.
directions	Airport: Jodhpur (40km, 40 mins). Train: Jodphur (43km, 50 mins).

Hotel

	Mr Pradhuman Singh Rathore
tel	+91 (0)2915 538 004
res. no	+91 (0)9414 477 694
mobile	+91 (0)9414 477 694
email	chandelao@rediffmail.com
web	www.chandelao.com

Map 3 Entry 103

Devi Bhawan
Ratanada Circle, Def. Lab Road, Jodhpur, Rajasthan

There's no dishonour in sounding the retreat back to the garden sanctuary of Devi Bhawan. No need to don the saffron robes of old and ride out to a certain fate if your attempt to conquer Jodhpur's mighty fort has failed. Instead, relax by the pool or on lounge divans, take dinner in the gazebo; even better, by candlelight in the garden. A series of cottages runs around the edge of this lush and immaculate scene, a century-old gift from the then Maharaja of Jodhpur. Some parts seem a mess of shrubs and plants overflowing from pots, half-hidden by neem trees; others are carefully ordered around trim lawns, an angel-shaped pond and a swing. Uncluttered rooms hold an integrity in their simple designs and teak furniture made by local craftsmen. Bathrooms are clean and marble fresh. A young and refined couple own the property, with noble connections to the royal family, not far away at Umaid Bhavan. Grandfather helps to look after the garden so expertly. It would be hard to find a more serene setting in Jodhpur; harder still to find better value for money.

rooms	14: 12 doubles, 2 suites.
price	Rs800–Rs900. Suites Rs1,200. Plus 10% tax. Peak season: November–February.
meals	Breakfast Rs150. Thali Rs150–Rs175. Dinner Rs200.
closed	Rarely.
directions	Airport/train: Jodhpur (1.5km).

	Mr Rattan Singh
tel	+91 (0)2912 511 067 or (0)2912 512 215
fax	+91 (0)2912 519 976
email	devibhawan@sify.com
web	www.devibhawan.com

Guest house

Map 3 Entry 104

Hotel Monsoon Palace
On Fort, Vyasa Para, Jaisalmer, 345 001 Rajasthan

In the backstreets of Jaisalmer where women beat their daily wash, you will be delighted to find – despite the name – a home and not a palace. Two townhouses, rather, are tucked quietly away: one a 600-year-old Brahmin's home, the other newly built in traditional fort style. Jain and Mughal influences are evident in the soft sandstone, ceilings are low, and packed earth floors lend a welcome simplicity to the old building. Bedrooms have been elegantly created in the space allowed through an awareness of light, colour and mirrored embroidery. The application of a little initiative will bring hot water to fresh bathrooms, two shared in the old house. Plan your desert safari from the cushioned rooftop terrace as a smiling Bapu brings your morning tea. At night the stars are amazingly clear. The two Brahmin brothers make for gentle and endlessly hospitable company: a multi-lingual Om is curious of European culture, while a younger Gitu is an excellent cook – and leads cookery classes. Meals are not served but many restaurants are nearby. Best of all, you'll probably have the place to yourself.

Homestay

rooms	4: 2 doubles; 2 doubles sharing shower.
price	Rs950-Rs2,050. Singles Rs1,200. Peak season: July-March.
meals	Restaurants nearby.
closed	Rarely.
directions	Airport: Jodphur (300km, taxi 5 hours). Train: Jaisalmer (2km, taxi 15 minutes).

	Om Prakash Kewalia
tel	+91 (0)2992 252 656
mobile	+91 (0)9414 149 631
email	monsoonpalacejsm@yahoo.com
web	www.indiamart.com/monsoonpalace

B 🎿 🏃 🦯 ✕ 🖃 👤 👟

Map 3 Entry 105

Hotel Killa Bhawan

On Fort, 445 Kotri Para, Jaisalmer, 345 001 Rajasthan

Killa Bhawan has gained quite a reputation since it opened in 1994, winning a coveted *Harpers & Queen* travel award and hosting a raft of visiting dignitaries. Perched on the edge of Jaisalmer Fort's ramparts and with unparalleled views, it's the baby of a French fashion designer: European and Indian influences create heavenly rustic-chic interiors. Bedrooms are gorgeous, everything beautifully chosen, from antique four-poster beds to wrought-iron lamps; most have dreamy views of the golden fort ramparts and the old city merging into the distant desert. Sunrises cast warm rays onto window seats piled high with vibrant silk cushions; later in the day the romance is enhanced by candlelight on a delightful roof terrace. Two rooms with their own bathrooms are in a separate annexe of the hotel with its own courtyard, dining room and roof terrace; ideal for families or honeymooners. Bathrooms are white marble and polished sandstone with luxuriously thick towels; funky printed cotton robes ensure stylishness in the communal bathroom. Achingly romantic – and a bargain to boot.

rooms	7: 2 doubles, 1 suite; 4 doubles sharing 1 bath.
price	Rs2,000-Rs2,700. Suite Rs4,500. Plus 10% tax. Peak season: November-February.
meals	Restaurants nearby.
closed	Rarely.
directions	Inside the Fort, near Little Tibet Restaurant, 1-minute walk from the main square & Grand Palace.

Hotel

	Mr Bharat
tel	+91 (0)2992 251 204
fax	+91 (0)2992 254 518
email	kbhawan@yahoo.com
web	www.killabhawan.com

B 🗎 ㅅ

Map 3 Entry 106

Shahi Palace Hotel

Opp. Government Bus Stand, Shiv Street, Jaisalmer, 345 001 Rajasthan

One of the nicest, friendliest and most stylish budget guest houses in the area. Cheerful, delightful Jora and his three brothers designed and built Shahi Palace to resemble a 500-year-old haveli – three years ago. All is bright, fresh, new, and yet has stacks of character. Jora visited hotels all over Britain picking up tips – including bathroom ones – and the attention to detail has paid off handsomely. Bedrooms are cheerful and comfortable – beds carved from stone or wood, polished sandstone floors, wicker chairs and soft uplighting – while bathrooms are a dream, all polished sandstone and gleaming fittings. Ask for a room with a view. You dine on the roof garden terrace with stunning views of the fort, equally fabulous by night, and are served vegetarian, multi-national dishes from a Nepalese chef. Should guests wish to eat with a family, Jora will escort you to his village home for dinner with his. A superb budget option, and an environmentally conscious one – the hotel lies just outside the fast-subsiding walls of the Fort. *Ask about camel & jeep safaris. Free pick-up from station.*

Guest house

rooms	16: 15 doubles, 1 single. Dormitory also available.
price	Rs250-Rs1,050. Dormitory Rs50-Rs100. Peak season: June-March.
meals	Breakfast Rs60. Lunch & dinner Rs120-Rs300 each.
closed	Never.
directions	A 5-minute walk from the Fort along Shiv Road. Airport: Jaisalmer (2km). Train: Jaisalmer (2km).

	Mr Jora Lal
tel	+91 (0)2992 255 920
mobile	+91 (0)9414 365 495
email	shahipalace@yahoo.co.in
web	www.shahipalacehotel.com

A 🕴 🖃 ⅄ 🚲

Map 3 Entry 107

Nachana Haveli
Goverdhan Chowk, Jaisalmer, 345 001 Rajasthan

The sandstone haveli, inhabited by the Jaisalmer Royal family, the Bhatis for 300 years, now run by a hip young two brothers and sister team, is more home than hotel. The central courtyard's languid bougainvillea, medley of war memorabilia and jostick'd barbecues encourage an off-beat nonchalance. High-ceilinged bedrooms are richly decorated in orange silk drapes, four-poster beds are elegantly furnished in silver-flower inlay and eclectic portraits hang, more forgotton than remembering. There may be a tiger skin in one room, a bear skin in another. Bathrooms, in spite of dignified old bath tubs, are less 'well appointed' than they once were. The fascinating but noisy market area is down below so steer away from the top floor suites – indeed, the smaller rooms are equally charming. Jaisalmer Fort is a five-minute walk; rest easy that you are not contributing to the subsidence effect of the too many water-reckless tourists who stay inside. Divya's treatments – herbal facials, hot turban head massages – are spoiling; the rooftop restaurant serves tasty food. *Adventure trips, camel safaris & dune dinners.*

rooms	13: 11 doubles, 2 suites.
price	Rs1,250-1,750. Suites Rs2,250-2,500. Plus 10% tax. Peak season: October-March.
meals	Breakfast Rs125. Lunch Rs275. Dinner Rs350.
closed	Rarely.
directions	In Jaisalmer's main square, 5-minute walk from the Fort. Airport: Jaisalmer (2km, 5 minutes). Train: Jaisalmer (2km).

	Mr Vikramaditya Singh
tel	+91 (0)2992 252 110
mobile	+91 (0)9414 149 311
fax	+91 (0)2992 251 910
email	nachana_haveli@yahoo.com

Guest house

Map 3 Entry 108

Fort Rajwada

1 Hotel Complex, Jodhpur-Barmer Link Road, Jaisalmer, 345 001 Rajasthan

Fort Rajwada does a fine job of looking and feeling like a 17th-century maharaja's palace – though it was finished in 2000. Every detail, from the carved sandstone balconies in the atrium lobby to the staff's turbans and saris, was created with a palace in mind. The whole place feels classic but contemporary, and was designed not by architects but by the owner, Dilip Singh Rathore, according to the Indian principle of 'vastu shastra'. The infinity pool, for example, is in the north-east corner of the hotel grounds – water works best at the point of sunrise. The elegant interior is the work of a French-German opera designer; bedrooms are big, stylish, with raw silk upholstery, marble floors and fresh flowers in the bathrooms; the hotel has a no-plastic rule. Sip an aperitif in the gorgeous bar – light, white and cream, with one wall lit at night by dozens of tiny lamps in alcoves. The staff are gracious and attentive, the atmosphere unstuffy and the sights and smells of Jaisalmer and 'real India' are a half-hour walk. *Desert treks & dinner on the dunes. Camel safaris & camel polo.*

Hotel

rooms	94: 90 doubles, 4 suites.
price	Rs4,950. Singles Rs3,900. Suites Rs9,500–Rs11,500.
meals	Breakfast Rs275. Lunch Rs500. Dinner Rs550.
closed	Never.
directions	3km from Jaisalmer Fort. Train: Jaisalmer (2km).

	Mr Dilip Singh Rathore
tel	+91 (0)2992 253 233
fax	+91 (0)2992 253 733
email	sales@rajwadafort.com
web	www.fortrajwada.com

C 🖃 🗋 🚶 🏊

Map 3 Entry 109

Apani Dhani Eco Lodge
Jhunjhunu Road, Nawalgarh, 333 042 Rajasthan

Here your conscience and your corpus can be at peace. The principles are 'eco' and 'low impact', rooted in Ramesh's deep concern for the disappearing local heritage and the damaging effects that tourism can have. Ramesh, the pioneer, lives here with his extended family, the sounds and smells of their lives providing a gentle backdrop to this beautiful and tranquil setting. The rooms are a cluster of traditional huts with mud-rubbed walls, thatched roofs and ruddy, earthy colours. Wooden furniture and intriguing *objets* in russet-toned alcoves create an understated, minimalist feel. Everything you need is here, including yoga and naturotherapy, though luxuries are few, and this is reflected in the price. The bathrooms are all gleaming white tiles and polished chrome. Seasonal, wholesome food is dished out on leaf plates under a bougainvillea-clad pagoda in the circular, crazy-paved courtyard that is the hub of the place. Visitors delight in Ramesh, a pleasant, well-travelled man of principle, who believes strongly in the importance of harmonious living. Superb cafetière coffee! *Guided excursions & great trekking.*

rooms	8: 4 doubles, 4 twins.
price	Rs750–Rs950.
meals	Lunch & dinner from Rs150 each.
closed	Rarely.
directions	Near Kisan Chatrawas off Nawalgarh bypass, on road from Sikar to Jhunjhunu.

Mr Ramesh C Jangid

tel	+91 (0)1594 222 239
fax	+91 (0)1594 224 061
email	enquiries@apanidhani.com
web	www.apanidhani.com

SPECIAL
GREEN ENTRY
see page 18

Guest house

A

Map 1 Entry 110

Hotel Mandawa Haveli
Near Sothaliya Gate, Mandawa, 333 704 Rajasthan

And so to bed. Heavily-studded double doors clunk and creak; lower your head and step over the wooden sill into a mysterious and magical interior largely unadapted – apart from the fact they've managed to sneak in a startlingly modern bathroom. Rooms on each floor lead off the heavily decorated central courtyard, most with windows to the streetside, small and low. Cultivated, delightful Dinesh seems tireless in his appreciation of his wonderfully preserved 1890s merchant's haveli, the first frescoed building en route into the old town, and will tell you all about it. You approach up steps, through a formal garden, and more steps... then choose an inviting corner in sun or shade and ponder awhile on the architectural gems. The whole place is relaxing and seductive, and the floodlit house an unforgettable backdrop to starlit dinners. Food is local, sometimes from the owner's own farm outside town, and the style of cooking traditional. And there's ayurvedic massage on an authentic wooden Kerala table. A heavenly haveli.
Camel rides & jeep safaris.

Hotel

rooms	22: 14 doubles, 4 suites, 2 singles, 2 rooftop tents.
price	Rs1,550. Suite Rs2,750. Plus 8% tax. Peak season: October–February.
meals	Breakfast Rs150. Lunch Rs250. Dinner Rs300.
closed	Rarely.
directions	From central bus stop in Mandawa, towards castle; hotel set back from the road up steps.

Mr Dinesh Dhabai

tel	+91 (0)1592 223 088
mobile	+91 (0)9629 193 798
fax	+91 (0)1592 224 060
email	hotelmandawahaveli@yahoo.com
web	hotelmandawa.free.fr

A 🖃 ᕱ

Map 1 Entry 111

Piramal Haveli

Bagar Shekhavati, Village Bagar, District Jhunjunu, 333 023 Rajasthan

Of the famous, frescoed mansions that punctuate the Shekhavati region, the Piramal Haveli is among the most gracious, its grandeur tempered by a touch of tongue-in-cheek kitsch. Once past the imposing entrance tower, built to honour the visit of the Maharaja of Jaipur in 1928, and beyond the green, wisteria-trailing façade, you enter a private world. Lovingly restored, the house gives you a taste of the life of a wealthy Marwari merchant in the early 20th century. Eight bedrooms with heavy doors and massive padlocks surround the pillared courtyards decorated with friezes of flying cherubs and gods in motorcars. Rooms are large and dark against the heat, decorated with 1930s colonial furniture and ageing portraits of British royalty. Facilities and service are basic, and language can be a bar, but staff are friendly and helpful. Meals take the form of platters of vegetarian *thali* infused with local herbs and spices. You can dine on the rooftop, serenaded by Rajasthani musicians and watch the exclusively male peacocks prance among the balustrades. *Treasure hunts can be arranged; picnics in the Thar desert.*

rooms	8: 2 doubles, 6 suites.
price	Rs1,500. Suites Rs2,000. Plus 10% tax. Peak season: September–March.
meals	Breakfast Rs100. Lunch & dinner Rs200 each.
closed	Rarely.
directions	In the main gate of Bagar. Haveli on left, set back from the road, beyond the gardens.

	Mr Sibhash Rai
tel	+91 (0)5972 221 220
res. no	+91 (0)1124 356 145
fax	+91 (0)1124 351 112
email	sales@neemranahotels.com
web	www.neemranahotels.com

Guest house

A 🖂 ⚚

Map 1 Entry 112

Bhairon Vilas Hotel

Next to Junagarh Fort, Bikaner, 334 001 Rajasthan

How to do justice to this funky, fabulous guest house? An oasis-like walled garden filled with birdsong and bougainvillea leads to an opium den of a reception room. Harshvardhan "Harsh" Singh is a charming host who treats you as an honoured guest at a special house party. His twin passions are entertaining and decorating. Unexpected steps lead to hidden doorways and terraces, and there's a small Hindu temple in the garden. Décor is decadent – lots of vibrant colours and creative re-upholstering using old sari material. Everywhere are amusing, quirky pieces; some family heirlooms, others hand-picked from markets. All bedrooms are delightful, but Room 101 (what a contradiction in terms) is the best, and the size of a suite. Pink walls are inlaid with dozens of small mirrors; peacock feathers sprout from vases beside comfortable armchairs. Outside, a sofa suspended from gold chains makes an irresistible swing seat. Staff are faultless: kind and attentive, humorous and relaxed, in keeping with the spirit of the place. All this and excellent food too. One-of-a-kind perfection.

Guest house

rooms	18: 13 doubles, 5 suites.
price	Rs800–Rs1,000. Singles Rs800–Rs1,000. Suites Rs1,200. Peak season: October–March.
meals	Breakfast Rs120. Lunch Rs200. Dinner Rs250.
closed	Never.
directions	500m from Bikaner train station, just behind Junagarh Fort in front of main post office. Airport: Jodhpur (4 hours).

	Mr Harshvardhan Singh
tel	+91 (0)1512 544 751
mobile	+91 (0)9828 544 751
fax	+91 (0)1512 520 435
email	hbhairon@rediffmail.com
web	hotelbhaironvilas.tripod.com

A ଶ ㄥ

Map 1 Entry 113

Bhanwar Niwas
Rampuira Street, Bikaner, 334 005 Rajasthan

This elegant family mansion is in Bikaner's most atmospheric quarter, among the narrow alleys and terracotta-and-pastel buildings of the old city. Look for an ornately carved red sandstone front, a smart doorman and a splendid 1927 Buick sitting at the entrance. Much of the furniture would look at home in a Parisian townhouse. The Rampuria family still occupies the top floor; Sunil Rampuria, the owner, is an occasional artist who painted the flowers on the walls of the 20-foot-ceiling dining room. Each room is different, but all have high ceilings, antique teak furniture and Belgian tiled bathrooms with huge tubs. A beautiful cloth-bound book on some of the writing desks, *An Indian Miscellany of Wise Nuggets*, is written by grandmother Chandra Rampuria; one of many family mementos. There's a luxurious sofa swing seat in an outdoor upstairs gallery, lit by soft lamps at night. Close your eyes and you'll hear birdsong and the faint tinkling of a courtyard fountain. A secluded slice of old-fashioned opulence close to the delights of Bikaner. *Painting classes with in-house artists. 'Desert nights' on dunes.*

rooms	27: 22 doubles, 2 singles, 3 suites.
price	Rs3,300. Singles Rs3,000. Suites Rs5,000. Plus 10% tax. Peak season: October–April.
meals	Lunch & dinner Rs400 each.
closed	Rarely.
directions	In Bikaner's old city, a 2-minute walk from City Kotwali Police Station. Airport: Jodhpur (4 hours).

	Mr Sunil Rampuria
tel	+91 (0)1512 201 043
fax	+91 (0)1512 200 880
email	bhanwarniwas@rediffmail.com
web	www.bhanwarniwas.com

Hotel

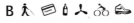

Map 1 Entry 114

Gujarat

Much of the architecture in Gujarat is Jain, Hindu and Islamic. Marvel at the holy pilgrimage site of Shatrunjaya – an awesome, hill-top mass of 843 Jain temples. Experience the exquisitely carved Moldhera Sun Temple, built in 1026 where the sun's rays travel through its chambers reaching the inner sanctum at high noon every day. Kick back and relax in the colourful seaside island of Dui (ex-Portuguese). Learn about the hand-made embroidery in the Kutch from an elaborately dressed villager in mirrorwork dresses and heavy silver bracelets. Skip through the bleached white salt plains and spot wild asses on Little Rann. Visit the Sasan Gir National Park – home to the Asiatic lion and leopard. Experience the Navrati Festival (Sep/Oct) where a whirling, clapping dance is performed in the mother Goddess' honour for nine nights. Visit the Calico Museum in Ahmedabad and see rare textiles, royal tents, silk brocades and costumes – this city has been a major centre for India's textile trade since the 15th century.

Gujarat is immensely friendly and off the tourist trail – it claims a third of India's coastline. It has a varied landscape too, from the choked capital Ahmedabad to the part-desert, tidal marshlands and salt flats of Kutch, forested hills and fertile plains in the east, remote coastal regions, and the industrial peninsula of Saurashthra with a major trading port at Surat and oil refineries. Gujaratis are hardworking and have since ancient times traded with the Persians, Arabs, Chinese and Indonesians. Their culture has been influenced by the Dutch, Portuguese, British, Mughal, Arabs and Parsis. The main religion is Jainism, based on the principles of non-violence, simple living, serving the community and high thinking. Mahatma Ghandi was from Gujarat and took many of these ideals to the independence struggle. So, too, are many of the Indians who ended up emigrating to E. Africa, and then England, Canada and New Zealand.

Best time to visit
Gujarat: October-March.

Photo top Michael Busselle
Photo bottom Laura Kinch

Old Bell Guest House

Sayla Circle, Ahmedabad–Rajkot Highway, P.O. Sayla, District Surendranagar, Gujarat

The colonial villa drips with remnants of British India with its overhanging creepers, sweeping drive, wide staircase and stately gardens. It was built in 1890 to house special guests of the state of Sayla; sepia-stained photographic — evidence of the original family's life, hunting parties and cherished vintage cars — line the veranda. Animal heads hang above doors, brass locks and old doorknobs still shine and bougainvillea splashes its colour among the garden greenery — it is very Raj but gently so. The bedrooms are generous: an extra room for luggage, four pillows of different colours, music and modern phone systems, comfort and charming simplicity. You may play tennis on the vintage court, practise your cricket at the nets or your chess on the outdoor board. The food is dependable and the staff bursting with good will. In the evening you see the Old Bell at her best — the turbaned guard at the gate, the lady by the flower pots greeting you with a *tikka*, high tea on the veranda, watching the sun set. *Latura-Katura wildlife sanctuary 45km.*

rooms	10 doubles.
price	Rs1,800. Single Rs1,500. Plus 15% tax. Full board Rs3,150 (for 2).
meals	Breakfast Rs175. Lunch Rs225. Dinner Rs275.
closed	Rarely.
directions	35km from Surendranagar train station. By road from Ahmedabad through Limdi to Sayla (135km), where the guest house is signed.

Hotel

	Yuvrani Prita Singh Jhala & Yuvraj Somraj Singh Jhala of Sayla
tel	+91 (0)2755 280 017
mobile	+91 (0)9426 302 856
fax	+91 (0)2755 280 357
email	spjhala@yahoo.co.in
web	www.ahmedabadcity.com/sayla

Map 4 Entry 115

Bhavani Villa

Danta Bhavangadh, District Banaskantha, 385 120 Gujarat

The old colonial villa sits high above the palace and the town. Maharana Mahipendra Singh, the 129th descendant of the founder of the Rajput dynasty, is passionate about animals, keeps a stud farm down below and breeds basset hounds at the villa. The quaint interiors have period furniture, plastic ceiling fans, the odd antique or hunting trophy and animal pictures galore. Guest bedrooms are in a new building: five big rooms with balconies and views (to scrubland hills on three sides, the town on the other). Dine on the terrace with the family; they are the nicest people and happy to serve the Rajput dishes that most guests prefer, though you may order western food too. Much of the produce comes from their own farm: poultry, milk, carrots, gourds, tomatoes, beans. Then explore the jungle and hills, on foot, bike, horse or by jeep; your host will be only too happy to place you in the saddle of one of his fine Marwari mares. You may expect to see partridges, peacocks, antelopes, bears, even a panther – it's a great place for wildlife.

rooms	5: 3 doubles, 2 suites.
price	Rs1,950. Suites Rs2,300. Plus 15% tax.
meals	Breakfast Rs150. Lunch & dinner Rs350 each.
closed	Rarely.
directions	On Palanpur-Ambaji road, 20km from Ambaji. Airport: Ahmedabad (170km).

Homestay

	Mr Mahipendra Singh
tel	+91 (0)2749 278 705
mobile	+91 (0)9426 567 166
fax	+91 (0)2749 278 759

A 🛖 🚜 🧍 🚲 👞

Map 3 Entry 116

House of MG - Metro Heritage Hotel

Opposite Siddi Saiyad Mosque, Lal Darwaja, Ahmedabad, 380 001 Gujarat

Mr Mangaldas Girdhardas (MG for short), a successful Ahmedabad business man and philanthropist, had a vision and built this grand house for his family in 1924. His grandson is realising another vision; now, after 12 years' hard work, the project is complete. This extraordinary Gujarati house has been beautifully restored, and its ornamental Baroque-influenced façade preserved – along with Italian mosaic marble flooring, stained-glass windows, courtyards and passages. It is a building with surprises round every corner. The Green House café serves Indian and continental snacks while the open kitchen and the more formal Agashiye terrace restaurant specialise in local dishes. The food is excellent. There's also a banquet 'facility' and a lifestyle store (so many people showed interest in the traditional décor used at the hotel that it made good sense to start selling similar items…), a movie and a reading club, an indoor pool, a gym and more. The 12 smart big bedrooms wrap themselves round an inner courtyard and have plush bathrooms and every mod con, including DVDs and wifi. *Heritage walks arranged.*

rooms	12 doubles.
price	Rs3,999-Rs6,999. Plus 15% tax. Peak season: October-March.
meals	Lunch Rs190. Dinner Rs250. Plus 4% tax.
closed	Rarely.
directions	In central Ahmedabad near the Old Town, near Rupalee cinema. Airport: Ahmedabad (7km). Train: (2km).

Hotel

	Mr Abhay Mangaldas (Manager)
tel	+91 (0)7925 506 946
fax	+91 (0)7925 506 535
email	customercare@houseofmg.com
web	www.houseofmg.com

Map 3 Entry 117

Gujarat

Rann Riders
Dasada, Surendranagar, 382 750 Gujarat

The sea receded a few hundred years ago and left this fascinatingly barren land of salt and desert: the Little Rann of Kutch. Many of the villages were once ports and you can see the old port walls, forts and entrances. It's hard to imagine making a living here, but the area provides much of India's salt and the people, many of them nomadic, bring survival skills and traditions from Rajasthan and as far away as Afghanistan; expect to see exquisite embroidered textiles, silver jewellery and pottery, and colourful festivals. There is also, astonishingly, a vast variety of bird and animal life: pelicans, flamingoes, nilgai, gazelle, wolves, jackals and wild asses. The 13 huts were created in Kutchi style, of mud and with roofs of terracotta tiles or grass. Inside are paintings on the walls and mirror-work on the wooden beams or doors, many of which are ornately carved. There are cane chairs and a writing desk, rugs on the floor and ample space; bathrooms have open-air showers. The staff are formal, helpful and charming, and the surroundng area rich in interest and history. *Spend a night camping with a nomad community.*

Safari lodge

rooms	13 cottages for 2.
price	Full-board Rs2,100. Includes safari. Plus 15% tax. Peak season: September-February.
meals	Full-board only.
closed	Rarely.
directions	Clearly signed just before entering Dasada. Airport: Rajkot (135km). Train: Surendranagar (35km).

Mr Amit Thakore
tel	+91 (0)2757 280 257
fax	+91 (0)2757 280 457
email	gopigroup@icenet.net
web	www.gopigroup.com

Map 3 Entry 118

Desert Coursers

Zainabad, Via. Patdi, Zainabad, District Surendranagar, 382 765 Gujarat

Dhanraj Malik has entertained National Geographic film crews, French photographers and Japanese equine researchers at his camp on the edge of Kutch, and is a charming and knowledgeable host. A member of the ruling family that once governed this former princely state, he grew up here and knows the country well. Set off by camel or jeep to discover the wildlife of Rann: wild asses, black bucks, desert cats, flamingoes, cranes, waterfowl. Or visit the nomadic tribes – cattle-hunters, hunters and musicians – for an insight into their colourful cultures. Camp Zainabad has been running for over 20 years; it's ethnic, well-organised and the local guides look after you with minimum fuss. Expect spotless linen in kooba huts with shower rooms attached, and concrete dormitory blocks for bigger groups. The restaurant – open sided with mud-coated seats and bright cushions – serves hot meals buffet-style. After which it's time to get cosy round the camp fire as darkness falls. Dhanraj will take you on as many safaris as you like and you'll probably tire long before him.

rooms	12 huts for 2. Dormitory room also available, sharing showers.
price	Full-board Rs4,000. Price includes safaris. Peak season: October-March.
meals	Full-board only.
closed	May-August.
directions	Train: Viramgram (45km). Frequent state transport buses run to Zainabad from Viramgram.

Safari lodge

	Mr Dhanraj Malik
tel	+91 (0)2757 241 333/335
mobile	+91 (0)9426 372 113
fax	+91 (0)2757 241 334
email	zainabad@hotmail.com
web	www.desertcoursers.net

B 人 👞

Map 3 Entry 119

The Palace Utelia

Via Lothal-Burkhi, Utelia, District Ahmedabad, 382 230 Gujarat

Dream of Saurashtra's princely past, and bask in the family's hospitality. Its ancestors founded the lovely, terracotta-roofed village of Utelia in 1646, and built the palace in Indo-Saracenic style a hundred years later. Its five domes, numerous pillars, arches and Gujarati haveli-style façades spring into view as you approach along the bumpy Ahmedabad road – the palace is quite a picture; indeed, impossible to miss with its commanding position over the fields. Yet it is all of a manageable size. A gallery leads into huge rooms with huge bathrooms that overlook the courtyard below; refreshingly cool in summer, this spills over with bougainvillea and shady trees. In the bedrooms are heavy carved doors, sweeping terracotta floors, splendid four-poster beds and cushioned alcoves by windows with long and peaceful views. After a walk in the village and a dip in the communal springs, return for daal, *raseele aalu* and mixed vegetables, charmingly served in the palace's nobly proportioned dining hall. It is a delightful place. *Jeep safaris to Velavader National Park.*

rooms	20 doubles.
price	Rs2,500. Plus 15% tax.
meals	Breakfast Rs250.
	Lunch Rs400. Dinner Rs425.
closed	Rarely.
directions	80km from Ahmedabad, near Lothal on the way to Bhavnagar & Palitana.

Hotel

	Mr Bhagirathsinhji of Utelia
tel	+91 (0)7926 445770
fax	+91 (0)7926 445770
email	utelia@icenet.net

B ♨ 👞

Map 3 Entry 120

Royal Oasis
Wankaner, 363 621 Gujarat

When the family's palace – Ranjit Vilas – grew too hot the family would retreat to the cool of the Oasis, on the banks of a river two miles away. Much rebuilding has happened and the rooms are luxurious with their own bathrooms and dressing rooms. There is Art Deco plastering around the door frames and along the walls and Rajasthani quilts decorate the beds. But the deepest lure of the Oasis is the stepwell, or Vaav, the last to be built in India in the 20th century, superbly carved and preserved. It has three stories underground, with fountains, and some fantastic sculptures and carvings. There is also a large Art Deco indoor pool. The food is western but this has its benefits: a grand opportunity to eat bread and butter pudding, maybe! The Wankaner family was – is – a remarkable family; after Independence their members were frequently elected to the state and national legislatures. If the Prince is here he often shows visitors around the palaces. All this and richly interesting Gujarat to visit, too. *Horse riding & land sailing available.*

rooms	14: 6 doubles, 2 suites. Annexe: 6 doubles.
price	Full-board Rs2,100. Plus 15% tax. Peak season: September-February.
meals	Full-board only.
closed	Rarely.
directions	Airport/train: Raijot (50km).

Mr Yuvraj Digvijay Singh

tel	+91 (0)7932 985 778
mobile	+91 (0)9879 305 778
fax	+91 (0)2828 220 001
email	info@wankanerheritagehotels.com
web	www.wankanerheritagehotels.com

Hotel

A

Map 3 Entry 121

Royal Residency
The Palace, Wankaner, 363 621 Gujarat

The king's palace – Ranjit Vilas – is vast and imposing, part museum and part king's domicile. The formalities of separate living are still observed, as are the memorabilia of royal life: huge ceilings, shadowy rooms, heavy furniture, billiard tables, a collection of vintage cars, animal trophies from all over the world. The late colonial-style Residency, built in 1882, adjoins it. It is only slightly less grandiose and guests of the palace often stay here, too. The rooms are named after ruling princes, a viceroy, the Duke of Connaught, the jeweller Jacques Cartier, Mahatma Gandhi's father and the first Governor-general of India, all of whom have been friends of the Wankaner royal family. The style is predominantly Art Deco, the quilts on the bed Rajasthani, and some bath tubs are old tin ones with ancient plumbing and showers above. There is a wonderful sense of space, an engaging mix of formality and laissez-faire and much to see. Luxury may not be the word, but elegance is, and a very modern royal family lives across the way. *Horse riding & land sailing available.*

rooms	14 doubles.
price	Full-board Rs2,500–Rs4,000. Singles Rs1,850. Plus 12% tax. Peak season: November–March.
meals	Full-board only.
closed	Rarely.
directions	Airport/train: Rajkot (50km).

Hotel

B 人 🏊

Map 3 Entry 122

	Mr Yuvraj Digvijay Singh
tel	+91 (0)7932 985 778
mobile	+91 (0)9879 305 778
fax	+91 (0)2828 220 002
email	info@wankanerheritagehotels.com
web	www.wankanerheritagehotels.com

Orchard Palace
Palace Road, Gondal, 360 311 Gujarat

The present owner is the descendant of that enlightened maharaja who transformed Gondal into a progressive princely state (out went purdah, in came roads, schools and electricity). The 19th-century villa is imposing, surrounded by orchards, gardens and lawns. Indulge in an early-evening chat on the upstairs terrace with the sociable Maharani, and watch the peacocks strut around the lotus pond; cuckoos, sunbirds and herons may also be seen. Your hosts share the same driveway as their guests, and the same excellent chefs. Other members of the family manage the place and your stay includes meals, viewings of the family's classic and vintage car collection, and tours of the town and the wonderfully carved Naulakha Palace. Huge bedrooms have 1940s décor and plumbing with a heritage feel; some have canopy beds, some are air-conditioned. There are sitting areas on both floors dotted with family photos, big glass ashtrays, the odd stuffed cheetah, a collection of miniature paintings. Trek off on a long-distance safari; birdwatching is excellent when the lake refills.

rooms	19 doubles.
price	Full-board Rs5,000. Plus 15% tax. Peak season: October-March.
meals	Full-board only.
closed	Rarely.
directions	A short walk from Gondal bus station.

	H H Kumud Kumari Jadeja
tel	+91 (0)2825 220 002
fax	+91 (0)7926 300 962
email	nwsafaris@hotmail.com
web	www.ahmedabadcity.com/gondal

Hotel

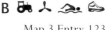

Map 3 Entry 123

Madhya Pradesh, Maharastra

Feel like an island king at the fantastic Orchha Palace, decorated with turquoise and lapis lazuli. Blush at the incredible erotic paintings of Khajuraho or come for the Festival of classical dance in February and March. Marvel at the medieval fort at Gwalior which stretches 3km across a giant rock plateau. There are many other gems in Madyha Pradesh (MP): the ancient Buddhist Stupa in Sanchi, tribal groups in the north-east and their beautiful crafts, and many ancient forts and temples. Tourists tend to overlook this state even though it has some of the best heritage sites in India and is friendly and relatively hassle-free. The hot, sunburnt central plains are landlocked by Bihar, Maharastra, Rajasthan, Gujarat, Chattisgarh and Uttar Pradesh. MP also has the highest percentage of forest in India and over 20% of the world's tiger population; you can see them in the four national Parks: Kanha, Panna, Pench and Bandhavgarh.

India's second most populous state, Maharastra, has a varied landscape with green hills, coastal plains and hectic industrial centres stretching from the Arabian Sea to the very centre of the country. Cotton, tobacco and fruit (chikoos, oranges, mangoes and strawberries) are all grown here. Once an important port, Mumbai (Bombay) is the glitzy state capital with skyscrapers, Victorian buildings, 16 million people, western luxuries, Bollywood films, vast slums and migrants who travel from each corner of India to make their fortune. Try the street food, or immerse yourself in the irresistible tangle of shops and bazaars. Head up to Pune, a prosperous hill station where Mumbai-ites go to cool down or dance at the Osho Meditation Resort. The twin World Heritage Sites of Ajanta and Ellora are astonishing. The sensational Ajanta Buddhist caves, some of which date back as far as 200 BC have intricate stone carvings and well-preserved cave murals set above a deep gorge with a tumbling waterfall. At Ellora 85,000 cubic metres were excavated to create a Hindu masterpiece; there are also a couple of Buddhist and Jain-style caves.

Best time to visit
Madyha Pradesh: September-February

Photos Laura Kinch

Ahilya Fort
Maheshwar, 451 224 Madhya Pradesh

Ancient Maheshwar is a sacred place, and Ahilya, perched high above the Narmada river where there's always a breeze, is an enchanting hotel. More home than fort, the building's pale stone floors, dark timbers and ancient shuttered doors have been exquisitely restored. Richard Holkar is the driving force behind Ahilya and the Holkars were the kings of Indore, though the family is more westernised today. Thanks to the Holkar Trust, the hand weaving for which Maheshwar was once famous is again thriving – you may visit the handloom centre nearby. Tranquil bedrooms have finely woven fabrics and views, an immaculate bathroom peeps through an arch, a white bloom graces a vase, and courtyards, gardens and pool drift serenely one into the other. Have buffet breakfast on the ramparts, lounge on silk cushions on the *jharokha* overlooking the water, dine on delectable (home-grown) food on the terrace, dream in the soft-lit magic. The two tents are as luxurious as the rest. Ahilya may not be cheap but it a place to treasure, and is run by delightful staff. *Two-day river trips & organic farm trips.*

rooms	11: 8 doubles, 1 suite, 2 tents.
price	Full-board €230-€350.
	Peak season: 15 October-31 March.
meals	Full-board only.
closed	May/June.
directions	Directions on booking. Ask for
	Maheshwar, then fort easy to find.
	Airport: Mumbai (95km, 2.5 hours).
	Train: Indore (91km, 2.5 hours).

Hotel

	Mr Richard Holkar
tel	+91 (0)7283 273 329
res. no	+91 (0)1151 551 575
mobile	+91 (0)1151 551 575
email	info@ahilyafort.com
web	www.ahilyafort.com

C ♿ 🧘 🏊

Map 4 Entry 124

Rashid Kothi
22 Yeshwant Niwas Road, Indore, 452 003 Madhya Pradesh

The moment you leave the town's main road and pass through the gates, you enter a hidden sanctuary. The large, sturdy house, surrounded by lush forest, was built in the 1940s. It belonged to Anu's grandmother and is still the family home, simply and beautifully furnished with a subtle luxury. Anu, Ashish and their parents are courteous, generous and good company: you're treated as an honoured family guest here. Ashish teaches physics and Anu runs a nursery in the grounds; they know the area well and can help you plan your tour. Three lavish, exquisitely prepared vegetarian meals (no alcohol) are served each day in the gazebo or on the dining room's petal-strewn table – and there's the delightful ritual of afternoon tea with the family. The two bedrooms have books and flowers; one is a leafy summerhouse in the garden. Both have ethnic bedspreads, pretty lamps and candles. Rainwater harvesting provides the showers. Frangipani and jasmine scent the air and the neem trees are revered for their revitalising properties – as we feel this house should be!

Homestay

rooms	2: 1 twin, 1 cabin for 2.
price	Full-board $100. Singles $60.
meals	Full-board only.
closed	Occasionally.
directions	From station, taxi to Rani Sati Gate. House next to motorcycle showroom, signed 'Playhouse Nursery'. Airport: Indore (8km, 25 mins). Train: Indore (2km, 10 mins).

	Ms Anuradha Dubey
tel	+91 (0)7312 434 377
email	ashanu@hotmail.com or rashidsufi@hotmail.com

B

Map 4 Entry 125

Ivy Suites

26 A Nadir Colony, Shamla Hills, Bhopal, 462 001 Madhya Pradesh

It is the last house on this prosperous residential estate, at the end of a long, meandering, lakeside road. The 1980s, ivy-clad home has been recently converted by its owners into a hotel – very welcoming, very homely. Hospitality is second nature to Mr and Mrs Sharma who delight in engaging guests in conversation over tea – or something stronger. Architecture, economics, the environment, food: all subjects are worthy of discussion. Indeed, you are encouraged to use their home as would a friend. Relax in the light-filled sitting/dining room with its marble floor, brass statuettes of dancing goddesses, coffee table books and fish-tank bar; the upstairs lounge with its smart settees, lush plants and wireless internet; or on the roof terrace, a fine spot for 8.30am yoga. And everywhere – big views through big windows of Bhopal's shimmering lake. Be sure to ask for a room with a view; the best are most definitely upstairs, two with their own sitting areas. Note: bathrooms and baths are pretty simple. Bhopal, on the other side of the lake, is a gentle green city full of lovely gardens and parks.

rooms	10: 1 double, 9 twins.
price	Full-board Rs 2,500. Singles Rs2,000. Plus 10% tax.
meals	Full-board only.
closed	Rarely.
directions	Airport: Bhopal (12km, 15mins). Train: Bhopal (5km, 15 mins).

Hotel

	Pramod & Manju Sharma
tel	+91 (0)7554 235 508
res. no	+91 (0)7554 234 753
mobile	+91 (0)9826 058 680
email	prashar26@yahoo.com
web	www.ivysuites.com

B 人 🖾 人 🚲 👞

Map 4 Entry 126

Hotel Jehan Numa Palace
157, Shamla Hill, Bhopal-13, Madhya Pradesh

Up a hill steep enough for rickshaw wallahs to appeal to your sympathy and purse, Jehan Numa Palace comes as a Bhopal surprise. Turning away from Upper Lake, a bold white façade greets you with 1890s colonial decorum, while columns and balconies are unmistakably Renaissance in style. The result is a relaxed, open-plan layout of lawns, quads and a superb swimming pool, all connected by covered walkways, hung with violet bougainvillea. Teak furniture in marbled bedrooms is comfortably austere and large beds are covered with muted patterns. With ambient music as you wash and all the frills of smart bathrooms, who could resist? Three good restaurants cater for every taste, including one of India's best attempts at an Italian trattoria. General Obaidullah Khan may have built the palace, but it was not until 1983 that his grandsons, the current owners, reinvented Jehan Numa. A charming duo, they'll happily tell you about the masses to do nearby. Find out too why the bars received their equestrian names – while drinking beer from the first pumps to offer draught ale in Madhya Pradesh.

Hotel

rooms	74: 72 doubles, 2 suites.
price	Rs2,250-Rs4,000. Plus 15% tax. Peak season: July-April.
meals	Breakfast Rs230. Lunch Rs425. Dinner Rs600.
closed	Rarely.
directions	Airport: Bhopal (12km, 15-20 mins). Train: Bhopal (5km, 10 mins).

	Nilay Poddar (Manager)
tel	+91 (0)7552 661 100
mobile	+91 (0)9303 134 756
fax	+91 (0)7552 661 720
email	jehanuma@sancharnet.in
web	www.hoteljehanumapalace.com

Map 4 Entry 127

Sheesh Mahal
Orchha, 472 246 Madhya Pradesh

You won't forget staying here — though you shouldn't consider it if you're after heritage-chic or bright uncomplicated luxury. The old town of Orchha lives up to its name — 'hidden place' — yet is awash with architectural gems, one of which is this palace. Arriving in an entrance courtyard, where the walls of a ruined fort rear up on either side, you are suddenly confronted by the full shabby grandeur of the façade. It is eerie, isolated, atmospheric... Inside, though the 300-year-old splendours have survived the transition to state-owned hotel, the air is one of melancholy and faint neglect. Yet the place has a character and eccentricity all of its own. The bedrooms range from the stiff splendour of the Maharaja and Maharani suites to a single room, its tiny proportions redeemed by access to an intriguing roof terrace (one of several). The baths, too, vary from vast grey marble affairs to bucket baths. The dining room may be forbidding but the Indian food is delicious — and very good value. The 'palace of mirrors' is supremely silent, with a spectacular view from every room. Let the peace wash over you.

rooms	8: 2 doubles, 3 twins, 1 single, 2 suites.
price	Rs890. Singles Rs490. Suites Rs2,490–Rs3,990. Plus 10% tax.
meals	Lunch & dinner, Rs250 each.
closed	Rarely.
directions	Airport: Khajuraho (173km, 3.5 hours). Train: Jhansi (20km, 35 minutes).

Guest house

	Mr Sanjay Malotra
tel	+91 (0)7680 252 624
fax	+91 (0)7680 252 624
email	hsmorcha@sancharnet.in or bcorchha@rediffmail.com

A

Map 4 Entry 128

Shergarh Tented Camp

Village Bahmni, Post Kareli, Tehsil Baihar, Kanha Tiger Reserve, 481 111 Madhya Pradesh

If you come across a small child climbing through nascent bamboo and swimming in rock pools, you might think you had found a real-life Mowgli on the edge of Kanha. It's easy to get caught up in the exhilaration of Katie and Jehan, young and newly wed, who have a deeply ecological vision for Shergarh. No more than six tents will be pitched here, so the impact is hardly apparent and the feel wonderfully natural. Two people are comfortably quartered under homely canvas, while two tents have family space. Zip open stone bathrooms and find constant hot water supplied by clean-burning LPG units. After a day's safari, everyone tucks into superb grub on the lodge veranda or under the stars by the lake; the food is fresh from the garden – even the hens. No waste here either for Katie is queen of composts. Light pollution is kept to a minimum to encourage wildlife and being on the less-busy Mukki side of the park, all is quiet. It would be hard to imagine a more magical environment to bring up Kai, their infant son, whose growth will be a reflection of Shergarh's own. *Spring-fed swimming pool.*

rooms	6 tents for 2-4.
price	Full-board Rs14,000. Singles Rs8,000. Safaris included.
meals	Full-board only.
closed	Mid-May-mid-October.
directions	Located at Mukki Gate. Airport: Nagpur (280km, 5.5 hours). Train: Gondia (140km, 3 hours).

Safari lodge

SPECIAL GREEN ENTRY see page 18

	Jehan & Katie Bhujwala
tel	+91 (0)7637 226 086/215
mobile	+91 (0)9324 331 583
email	enquiries@shergarh.com
web	www.shergarh.com

D 🏕 🚜 🏊 ◌◌ 👟

Map 4 Entry 129

Krishna Jungle Resort

Mocha, Mandla District, Kanha National Park, 481768 Madhya Pradesh

Sit up straight and pay attention to your jungle orientation lesson. Straight-talking manager Sanjeev Kulhalli isn't actually that strict and will happily tell you about the camp's exemplary attitude towards the environment, down to the eco-orange hue of the buildings – among enough shrubbery to bring the jungle back to your doorstep. There's an easy-going feel here with several communal areas; most popular, unsurprisingly, is the outdoor bar where you mix company with other guests – groups come here – and amusing naturalists. Cool off later in the pool. Rooms are whitewashed simple affairs, splashed with the occasional tiger motif, comfortable not luxurious. Bathrooms are whiter-than-white sepulchres with hot water. Chilly dawn safaris don't allow for any idling about – the tigers certainly don't at that time – but if you focus only on the trophy animals you miss the real beauty of Kanha, its pulsing green and spectacular views of untrammelled land. Swap stories of success and failure back at camp; you'll treat the two just the same once the food arrives. And the food is delicious.

rooms	31 doubles. Tents available.
price	Full-board £120. Safari included. Peak season: November–March.
meals	Full-board only.
closed	July–September.
directions	Airport/train: Nagpur (5 hours), Jabalpur (2.5 hours).

Safari lodge

Mr Neelesh Agrawal

res. no	+91 (0)7614 004 023/024
fax	+91 (0)7612 412 253
email	krishnahotel@hotmail.com or info@krishnahotels.com
web	www.jungleresort.in

C &. ℱ 🏊 ⚲ 👟

Map 5 Entry 130

Kipling Camp

Mocha Village, Kanha National Park, Mandla District, 481 768 Madhya Pradesh

Look out of the window and hold your breath for wildlife. The hum and chirrup of insects and birds continues through the day and into the night. In spite of being one of the most inaccessible places on the planet, Kipling Camp, created by Anne and Bob Wright in 1990, is still a magnet for conservationists and nature lovers. The cottages sit in a *Jungle Book* clearing, a jeep-ride away from breathtaking views of untrammelled land – and pre-dawn rises are required for inspiring sightings of barasingha, jackals, leopard and even tiger. It may not be the lap of luxury, but the whitewashed mud structures have a simple elegance. Coolish throughout the day, they come with shower rooms and electric coolers for summer; large raised beds are comfortable and enclosed by meshes of mosquito netting. There is a house-party feel, and dinner is sometimes around the camp fire. The camp is also home to Tara, star of Mark Shands' *Travels on My Elephant*; her daily bath in the river is one of the highlights of the trip. Responsible tourism at its most seductive.

Safari lodge

rooms	19: 3 doubles, 14 twins, 2 singles.
price	Full-board Rs6,600 p.p. Safaris included. Peak season: December; February; March.
meals	Full-board only.
closed	Mid-May–September.
directions	Airport/train: Nagpur (5 hours), Jabalpur (2.5 hours).

	Ms Anne Wright
tel	+91 (0)1155 196 377
fax	+91 (0)1126 803 240
email	info@kiplingcamp.com
web	www.kiplingcamp.com

D 🚶 🛶 🚴 👟

Map 5 Entry 131

Camp Mewar On Ketkiya

Tala Bandhavgarh P.O., District Umaria, Madhya Pradesh

Furthest from the tiny village of Tala, Camp Mewar is a 4x4 ride into the thick of things at Bandavgarh National Park. An excursion takes you to within a wire's breadth of the wild, and drivers are warned not to stop their vehicles. You'll feel safe, though, in your thatched cottage or Shikar tent, raised on wide granite platforms and densely hidden by bamboo. Light filters through slatted blinds, dappling safari-smart interiors of cushioned twin beds and portraits of bearded monkeys. No need to squabble over which bed as both sides have their own writing desk, dressing table and entrance to the bathroom – a surprise of copper and marble and piping hot water. As he warms his whisky by the log fire in the communal lodge, the owner's easygoing charm belies an outspoken personality, most vehemently on preserving the indigenous life of the park – beginning with his camp. Excellent buffet meals are relaxed gatherings when guests regale each other with rare – or not so rare – sightings over mouthwatering tandoori. Even if you don't manage to see Mr Tiger, rest assured, he has seen you.

rooms	12: 5 tents for 2, 4 lodges for 2, 3 huts for 2.
price	Full-board $280. Singles $160. Extra person $100. Two safaris included.
meals	Full-board only.
closed	15 April-end-October.
directions	Airport: Jabalpur (4.5 hours), Kajuraho (6 hours). Train: Umaria (1.5 hours).

Safari lodge

	Mr Arjun Singh
tel	+91 (0)7627 265 395
mobile	+91 (0)9414 159 797
email	campmewar@gmail.com
web	www.campmewar.com

Map 5 Entry 132

Gordon House Hotel

5 Battery Street, Appolo Bunder, Colaba, Mumbai (Bombay), 400 039 Maharashtra

You'd never guess what lies behind the façade of this white tower block: a restaurant with Asian fusion food, a buzzing night club on the ground floor, bedrooms above and an easy-mannered young staff in white suits and bright shirts. If the idea of a stylish themed hotel fills you with dread, fear not – the place does not take itself too seriously. A tapestry in the Versailles suite reads 'It ain't easy being King' and the Mediterranean, Country and Scandanavian interiors differ only in clever twists on the detail; a ruffled curtain or a wicker blind, plain white bathroom tiles or colourful florals. The rooms, not huge, come with little treats: a bowl of sweets by the bed, good toiletries in the bathroom, a CD player. The three storeys wrap themselves around a central atrium that floods the jazzy reception area with natural light. Stylish and pristine, this place may not give you the most Indian of experiences but it does guarantee you a stylish and spotless one. And India Gate, the city's principal landmark, is just around the corner. The doorman will book you a taxi or tell you the best places to shop. Young and fun.

rooms	29: 28 doubles, 1 suite.
price	Rs5,000. Suite Rs10,000. Plus 6.3% tax.
meals	Lunch from Rs300. Dinner from Rs350.
closed	Rarely.
directions	Right behind Colaba's Regal Cinema, very near India Gate.

Hotel

	Ms Gayle Almeida
tel	+91 (0)2222 871 122
fax	+91 (0)2222 872 026
email	dutymanager@ghhotel.com
web	www.ghhotel.com

C 🛏 🍾 👤

Map 3 Entry 133

The Verandah in the Forest
Barr House, Matheran, District Raigarh, 410 102 Maharashtra

Deep in primary forest, reached only by foot, palanquin or horse, this small hotel is well named. And the veranda is a fancy one, framed in decorative white wooden balustrades and tiled in large floral-shaped terracotta tiles – perfect camouflage for the forest's pervasive red dust. Here you may lounge on planters' chairs, lime soda in hand, and stretch your eyes over the view. You dine here or indoors, sharing a long table with other guests. The food is delicious. The airy drawing room echoes beneath a huge vaulted ceiling and has many coffee-table books on the region. Matheran is the last pedestrian hill station in Asia, and the house was built in 1852 by a British colonel to escape the Bombay heat – an hour's drive yet a world away. The hire of a horse – whether pony or racehorse – can be arranged, and there are many beautiful walks, including a trek to the Khandala lookout point. Retire to a four-poster bed in a large, simple room and sleep soundly... you may be woken by monkeys scrabbling over the rooftop at dawn. Note: the journey to get here is not for the timorous!

rooms	11: 8 doubles, 3 suites.
price	Rs2,000–Rs4,500. Suites Rs2,500–Rs4,500. Plus 6% tax. Peak season: September–March.
meals	Lunch Rs275. Dinner Rs325.
closed	Rarely.
directions	150km from Mumbai.

Hotel

	Mr Kiran
tel	+91 (0)2148 230 296
res. no	+91 (0)1124 356 145
fax	+91 (0)1124 351 112
email	sales@neemranahotels.com
web	www.neemranahotels.com

C

Map 3 Entry 134

Captans

Rajmachi Road, beyond Tungarli Dam, Thakuwadi, Lonavala, Nr. Pune, 401 401 Maharashtra

The British may have gone, the daring forts of the Rajmachi lie deserted, but here the legacy of hill stations survives. Travellers coming from Mumbai will notice the cool, clean air on arrival; doubly refreshing to breath easy after the challenging 4x4 journey from Lonavala. Further rewards come with the sense of intimacy, the freshness of the greenery, the abundant birdsong, the palm-shaded pool. Inside a modern colonial chalet of Indian hardwoods, you find unusual Japanese-styled rooms of polished teak attached to large but not luxurious bathrooms. The style is pure, uncluttered. Garden cottages offer more private quarters and still the oriental simplicity (some simpler than others), electricity and hot water. Finding your way back at night along romantic, lamp-lit paths is easy. Owner and property namesake Captain Mohan Chabba spent many years in the Merchant Navy before happily turning landlubber — and yoga-adept — here in the hills. Dinner (served by uniformed staff) in the company of his friends promises colourful conversation and tasty tandoori. *Trekking, healing & meditation courses.*

Guest house

rooms	3 + 7: 2 doubles, 1 suite. 7 cottages: 4 for 3, 3 for 2.
price	Rs3,500. Suite Rs4,000. Cottages Rs2,400-Rs2,800. Peak season: Nov-Jan; June-August.
meals	Lunch £3. Dinner £4.
closed	Rarely.
directions	Mumbai-Pune highway, exit Lonavala/Khandala. At BP petrol pump in Lonavala (opp. Surya Resorts) take road to Tungarli Dam; 2km.

	Capt Mohan Chabba
tel	+91 (0)2114 271 313
res. no	+91 (0)2114 326 884
mobile	+91 (0)9850 100 331
email	captans@vsnl.net
web	www.captans.com

B 🚶 🍴 💳 🧘 🏊 👟

Map 3 Entry 135

Goa

With its laid-back attitude, this is a superb place to unwind and relax. Goa, the smallest state in India, hugs the Konkan coast and has beautiful palm-fringed beaches and secluded coves. The distinctive culture comes from its colonial past – it was ruled by the Portuguese for more than 400 years. This influence remains and can be seen in the language, dress, architecture, cuisine, religion and music. Music is a blend of Konkani folk songs and evocative Portuguese Fado. There are whitewashed churches, crumbling forts and yellow, ochre, green or indigo houses with white trims. Women prefer skirts to saris, and food is a fusion of meat, seafood and fresh fish with a heady mix of spices (originally brought to India by the Portuguese traders). Portuguese is the lingua franca among Goa's elite and a third of the population are Catholics. The main jobs here are fishing and tending to coconut plantations, rice paddies and tourism.

The Goans are extremely friendly and make tourists very welcome. The state is divided into the northern and southern areas. The state capital, Panaji (Panjim) is in the northern part and has a mix of Catholic churches, cathedrals and convents attracting many of India's Catholic pilgrims. Old Goa is a World Heritage Site and the magnificent Basilica de Bom Jesus and the grand Sé Cathedral should not be missed. The market town of Mapusa and the colourful flea market at Anjuna are also northern highlights and it is here that the 'traveller' population congregates. In the south, tourist development is less intense and so this area tends to be more relaxed. At beaches such as Colva and Benaulim, you find the upmarket resorts; Palolem beach is renowned for its beauty. Head inland and explore Goa's wildlife sanctuaries and the splendid Dudhsagar Falls. A chance to explore the colonial landowner mansions in Chandor near Margao is worth the trip. Come in February for the annual carnival – a colourful extravaganza with floats and masked dancers.

Best time to visit
Goa: October-March

Photo top Indian Tourist Board
Photo bottom Brian Kinch

Fort Tiracol

Tiracol, Perney, 403 524 Goa

You might expect a fort to be austere and uncluttered – but not this one. It's a national monument, with all the restrictions on change that that implies, yet they have managed to repaint and refurbish every corner, and the yellow walls and wrought-iron furniture create a mood of elegance. Each bedroom gets its own balcony – and the best views in Goa. The building stands on a river estuary so you can see along a length of coast and out to sea; it is breathtaking. Watch the fishermen at work on the sandbanks or the dolphins out at sea (boat trips are bookable). From the rooftop restaurant/café are the same eye-stretching views. Within the fort's compound is an old chapel to which the townspeople still hold the keys and where Mass is held on weekends and Wednesdays. The owners live away but the manager is friendly and helpful, and the whole place is open to tourists so there's a constant to-ing and fro-ing. A busy and unusual place – and more like a Portuguese pousada than anything you might expect in India.

rooms	7: 4 doubles, 2 suites, 1 family room for 4.
price	Half-board $110. Plus 10% tax.
meals	Half-board only. Lunch $10-$20.
closed	Rarely.
directions	From Panjim head for Calangute, then Siolim, then Tiracol.

Hotel

	Mr Vivek Tiracol
tel	+91 (0)8322 276 793
fax	+91 (0)8322 276 792
email	nilaya@sancharnet.in

B 🖃 🛢

Map 8 Entry 136

Otter Creek Tents
Mandrem, Arambol, 403 801 Goa

Sip morning tea by your private bamboo jetty and watch an otter slip by. Walk on the beach and see only fishermen's footprints. Magical things happen at this singularly seductive hideaway cut off from the rest of Goa's glorious (but popular) beaches by a bamboo footbridge. This privately owned spit of land has a tiny 'hotel', the Beach House (entry 138) but for privacy and a close-to-nature feel, why not sleep under canvas? Banish thoughts of groundsheets and sagging tent poles: these sugar-almond mini-marquees come with bamboo four-posters, drifts of muslin and elegantly spare furnishings. Tucked amongst coconut palms, each has a tiny bathroom as well as a small terrace leading to a jetty over Otter Creek. (And the otters are often spotted.) The white sands are a flip-flop away from the other side of the tent, there's a cook to hand, and a car and driver to whisk you to Goa's more raucous pleasures – but you'll soon hurry back. Birds to spot, turtle eggs to watch hatching (in season), beaches to amble and an ocean to stare at. What more does a hedonist need?

rooms	3 tents for 2.
price	£182–£280 per week. Peak season: November–February.
meals	Breakfast £2.50. Lunch & dinner £3.25 each.
closed	Rarely.
directions	Cross Siolim Bridge, for Morjem, then Asvem. Ask for house of Juse Calisto. Advisable to call first. Airport: Dabolim (60km, 75 mins). Train: Pernem, Goa (35km, 45 mins).

Under canvas

	Mr Denzil Sequeira
tel	+91 (0)8322 247 616
res. no	+91 (0)9326 020 701
mobile	+91 (0)9820 037 387
email	gaze@aseascape.com
web	www.aseascape.com

Map 8 Entry 137

The Beach House
Mandrem, Arambol, 403 801 Goa

The road brings you to a rickety bamboo footbridge across a saltwater creek. On the far side stretches a ten-acre spit of land thick with coconut groves and banyan trees, one tiny house and, just possibly, the emptiest beach in Goa. Little has changed since the beach house was built in 1886. Thick-walled and rusty red with white-pillared veranda and faded blue shutters, it gazes over the Arabian Sea. Still belonging to the same family, it has been subtly modernised to give rooms of simple luxury. Open to the rafters, bedrooms are cool and white with tiled floors, hand-made four-poster beds and a few, well-chosen pieces of rustic furniture. Decoration is spare – a pretty mirror, a striped bedcover, a woven basket – and in the sitting room are digital satellite radios and good books. Cook will rustle up Goan fish curry and pancakes or you can do your own thing over a campfire on the beach. There are a car and driver to take you sightseeing – but why leave such a perfect place? Walks, wildlife, turtles if you're lucky, an ocean to stare at and not a hawker in sight. *Minimum stay seven nights.*

Catered cottage

rooms	House for 6 + child.
price	£735–£994 per week. Peak season: November-February.
meals	Breakfast £2.50. Lunch & dinner £3.25 each.
closed	Rarely.
directions	Cross Siolim Bridge towards Morjem, then Asvem. Ask for the house of Juse Calisto. Advisable to call first. Airport: Dabolim (60km, 75 mins). Train: Pernem, Goa (35km, 45 mins).

Mr Denzil Sequeira

tel	+91 (0)8322 247 616
res. no	+91 (0)9236 020 701
mobile	+91 (0)9820 037 387
email	gaze@aseascape.com
web	www.aseascape.com

D

Map 8 Entry 138

Laguna Anjuna
Soranto Vado, Anjuna, 403 509 Goa

Lazy days! This funky, architect-designed resort-hotel is the ultimate, laid-back place to stay. It sits in a coconut grove verdant with bamboo, frangipani, banana and mango, there's an intimate central courtyard, rustic cottages to retreat to, mud baths and massages and a meandering pool. The cottages differ in shape and size but all have whitewashed walls, wooden rafters, pillars, arches, domes, split levels and space. Furniture is wrought-iron, colours bright, materials natural. The hands-on owner/manager Farrokh is as relaxed as can be, the staff are friendly but unobtrusive and guests are an eclectic mix: a biker in studded leather, a world-class chef, a visiting DJ (welcome to perform in the bar). Views stretch from paddy fields to the hills, and there's a sociable restaurant that has old-world style and grace; don't miss the weekend Thai buffets. The whole place is perfect for Anjuna, Goa's hippy heart – and, should you tire of the easy living here, the beach is a jog away. Ideal for those who thrive on informality and spontaneity. *Ask about water sports, cycling, casino trips.*

rooms	25: 19 cottages for 2, 6 cottages for 4.
price	Rs7,500 for 2. Rs10,500 for 4. Peak season: 20 December–15 January.
meals	Lunch & dinner Rs350 each.
closed	Never.
directions	Ask for directions in village.

	Reception	
tel	+91 (0)8322 274 305	
fax	+91 (0)8322 274 305	
email	info@lagunaanjuna.com	
web	www.lagunaanjuna.com	

Resort

Map 8 Entry 139

Yogamagic Canvas Ecotel

1586/1 Grand Chinvar, Close to Bobby Bar, Anjuna, North Goa, 403 509 Goa

Spot the tents and flags from a distance — splashes of colour amid the palms, paddy fields and strolling buffalo. British Phil and Juliette greet you warmly — both are passionate about their natural retreat. In the bamboo, rammed-earth and palm-leafed restaurant, relax on soft cushions and watch the kingfishers, humming birds, bathing animals and local people. Floating flowers, water candles, a Buddha statue, soft Indian music and delicious treats are here — from fresh juices to perfect eggs florentine to generous vegetarian buffets. The style combines rural India with contemporary minimalism. Be inspired by the use of local wood and cotton, solar-power, recycling, and organic fruit and veg. The peaceful and luxurious suite is inside, while the Rajastani hunting tents, each lined with a different colour to represent one of the *chakras*, reveal comfy beds, wardrobes, a sink, a terrace and a composting loo. Flower- and tree-filled gardens and outside showers are a short stroll. There's yoga by day (should you choose it) and a pool; fires and musical performances by night. A small piece of paradise.

rooms	8: 7 tents sharing showers; 1 suite.
price	£50. Suite from £70. Plus tax 3%-10%. Peak season: mid-Dec-mid-Jan.
meals	Dinner £4.50.
closed	April-October.
directions	Airport: Dabolim, Goa (48km, 1 hour). Train: Thivim (16km, 20 mins).

Under canvas

	Phil Dane & Juliet Leary
tel	+91 (0)8325 623 796
mobile	+91 (0)9370 565 717
email	info@yogamagic.net
web	www.yogamagic.net

C ☙ 👟

Map 8 Entry 140

Palacete Rodrigues
Mazal Vaddo, Anjuna, 403 509 Goa

Mrs Iria Da Costa celebrated her wedding here; 40 years on she lives with her grandson and shares her much-loved home with guests. A watercolorist whose paintings decorate the corridors, she is proud of the 200-year-old Portuguese mansion and full of stories about the old days – the place resonates with family history. High-ceilinged bedrooms have polished red floors and soft lighting; some have four-posters with canopies, others open to the veranda. Large living rooms are busy with carved and polished pieces and small collections to take your fancy – shells, ceramic hot-water bottles, old terracotta jars. There are plants everywhere, an inner courtyard garden, a lawn with plastic chairs, and an imposing 'conference room' for dinner parties on busy nights. You are in a quiet part of town, yet the famous beaches are a walk away. It is a homely and comfortable place to stay, and 'Madam' and her staff are lovely. Make sure you spend some time with this gentle lady: it will be both educational and entertaining. *1.5km from Anjuna beach.*

rooms	15: 11 doubles, 3 suites, 1 single.
price	Rs650. Single Rs550. Suite Rs750-Rs850. Peak season: December-March.
meals	Anjuna's cafés are a short walk.
closed	Rarely.
directions	9km from Mazal. Airport: Dabolim (50km, 1 hour). Train: Thivim (16km, 30 minutes).

Guest house

	Mrs Iria Da Costa
tel	+91 (0)8322 273 358
email	palaceterodrigues@hotmail.com
web	www.palaceterodrigues.com

A 人 👞

Map 8 Entry 141

Hotel Bougainvillea/Granpa's Inn

Gaun Wad, Anjuna, 403 509 Goa

It doesn't matter what you call this place, it will soon feel like home – thanks to the delightful Lucindo and Betina. He is a descendant of the family that built this old, Portuguese-styled Goan mansion and you can see the ancestral portraits inside; Lucindo knows all the history. The house has recently been modernised but the old terracotta tiles, lofty rooms and stained-glass windows remain. It's a cool, rustic hotel whose good-sized rooms are clustered around a central courtyard; light and airy, they have cheerful bedspreads and plants and open to the veranda, while the poolside suites have private courtyards with extra outdoor showers. There's no-one to rush you, breakfast lasts as long as you like and the food is good. On some days there are barbecues and a band. Cool off with a cocktail by the pool, lounge in the lush gardens, wander indoors for billiards, massage or yoga, spin off on a bike to discover Anjuna's flea-market – and the heady, hippy delights of the coconut-palm-fringed beach. *Go-karting & elephant trails.*

Guest house

rooms	14: 6 doubles, 1 single, 7 suites.
price	Rs1,200. Suites Rs1,800-Rs2,500. Peak season: October-March.
meals	Lunch Rs175-Rs250. Dinner Rs300.
closed	Rarely.
directions	1km from Anjuna church on Mapusa-Anjuna road; 7km from Mapusa town. Airport: Dabolim (50km, 1 hour). Train: Thivim (16km, 30 minutes).

	Mr Lucindo & Betina Faria
tel	+91 (0)8322 273 270/271
fax	+91 (0)8322 274 370
email	granpas@hotmail.com
web	www.goacom.org/hotels/granpas

A 🖻 🍶 🏊 ᴓᴓ

Map 8 Entry 142

Nilaya Hermitage
Bhati, Arpora, 403 518 Goa

A star-spangled retreat on the crest of a tropical hill. The hotel was designed by
Goan architect Dean D'Cruz; German designer Claudia added the final touches.
Cosmically themed with fantasy elements, bedrooms have vibrant colours, white
muslin, bathrooms of mosaic; all are large, cool, chic and connect around a
curving central pool. Be seduced by bowls of floating flowers, sun-shaped lamps,
teak columns from a temple in Kerala… and views over paddy fields and wooded
hills to a glittering sea. The stylish owners, Hari and Claudia Ajwani, are not
always present but young staff in blue kurtas and white saris look after you. Food
is a subtle blend of eastern and western flavours overseen by a French chef.
There's no starched formality and the atmosphere is house party not hotel; dine in
your sarong by the langorous decked pool, or in your room. Breakfast lasts as long
as you like. And, should you finally tire of the pleasures of the gym, steam room,
sauna and ayurveda – and the beautiful people – the coast is a ten-minute drive.
Children over 12 welcome. Minimum stay three nights.

rooms	14: 10 doubles, 4 tents for 2.
price	Half-board €290.
	Christmas & New Year up to €450.
	Airport transfer included.
meals	Half-board only.
closed	Rarely.
directions	Hotel staff pick you up from Arpora airport.

	Hari and Claudia Ajwani
tel	+91 (0)8322 276 793/4
fax	+91 (0)8322 276 792
email	nilayahermitage@sify.com or
	nilaya@sancharnet.in
web	www.nilaya.com

Hotel

E 🖻 🍷 🧍 🏊

Map 8 Entry 143

Casa Palacio Siolim House
Waddi, Siolim, Bardez, 403 517 Goa

Much-travelled Varun Sood discovered the neglected 300-year-old villa on one of his travels, then transformed it into a luxurious haven. Once belonging to the Governor of Macau, the *casa de sobrado*-style building has been properly renovated with walls of shell and lime plaster and windowpanes of oyster shell. It's a spoiling place – seven big suites named after 17th-century trading ports, fabulous food, solicitous staff. Terracotta pots sit under shapely white pillars in the central courtyard with fountain and bougainvillea; more pots nudge the pool. Bedrooms, two on the top floor, some around the courtyard, have white walls, dark wooden or tiled floors, rosewood cupboards and wrought-iron beds hung with muslin. There are a sitting room and a library with chess, and a restaurant with glass-topped tables. Dine on caught-that-day fish: pomfret, snapper, bass, mussels, crab and the biggest prawns ever seen. Siolim is a small village with a large Catholic church (services are in English at weekends), bustling Anjuna is three kilometres away, Calangute beach ten. *Tailor-made local tours.*

rooms	7 suites.
price	Rs3,000. Plus 3% tax. Peak season: 19 December–10 January.
meals	Lunch & dinner $15 each.
closed	Rarely.
directions	At entrance to Siolim village just north of Chapora river in north Goa.

Hotel

	Mr Varun Sood
tel	+91 (0)8322 272 138
mobile	+91 (0)9822 584 560
fax	+91 (0)8322 272 941/138
email	info@siolimhouse.com
web	www.siolimhouse.com

B 🖃 🛈 👤 🏊

Map 8 Entry 144

Panchavatti

Kolo Muddi, Corjuem Island, Bardez, 403 508 Goa

The choice of setting for 'Sacred Five Trees' is inspired and the 40m-long covered veranda is a place to sit and dream – amid the sweet scents of jasmine and frangipani. Unfussy decorative touches – copper pots, bowls of floating flowers, cane lampshades – soothe, as do the views of the river, the buffalos grazing and the distant forest. You breakfast on homemade strawberry jam, lashings of real coffee and Goan bread. Belgian by blood, Goa-born and convent-eductated in Surrey and Bombay, Lulu's approach to guests is wise and warm; nothing is too much trouble and her new venture looks set to be a success. Only traditional materials have been used (apart from in the bathrooms): laterite stone, high wooden ceilings and tiled roofs. All the furniture, divans and charpoys, has been copied from old designs in order to preserve traditional techniques. Bedrooms, each with a private balcony, wrap around an inner courtyard where fountains play; there is a constant sound of flowing water. The serene new swimming pool is the final treat. *Ask about cookery courses, concerts & yoga.*

rooms	4 doubles.
price	Full-board from Rs6,000.
meals	Full-board only.
closed	June-September.
directions	From Aldona, signs to Aldona Bridge for Corjuem Island. Left after bridge; 2nd road on left (striped telegraph pole); 1st mud road on left; along wall and through gates. No signs! Airport: Dabolim (1 hour).

Guest house

Ms Isla Maria 'Lulu' Van Damme

tel	+91 (0)9822 580 632
fax	+91 (0)9823 026 447
email	info@islaingoa.com
web	www.islaingoa.com

B 人 ⌐

Map 8 Entry 145

Godfrey's Indian Retreat

Sal Village, P.O. Assanora, Bardez, 403 503 Goa

Godfrey 'Goofy' Lawrence discovered these 20 acres while scouting for film locations in an earlier life. Now he has his own inland paradise, minutes from beaches and at the end of a red dirt road. The cluster of one-storey cottages blends quaintly into the landscape – at its most lush and most peaceful in the monsoon months. Comfort is ethnic within your four mud walls – hessian curtains, terracotta lamps, beds "big enough for foreigners" and blue-tiled bathrooms. The *machhan* (treetop house), perfect for honeymooners, has dreamy views. Then dine in the grass-roofed restaurant with a safari feel… on okra, rice, king fish and prawns. Much of the produce comes from the farm, including the Jersey milk and fresh herbs. Goofy sorts plastics, returns organic waste to the soil, redirects water to the gardens and has made sure the pool is chlorine-free (it's ionised instead). De-stress with a relaxing dip in the jacuzzi. No loud music, no TV, just the odd piping of the flute as you sip a cool beer and relax. When you leave, plant a sapling in memory of your stay. *Ask to visit the waterfalls nearby.*

Resort

rooms	12 cottages for 2.
price	Full-board Rs6,000–Rs11,000; includes elephant safari (Nov–May). Singles Rs4,000. Peak season: October–April.
meals	Full-board only.
closed	Rarely.
directions	Train: Thivim (12km), Mapusa (20km). Airport: Dabolim (65km, 90 mins).

	Godfrey Laurence
tel	+91 (0)8322 389 231
email	safari@goaecoretreat.com
web	www.goaecoretreat.com

C 📖 🛢 ⛷ 🏊

Map 8 Entry 146

Kerkar Retreat

Gaurawaddo, Calangute, 403 516 Goa

A dose of culture in the big beach party that is Goa. Years ago Subodh Kerkar swapped medicine for art – sculpture, furniture, painting, architecture – and here are the results. On the ground floor of the Indo-Portuguese-styled house are a gallery and a café – all blue walls and metal chairs, inspired by the sea. Upstairs, generous, colourful bedrooms have big beds on glazed floors, soft lights, paper lanterns, gauze curtains and art by Subodh and his father. The fish and vegetable curries are delicious and there's a kitchen should you wish to rustle up your own king prawns and crabs (fresh from unpolluted Goan waters). Choose a book on philosophy or art from the library; relax with a drink from the honesty bar; salute the sun on the rooftop terrace under the shady palms. There's even a studio where you can show off your pottery or painting skills and, in summer, open-air performances of music and dance. No matter if the electricity fails, they'll carry on by candlelight! Staff are helpful and friendly and the bustling, beautiful beach is 300 metres away.

rooms	5 doubles.
price	Rs4,000. Peak season: 20 December–10 January.
meals	Breakfast Rs250. Lunch & dinner Rs250 each.
closed	Rarely.
directions	Airport: Dabolim (40km). Train: Panaji (15km).

Guest house

	Dr Subodh Kerkar
tel	+91 (0)8322 276 017
fax	+91 (0)8322 276 509
email	subodhkerkar@satyam.net.in
web	www.subodhkerkar.com

B ▭ ◊ 人

Map 8 Entry 147

Marbella Guesthouse
Sinquerim-Candolim, 403 515 Goa

The house was built not so long ago, and resembles an old Goan mansion. Dian recycled the white roof borders, the pillars and some of the furniture, the tiles on the courtyard table come from North Goa and the flooring was laid by a company that uses old stencils from houses built at the turn of the last century. The whole place is unashamedly romantic, its luxurious suites individually decorated and named (Bougainvillea, Moghul etc). The Penthouse is especially lavish, with marble floors and huge views. There's plenty of space, and you can mingle with other guests in a wonderfully lush central courtyard. Cats and dogs doze in and around the house – and the kitchen is open so you can watch the chefs prepare your meal. The whole heavenly place awaits down a quiet lane on the edge of Candolim village, away from the tourist hum. There's a touch of the exotic at play, which may stem from Dian's half-German background and his passion for the guitar – rock, jazz and blues. Come and join in.

Guest house

rooms	6 suites.
price	Rs1,150–Rs3,800.
meals	Breakfast Rs150.
	Lunch & dinner Rs250 each.
closed	Rarely.
directions	Turn right at Joe Joe's on main road towards Fort Aguada Beach Resort. Guest house 500m along, one of the last on the right. Take a taxi.

Dian Singh

tel	+91 (0)8322 247 9551
mobile	+91 (0)9822 400 811
email	marbella_goa@yahoo.com

B 🍴 ⛷ ♿

Map 8 Entry 148

Panjim Peoples

31st January Road, Fontianhas, Panaji, 403 001 Goa

Sleepy, cobbled Fontainhas is a legacy of Goa's past; it's unlike anywhere else in India. And it's more lively than sleepy in the mornings when the neighbouring high school gets into swing. Panjim Peoples was itself a school (Jack's mother was educated here) and the big corner-shaped building keeps its colonial feel. Come to Peoples if you like to see how the locals live; the welcoming Sukhija family have been taking in guests for years. There's no sitting room, nor garden, and the house is not outstandingly cosy – it was a school, after all – but the red-tiled guest bedrooms are large and lofty and furnished with framed maps of the world and antique rosewood beds – among the finest (and most comfortable) we've seen. Bathrooms are whimsically, eccentrically mosaic'd, with deep tubs and western loos. There's a gallery below displaying contemporary art and you have all the advantages of the Inn next door with its friendly restaurant; guests have been known to lend a hand in the kitchen. Interesting, too, to live in Asia's only Latin Quarter where Portuguese is still the first language.

rooms	4 doubles.
price	Rs3,000-Rs5,400. Plus 3% tax.
meals	Lunch & dinner Rs200-Rs250 each (at Panjim Inn).
closed	Never.
directions	In Fontainhas (the Latin Quarter of Panjim) next to the People's High School, opposite Panjim Inn.

Guest house

	Mr Ajit Sukhija
tel	+91 (0)8322 226 523
res. no	+91 (0)8322 435 628
fax	+91 (0)8322 228 136
email	info@panjiminn.com
web	www.panjiminn.com

Map 8 Entry 149

Panjim Inn & Panjim Pousada

E-212 31st January Road, Fontainhas, Panjim, 403 001 Goa

These two are perfect if you want a taste of Panjim's Portuguese past. They are both in Fontainhas, the throbbing heart of the Latin Quarter; an area of sleeping dogs and gonging chapels. The Inn is Goa's first and only official heritage hotel, a 300-year-old mansion built by the owner's family and graced with colonial rosewood furniture. Most rooms have four-poster beds with colourful covers and curtains billowing from wooden lattice windows; two upstairs rooms have private balconies. There's also a large veranda restaurant; the food is Goan or international, and good. The nearby Pousada – quieter than its neighbour – is a Hindu house in a largely Catholic area, and has been renovated and decorated by Mr Sukhija in a similarly elegant fashion. Downstairs rooms open to the garden and to an interior courtyard – a delightful comtemporary art gallery; upstairs rooms share a balcony overlooking the garden. Mr Sukhija is as interesting as his houses; you'll probably find him sipping a watermelon juice with guests on the first-floor veranda of the Inn. *Ask about dolphin watching & bird spotting.*

Hotel

rooms	Inn: 14 doubles. Pousada: 8 doubles.
price	Rs1,440-Rs2,610. Singles Rs1,260-Rs1,440. Plus 3% tax. Peak season: 21 December-2 March.
meals	Breakfast Rs150. Lunch & dinner Rs200-Rs250 each.
closed	Rarely.
directions	In Fontainhas (the Latin Quarter of Panjim) opposite the People's High School.

	Mr Ajit Sukhija
tel	+91 (0)8322 226 523
fax	+91 (0)8322 228 136
email	panjimin@sancharnet.in
web	www.panjiminn.com

B 🖾 ▯ 丄

Map 8 Entry 150

Coconut Creek
Bimmut, Bogmalo, 403 806 Goa

'Paradise', says the brochure, and paradise it is. These ten houses lie among swaying coconut palms near the sea; be lulled to sleep by the rustling wind. It is ineffably lovely: state-of-the-art new, yet respectful of the environment and the essence of Goa. Lynne and Agnelo are a Scottish-Goan couple who have poured love and energy into creating Coconut Creek. It is a 'resort', so you may expect quiz nights, darts and pool, but it is exquisitely put together and some of the profits go to a local orphanage. Each house has two storeys; the ground floor bedrooms are air-conditioned, those on the upper floors have ceiling fans and generous French windows. The style is minimalist yet exotic. One bedroom has a mattress on a wide wooden platform and pale yellow walls with niched arches for candles and flowers. Bed linen is crisply white. You cross the lovely pool on wooden bridges; the sea and Bogmalo's unspoiled beach are two minutes away. Lynne is a wonderfully friendly, down-to-earth hostess, on hand to help in any way, and the food is delicious.

rooms	20: 16 doubles, 4 twins.
price	Rs4,500–Rs5,500. Peak season: October–April; Christmas & New Year.
meals	Lunch from Rs150. Dinner from Rs310.
closed	Never.
directions	Airport: Dabolim (3km, 5 minutes). Train: Vasco-da-Gama (6km, 15 minutes).

Resort

	Lynn & Agnelo D'Cruz
tel	+91 (0)8322 538 100
res. no	+91 (0)8322 538 090
fax	+91 (0)8322 538 880
email	joets@sancharnet.in

Map 8 Entry 151

Joet's

Baillichad Ward, Bogmalo, 403 806 Goa

Right on the beach at Bogmalo, with Coconut Creek a few yards down – owned by the same delightful people – is an unusual meeting of Scotland and Goa. The place is run by Agnelo's brother Selvy who goes to the fish market daily so there is a constant supply of prime fish to the restaurant: prawns, shark, kingfish, crab… no wonder people come from far and wide to eat here. Joet's is a guest house, a Coconut Creek on a modest scale, and you may share the swimming pool if you tire of the sea. Café-bars play western music but Bogmalo is still a small-scale resort, and the guest house still stands among battered fishing boats and wind-bent palms. It's been a huge success considering it started life as a fisherman's shack – and the beach is pretty much yours: a treat in Goa. The interiors are light and colourful, simple and charming: blue tiles in the restaurant, blue spreads on the beds, tiled floors, fans and mini-bars, tea and coffee trays and small balconies for the upstairs rooms. All have their own separate living room. The noise of giant waves tumbling onto the sands guarantees deep sleep.

rooms	7 suites.
price	Rs2,500–Rs3,500. Peak season: October–April.
meals	Lunch £2. Dinner £4.
closed	Never.
directions	Airport: Dabolim (3km, 5 minutes). Train: Vasco da Gama (6km, 15 minutes).

Guest house

	Lynn & Agnelo D'Cruz
tel	+91 (0)8322 538 036
fax	+91 (0)8322 538 880
email	joets@sancharnet.in

B 🚶 📖 💧 ⛲ 🏊

Map 8 Entry 152

Bhakti Kutir
296 Patnem, Colomb, Canacona, 403 702 Goa

Ute has started a school on the premises for her children; yours may wish to join in. German-born, she has become engagingly Indian after many years here. She and Panta have created a remarkable place: 22 thatched eco-cabanas, some of them two-storey, in surroundings teeming with birdlife at the southern end of Palolem beach – a five-minute walk from the town. There are candles and mosquito nets, hessian curtains and low divans, stone floors inlaid with shells. All have their own bathrooms, some outside but still private. Ute and Panta are serious about environmental sensitivity amd the loos use a biodegrading system, much to the delight of visitors. Bathrooms are 'bucket bath', vegetables – and wheatgrass juice – are organic and home-grown, fish is caught that day. On site are a tailor and clothes craftshops, a library and a concert area, mud baths, steam baths and ayurvedic massage. Everything is made from eco-friendly and local materials – mud, coconut wood, eucalyptus, bamboo – and it works brilliantly. *Dolphin watching & fishing.*

rooms	27 huts: 24 for 2, some sharing baths; 3 family.
price	Rs1,500–Rs2,000. Singles from Rs1,200. Plus 8% tax. Peak season: November–March.
meals	Breakfast Rs150–Rs200. Lunch & dinner from Rs80 each.
closed	During monsoon.
directions	Airport: Dabolim (72km, 1.5 hours). Train: Chaudi, Canacona (3km, 5 minutes).

	Ute & Panta Ferrao	Resort
tel	+91 (0)8322 643 469	
mobile	+91 (0)9822 380 229	
email	info@bhaktikutir.com	
	or bhaktikutir@yahoo.com	
web	www.bhaktikutir.com	

SPECIAL GREEN ENTRY
see page 18

B 🍶 🚜

Map 8 Entry 153

Casa de Morgado
House 115, Sontrant, Cortalim, 403 710 Goa

This 'house of friendly spirits' is just that. Beaming Beulah runs it with her mother, two cricket-mad sons and friends as backup. She does everything – scooter pick-ups, housework, room design. There's a lovely family feel at Morgado. Beulah, a traditional Catholic, prefers quiet after 11pm, but you really can come and go as you please. This is also a rare chance to experience one of the oldest houses in Goa. The 400-year-old ancestral home, part Portuguese, part Moorish, has been declared an official heritage house. It sits at the foot of a hill, overlooking an expanse of green paddy fields, and is a mile from the village where friendly locals take your hand and wish you well – in Konkani. It's the best way to get a taste of Goan village life. Bathrooms are modern, bedrooms are a good size with white walls, red-oxide floors, plain wrought-iron beds, and share a veranda that encircles the place. Breakfast is fruit and eggs several ways; there's home-cooking for dinner, red wine and fruit. Beulah, kind and helpful, provides excellent daily itineraries. *Boat rides on the river. Hire car available.*

Homestay

rooms	3 doubles.
price	Rs1,220. Peak season: September-March. Cancellation fee 25%. Peak season: November-March.
meals	Breakfast Rs100. Lunch & dinner Rs300 each.
closed	Rarely.
directions	Midway between Panjim & Margao; call for directions. Pick-up charged at government rate. Airport: Dabolim (12km).

	Mrs Beulah Athayde Gomes
tel	+91 (0)8322 550 216
mobile	+91 (0)9822 586 923
email	beula_h@yahoo.com

A 🕴 👶 🚲 👟

Map 8 Entry 154

Kerala

A narrow strip of land between the Arabian Sea and the Western Ghats, Kerala is a mosaic of inland waterways and lakes smothered in lilac water hyacinths, swaying palm trees by lime green paddies, heady spice plantations and fascinating rituals. Its communist government, elected in 1957, has created a more even spread of wealth and land as well as excellent healthcare and education systems. It has the highest literacy rate (91%) and the lowest infant mortality rate in the country. This is India's most densely populated state – some Keralans (or 'Malayalis') head to the Middle East and add their remittances to the tourist income of this already prosperous state.

An idyllic way to travel from Alappuzha (Alleppey) is by rice barge – large, thatched houseboats which wend their way past villages and school children through rural Kerala. In Kochi (Cochin) you can forage in the antique shops for a glimpse of Jewish, Keralan, Portuguese and British culture or watch fishermen demonstrate their ingenious Chinese fishing nets. Head for the hills and the spice plantations and see how tea, coffee, vanilla, cloves, cardamom, rubber and pepper grow. Watch the Kattakali dance where heavily made-up male artists dance out a bizarre pantomime. In villages further north you may see the Theyyam, an all-night holy dance where the performers experience a trance-like state. Here, visit thriving Kozhikode (Calicut), the remote northern beaches and the tourist-quiet Wayanad Wildlife Sanctuary.

In southern Kerala, chill out on the relaxed, palm-fringed beaches at Varkala and Kovalam and book in for some herbal ayurvedic massage to rub away any remaining tension. Snorkel in the unspoilt Langshadweep Islands, part of Kerala – its coral atolls have 600 varieties of reef fish including purple-lipped giant clams, sea anemones, ink-blue starfish and multicoloured clown and parrot fish.

Best time to visit

Photos Laura Kinch

Kerala

Costa Malabari
Near Adikadalayi Temple, Kannur, 670 007 Kerala

If you seek somewhere off the tourist trail and are a fan of 'small is beautiful', you'll love Costa Malabari – hemmed in by cashew and coconut plantations it's an idyllic five-minute stroll from golden beaches (and dolphins). Once a power shed, then a coconut-oil processing outfit, this unpretentious guest house still has a lofty warehouse feel; don't come looking for luxury. Pastel pink walls soften the cavernous dining hall while a warm yellow washes the four snug and simple bedrooms. Mr Kurien is intelligent and welcoming and his inventive twists on traditional recipes make each meal a feast – the tropical fruit ice creams are delicious. Ingredients are bought locally, staff are from the neighbouring village, and the guest house hasn't expanded in its eight years – the result is a respectful, easy and unobtrusive relationship with the community. You may get invited to local events or weddings and are well placed to find out about Keralan festivals. A getaway in the best possible sense, wonderful people, a great ethos. Of the owner's various properties, this is the one we recommend.

Guest house

rooms	4 doubles.
price	Full-board Rs2,000. Peak dates: 15 October-14 February.
meals	Full-board only.
closed	June/July.
directions	8km south of Kannur train station, near Adikadalayi Temple. Please call before arrival.

	Mr P.J. Varghese (Manager)
res. no	+91 (0)4842 371 761
mobile	+91 (0)9847 044 688
email	touristdesk@satyam.net.in
web	www.costamalabari.com

A 🚶 👟

Map 8 Entry 155

Ayisha Manzil

Court Road, Telicherry, 670 101 Kerala

The 'house on the hill' was built by an English colonel-turned-cinnamon-planter in 1862. In 1900 it was bought by Mr Moosa's grandfather. The house is neither large nor exceptional, though the bedrooms and bathrooms are on a grand scale, and it is elegantly adorned with the original furniture. Come for Mr Moosa – a lovely man, passionate about Keralan culture and proud of the celebrated local martial art displays that he organises for guests. He is a resourceful and engaging host – make the most of him. You eat well here, too: Mrs Moosa specialises in Mapalla cuisine, the local Muslim food served at a shared table in the garden. This coastal area is where the old British trading ports used to be; now this special heritage homestay is beginning to put the region back on the map. Ayisha overlooks the vast Arabian sea, with a glorious stretch of unpopulated virgin beach nearby. You are just outside Telicherry so might hear the road below or the odd train. Do visit the 1750 Protestant church, and the family-owned 450-year-old mosque, built of rosewood and copper. *Cookery courses.*

rooms	6 doubles.
price	Full-board from $200. Peak season: April-August.
meals	Full-board only. Lunch & dinner from $15 each.
closed	Rarely.
directions	Close to Telicherry town. Take Calicut road, Sea View Park on left, turn right and house uphill. Airport: Calicut (90km).

	Mr & Mrs Moosa
tel	+91 (0)4902 341 590
fax	+91 (0)4902 341 590
email	cpmoosa@rediffmail.com

Homestay

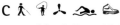

Map 8 Entry 156

Vythiri Resort

Vythiri, Lakkidi P.O., Wayanad District, 673 576 Kerala

The mild misty green of the Wayanad forests provide a deep, cool relief from the oppressive heat of the plains. The Paadi rooms were once watering holes for plantation workers; now they are cossetting bedrooms perfect for families, their beds raised 30cm off the floor, their small arches leading to shower rooms. The huts and cottages have been recently built but the surrounding forest is otherwise undisturbed; polished bamboo doors lead into wonderfully comfortable rooms that you may share with a tree or a huge slab of rock. Local, naturally tinted mud dresses each cottage in vast orange swirls; stylish-rustic is the feel. No plastic in sight, just terracotta water jugs and mugs and bamboo light fittings. The cottages face the racing river and have vast balconies where monkeys tumble gaily. The food is delicious, and the 'resortiness' subtle and unobtrusive, the presence of health spa, business centre and TV room detracting not a jot from the arresting – and remote – beauty of the place. There are wonderful walks to natural pools and waterfalls... but don't forget the leech socks. *Serena Spa treatments available.*

Resort

rooms	36: 6 family rooms, 18 cottages for 2, 12 huts for 2.
price	Full-board $75-$90.
meals	Full-board only.
closed	Rarely.
directions	A jeep takes you the few bumpy miles from Vythiri town to the resort, or pick-up can be arranged from station or airport. Airport: Calicut (85km, 1.5 hours).

	Mr Roy Chacko
tel	+91 (0)4936 255 366
res. no	+91 (0)4842 356 249
fax	+91 (0)4936 255 368
email	vythiri@serenaspa.com
web	www.vythiriresort.com

B 🖂 🏊

Map 8 Entry 157

Rain Country Resorts
Lakkidi, Wayanad District, 637 576 Kerala

Swirling mists and echo-ing monkey calls weave through the majestic Wayanad valley, low lamps illuminate the dirt trail that carves its way through the un-resorty 'resort'. It is a splendid departure from the world of 'pack 'em in'; Rain Country's 20-acre valley is shared by several cottages but you'd have to yodel to be heard by your neighbour. Tiled roof cottages are simple (limited electricity, no phones) yet comfortable 'heritage' affairs with one or more double rooms. Less private, the bigger cottage makes interesting use of the space; its bathrooms are semi-open and its *charupadi*, or porch, juts out from the veranda. Potter across a wooden bridge to the small thatched dining room – the resort's kitchen will spice up any successful catches you may have made from the natural pool (also good for swimming). Stroll undisturbed through the grounds or attempt one of the stunning walks. Die-hard trekkers should try the Chembra peak; at 2,100m, the highest in Wayanad. It's impossible to feel rushed at Rain Country. Just pause and take a deep breath – and what good air it is! We love this place.

rooms	5 cottages: 1 for 6, 2 for 4, 1 for 2.
price	Rs2,500–Rs3,500. Peak season: October–May.
meals	Breakfast Rs100. Lunch & dinner Rs150 each.
closed	Rarely.
directions	Pick-up from Lakkidi, 3km from resort. Airport/train: Calicut (85km, 1.5 hours).

Resort

	Mr E K Anil
tel	+91 (0)4936 205 306
mobile	+91 (0)9447 245 288
fax	+91 (0)4936 255 306
email	resorts@raincountryresort.com
web	www.raincountryresort.com

B

Map 8 Entry 158

Tranquil, Plantation Hideaway

Kuppamudi Coffee Estate, Kolagapara P.O., Wayanad, 673 591 Kerala

Three thousand feet up in the Western Ghats, this smart guest house sits hidden among the coffee bushes and unspoilt rainforest of the Kuppamudi Coffee Estate. The 70-year-old plantation bungalow has been beautifully restored; enormous bedrooms have thick cotton sheets, patterned bedcovers and extremely comfortable beds. Expect hotel-smart furniture, TVs and floral curtains, and huge bathrooms. A breezy veranda runs outside. Best of all is the sturdy tree house, entirely constructed from natural materials – bamboo woven walls, coffee roots for tables and shelves, and a branch growing inside; there's also a secluded terrace for fabulous forest views. Victor and Ranjini sweep you into their lives – you may meet the grandchildren. There's a shady platform for a nap, hammocks and pool-side loungers – a sense of calm pervades. Guests can enjoy Indian and continental buffet dinners around the big table. Hill-top breakfasts and plantation walks are easily arranged; the Eddakal Caves are a ten-minute drive. *Children by special arrangement. Trekking & birdwatching in Wildlife Sanctuary.*

Guesthouse

rooms	9: 6 twins, 1 double + sofabed, 1 suite + sofabed, 1 tree house.
price	Full-board €170–€340. Singles €130–€190. Tree house: €220–€300. Peak season: December–March.
meals	Full-board only.
closed	July.
directions	1.5km off Mysore-Calicut highway. Turn at Kolagapara Junction onto road leading to Edakkal caves; house signed on left.

	Mr V K Rajaram
tel	+91 (0)4936 220 244
mobile	+91 (0)9847 865 824
fax	+91 (0)4936 222 358
email	tranquil@satyam.net.in
web	www.tranquilresort.com

Map 8 Entry 159

Harivihar Ayurvedic Heritage Home
Bilathikulam, Calicut (Kozhikode), 673 006 Kerala

Lush lawns tumble around this horseshoe-shaped house and if you can resist the charms of the natural rocky pool there are many shady spots under the jackfruit and mango trees. Inside, an oasis of calm: oceans of gleaming red oxide floors beneath fresh white walls, and veranda oil lamps spilling light onto huge bright canvases of temple icons and dancing forms. Bedrooms are sober and charming, some with great garden views. A lofty dining room opens to the lawn and a meditation and yoga room on the top floor resides serenely over all. So tranquil is it that's it's easy to forget you're in the centre of Calicut – and hard to believe that until the early 1980s almost 60 members of Neethi's extended family called this home. Neethi has returned here with her husband Dr Srikumar and they have carved out this little sanctuary – a committed centre of treatment and learning. Join talks on Indian culture and philosophy; immerse yourself in ayurveda. Balm for the soul.

rooms	8: 5 doubles, 3 singles.
price	Full-board from €90. Singles from €65.
meals	Full-board only.
closed	Mid-April-mid-May.
directions	A 15-minute drive from Calicut train station.

Guest house

	Dr G Srikumar
tel	+91 (0)4952 765 865
email	admin@harivihar.com
web	www.harivihar.com

B ✕ ⅄ ⟿

Map 8 Entry 160

Tasara, Centre for Creative Weaving
North Beypore, 673 015 Kerala

Piles of plush fabrics cover tables and floors, the weaving studio clatters with activity, and fantastical completed pieces are showcased in the new whitewashed exhibition building. (The weavings are sold worldwide.) There's a real working atmosphere here; the ethic was clear long before Mr Vasudevan explained (tongue only slightly in cheek) that "we don't like idle people". He shares the house with five siblings, two children, a pair of bounding dogs and any number of artistically inclined guests. Bedrooms in the exhibition building are less bustling than those of the family house, but all are simple and vary considerably in size. Things here may be a bit too shambolic and high energy for some and it's definitely not the spot to tick 'quality lazy time' off your holiday wish list. But, if you love people, creativity and bustle, you'll relish carving out a happy niche in this busy family den. If not to weave, come to write, paint, cook and create in what must be one of the most truly unique of Keralan homestays. Eccentric and intriguing. *Weaving courses & vegetarian cookery classes all year round.*

rooms	8 doubles.
price	Full-board €100. Singles €50–€70. Includes use of studio facilities.
meals	Full-board only.
closed	Rarely.
directions	Airport: Calicut (21km). Train: Calicut (7km).

Guest house

	Mr V Vasudevan
tel	+91 (0)4952 414 233
email	tasara@sancharnet.in
	or vasudevantasara@yahoo.com
web	www.tasaraindia.com

B 🛗 ✕ òò

Map 8 Entry 161

Tharavad

Kandath Tharavad, Thenkurussi, Palakkad, 678 671 Kerala

Nearly all the agricultural land you pass on the route from Palakkad belonged to the Kandath family. Their impressive ancestral home was built in 1794 on part of the estate, of mud and teak. Much of the land has since been redistributed but Tharavad seems unwilling to relinquish the splendour of its glory days. However, renovation has added creature comforts, and the presence of Mr Bhagwaldas and his family memorabilia lends it a homely air. Bulbous carved teak pillars frame the colourful naturally dyed tiles of the raised *purathalum*, where Bhagwaldas's grandfather perched to conduct his money lending. Little carved wooden doors draw you to a smaller *purathalam*, traditionally the female domain. Although only seven metres apart, neither group was required to mince their words: not a sound can be heard between the two. Conversation is still important at Tharavad, where guests enjoy shared meals with their quietly intelligent host, perhaps round candlelit tables on the lawn. A fascinating home.

rooms	6 doubles.
price	Full-board Rs7,000.
	Peak season: October-March.
meals	Full-board only.
closed	Rarely.
directions	10km from Palakkad; call to be picked up.

Homestay

Mr Bhagwaldas Sudevan
tel   +91 (0)4922 284 124
email   tharavad15@yahoo.com
web   www.tharavad.info

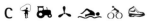

Map 8 Entry 162

OlappamannaMana

Vellinezhi, District Palakkad, 679 504 Kerala

In the 18th century this was a feudal lord's house with a Hindu family deity, a bathing tank and separate quarters for men and women. Over the years additional structures sprang up, and it became an important seat of learning for Kathakali, classical Keralan dance and traditional Veda and Sanskrit. The main building is where you can watch the *puja*: dance, prayer and drumming around a giant sand painting of the Goddess Kali. Upstairs are two clean and simple bedrooms (own wcs, shared bathroom downstairs) panelled in dark rosewood and teak. In a newer building are two more, cheerful with antiques and sharing a kitchen and large veranda. Guests alone stay in these buildings; choose the new rooms if you prefer a lighter atmosphere. Mr Damodoran and his smiling wife Sreedevi live a five-minute stroll away though coconut palms and will show you the family antiques and decorative festival elephant attire. They also serve authentic and delicious south Indian vegetarian food. A most unusual and traditional place. *No alcohol. Thayampaka drumming & Kathakali dance performances — ask for prices.*

Homestay

rooms	4: 2 twins sharing bath. New building: 1 double, 1 family room.
price	Full-board $70-$100. Family room $125-$150. Peak season: November-May.
meals	Full-board only. Packed lunches available.
closed	Rarely.
directions	From Palghat, 43km, take Calicut Rd (Cherepalchery route). Airport: Calicut (50km, 1.5 hours). Train: Palakkad Jn, Shoranur (25km).

	Mr Nayayan Damodaran
tel	+91 (0)4662 285 383/797
email	olappamannadamodaran@gmail.com
web	www.olappamannamana.com

B 🚶👟

Map 8 Entry 163

Kadappuram Beach Resort
P.O. Nattika Beach, Trichur, 680 566 Kerala

From the air, the eco-resort of Kadappuram is indistinguishable from the fishing villages scattered along the coast, its cottages, long and low, constructed of coconut thatch, wood and bamboo. In 'The Land of the Coconut Palm' there's little reason to build any other way. Here, a number of attractive cottages (some with two double rooms) sprawl across a sandy seven acres, the golden beach 200 metres away. The bamboo-mat walls form a restrained backdrop to simple luxuries — cascading mosquito nets hang over the crisp white sheets of dark four-posters, while polished wooden steps either side of the bed add further grandeur. Small details combine to create a special whole: incense wafts through the rooms each evening, palm leaf origami figures hang from verandas and dance on the warm evening air. And the sweet smell of ramacham roots stuffed into the thatched roofs infuses the rooms when the rains and winds come. The restaurant serves authentic Keralan food, and you can snack throughout the day at no extra cost. Bliss. *A strong ayurvedic focus; any diet can be catered for. Minimum stay 14 nights.*

rooms	27: 24 doubles, 1 triple, 2 tents for 1.
price	Full-board €95. Plus 7.5% tax. Peak season: October-30 April; 21 December-3 January.
meals	Full-board only.
closed	Rarely.
directions	On Kochi-Calicut highway; well-signed from Nattika junction. Airport: Kochi (65km). Train: Trichur (25km).

Mr M R Gopalakrishnan

tel	+91 (0)4872 394 988
mobile	+91 (0)9447 139 498
fax	+91 (0)4872 394 988
email	kadappuram@sancharnet.in
web	www.kadappurambeachresorts.com

Resort

B

Map 8 Entry 164

Mundackal Homestay

Mundackal Estate, Pindimana PO, via Thrikariyoor, Kothamangalam, 686 698 Kerala

You approach along a bumpy farm track that winds through a rubber plantation on the edge of the Salim Ali Bird Sanctuary. Seeing no official boundaries, birds of every description come to sing over breakfast – the only disturbance in this lush oasis. Daisy and Jose, whose father was a leading Keralan politician, are a warm and generous pair – perhaps a little too eager to make you leave feeling more circular than when you arrived. This is a genuine Indian homestay. The décor is unremarkable with splashes of kitsch, you sleep in bare but adequate bedrooms, and feast on mountains of food! (Daisy can teach you a few culinary tricks.) The setting – secluded, green and with birds to excite twitchers – is wonderful, and don't miss out on Jose's plantation walk: you'll learn how rubber is tapped and turned into sheets, and spot eastern spices growing wild. An engagingly Indian experience, particularly for anyone with ornithological or gastronomic leanings – and a rare chance to dip your toes into the lives of a working plantation family. *Kodanad elephant training camp nearby.*

Homestay

rooms	5 doubles.
price	Full-board $125-$140.
meals	Full-board only.
closed	Rarely.
directions	Kothamangalam is 57km from Kochi. Plantation House is 7km from Kothamangalam. Don't try to find it on your own!

	Jose & Daisy Mundackal
tel	+91 (0)485 2570 717 or (0)485 3202 000
mobile	+91 (0)9388 620 399
email	nestholidays@hotmail.com
web	www.mundackalhomestay.com

B 🚶 🍴 🚜 🧘

Map 8 Entry 165

Periyar River Lodge

Anakayam, Kuttampuzha PO, Thattekad, Ernakulam District, 686 691 Kerala

The views from this simple teak-built lodge on the banks of the serene Periyar river soothe the soul. On the doorstep of the Thattekad Bird Sanctuary – home to some 270 bird species – the guest house has a laid-back, simple feel. And you're in the midst of it – among rubber plantations – so this is a great place for people-watching and taking in village life. Inside is a sunken central courtyard where a leafy palm reaches for the sun. A small seating area with subdued cosy lighting and bamboo seats with stripy red and burnt-orange cushions lies on one side; a small kitchen and dining room lie on the other. A local lady cooks delicious south Indian meals, served by your attentive, eager-to-please host Paul. Several windows throw light into the bedrooms which have been designed with a stylish hand. Rattan blinds, decorated terracotta lamps, red and cream bedspreads on comfy beds – all look beautiful against the backdrop of rich teak walls. Best of all are the bathrooms with open-air showers. The birds will wake you, the insects will sing you to sleep. *Boat trips, bicycle tours & guided walks.*

rooms	2 doubles.
price	Full-board Rs3,200.
	Whole lodge Rs5,200.
	Peak season: October–March.
meals	Full-board only.
closed	Rarely.
directions	Near Thattekad Bird Sanctaury.
	Airport: Kochi (50km, 1.5 hours).

Guest house

	Mr Eldho Kuruvilla
tel	+91 (0)4842 207 173
mobile	+91 (0)9447 707 173
fax	+91 (0)4842 207 173
email	info@periyarriverlodge.com
web	www.periyarriverlodge.com

Map 8 Entry 166

Windermere Estate
Pothamedu, Munnar, 685 612 Kerala

What cool, green relief from the heat and stickiness of the coast, here in Munnar. Sprays of bougainvillea and morning glory cover the garden walls of this stunning spot, perched above miles of steep-sided tea estates and wooded slopes. It is green beyond imagination and as colourful as a Devonshire spring garden. The chalet-like buildings are simple but comfortable and gently suffused with the scent of cardamom. There is a long shaded terrace with wicker chairs in which to read, and gardens in which to stroll. You might find an embroidered alpine milkmaid watching you from the dining room wall, but the setting is stunning, the tranquillity total and the early morning or evening walk through the cardamom forest takes you into another world of birdsong and arboreal paradise. The trees are vast buttressed giants that play host to hundreds of species of birds and wild bee colonies, beneath which sprout the jungle-like cardamom plants. Windermere is intimate if not entirely Indian – one of those rare finds which you are reluctant to share. Be sure not to miss sunrise from the hilltop lookout.

Guest house

rooms	15 doubles.
price	$125–$195. Plus 10% tax. Less 25% May–July. Peak season: October–March.
meals	Lunch $7. Dinner $10–$15.
closed	Rarely.
directions	From Kochi, right after narrow bridge 2km before Munnar; towards Pothamedu viewpoint; 500m, entry through tea garden entry. Airport: Kochi (160km, 3 hours).

	Dr Simon John
tel	+91 (0)4865 230 512
mobile	+91 (0)9447 025 237
fax	+91 (0)4865 230 978
email	windermere@satyam.net.in
web	www.windermeremunnar.com

D 🚜

Map 8 Entry 167

Gramam Homestay

Neduveli House, North Kumbalangi Island, Kochi, 682 007 Kerala

From a bamboo swing, experience the gentle pace of backwaters life on this small island; hard to believe this is only 10km from Fort Kochi. From this sweet and simple homestay wander through the sloping garden, past mango trees and coconut palms, down to the water's edge. Jos, his wife, mother and two sons live here – all are friendly and welcoming. Light-filled bedrooms have comfy wooden beds and shutters, patterned wall hangings, crisp sheets, fans and mosquito nets. Old mango pots used for salting and storing fruit have been artfully turned into lamp bases and luggage racks have been created from bamboo. The bedroom at the back of the house is more private, with its lovely terrace and antique snoozing chairs. Fresh bathrooms are small with hot showers. The family take their environmental responsibilities seriously, support the local community and are building a new eco cottage under the palms at the edge of the backwaters. Watch the toddy-makers at work, go fishing with the locals, spin off on a bike. And the fresh, homemade fish, prawn and crab curries are delicious. *Cookery courses.*

rooms	2 + 1: 2 twins. 1 self-catering cottage for 4.
price	£40-£50. Cottage £60. Peak season: September-March.
meals	Breakfast included. Lunch & dinner £6 each.
closed	Rarely.
directions	On North Kumbalangi Island, 10km south of Kochi.

Homestay

	Mr Jos & Lyma Byju
tel	+91 (0)4842 240 278
mobile	+91 (0)9447 177 312
email	keralagramam@vsnl.net or keralagramam@hotmail.com
web	www.keralagramam.com

Map 8 Entry 168

The Brunton Boatyard

1/498 Fort Kochi, Kochi, 682 001 Kerala

The hotel is at once big, grand and simple — like a plantation owner's house. A further appeal lies in its handsome dominance of the waterfront and its setting near the Chinese Fishing Nets. (Permission to build in this preservation area is tightly controlled, which says something for the integrity of the Casino Group who own the place.) This is history recreated and the large, serene spaces resemble a museum of Dutch colonial living — though they are far more comfortable. The vaulted lobby walls read like a gallery of the major players in Cochin port's life, while the ceiling is overhung with enormous old-fashioned fans of Indo-Portuguese origin. Open walkways encircle the central courtyard with its vast rain tree; behind, every room's balcony faces the busy shipping channel, where tankers cross wakes with ferries and fishing canoes plying their way to the islands beyond — a scene you don't tire of watching. The pool area is hotel-standard and large, the restaurants a little soulless, but beautiful bedrooms have antique bedsteads and bathrooms are truly sensual. *Free sunset cruises.*

Hotel

rooms	22: 12 doubles, 6 twins, 4 suites.
price	$360. Suites $410. Plus 15% tax. Peak season: February; 21 December–10 January.
meals	Breakfast $8. Lunch & dinner from $12 each.
closed	Rarely.
directions	At the mouth of the harbour next to Fort Kochi bus station.

Mr Sunil Varghese (Manager)

tel	+91 (0)4842 215 462
fax	+91 (0)4842 215 562
email	bruntonboatyard@cghearth.com
web	www.cghearth.com

E ⊠ ♨ 人 ≋

Map 8 Entry 169

Trinity House
Parade Road, Fort Kochi, Kochi, 682 001 Kerala

The onetime Indian headquarters of the Dutch East India Company has become a voguish little bolthole exuding privacy and peace – ideal for families and stylish groups of friends. It's a young offshoot of Malabar House (see entry 171) – an intimate, unhotelly and seductive place to stay. The three suites sing with Anglo-Indian good taste: coloured silk cushions on raised double beds, original art, luxurious linen, controlled blinds, outside bathrooms with sunken showers encircled by pebbles. Two suites have an extra bed on the mezzanine, the smallest has an outdoor deck. For views, seek out the balcony that overlooks the parade ground – mellow-yellow in the early evening light. Breakfast when you please, on fresh breads and pastries, fruit and eggs and banana and coconut pancakes, smilingly served. For Indian designer clothing, there's an on-site boutique. For dinner – and massage – there's Malabar House. For sport – bikes and a tiny pool. Then retire to the dining/sitting room, chic and inviting with deep orange chairs, books, DVDs, internet and large, lush bowl of fruit.

rooms	3: 1 suite, 2 family suites.
price	€170-€250.
meals	Meals at Malabar House.
closed	Rarely.
directions	In Fort Kochi, 200m across Parade Ground from its sister hotel, Malabar House. Airport: Kochi (1 hour).

Mr Mervin Issac (Manager)

tel	+91 (0)4842 216 666
fax	+91 (0)4842 217 777
email	reservations@malabarhouse.com
web	www.malabarhouse.com

Hotel

Map 8 Entry 170

Malabar House

1/268 & 1/269 Parade Road, Fort Kochi, Kochi, 682 001 Kerala

Joerg Drechsel, an ethnographic exhibition creator of taste and style, has created a slice of heaven. Old temple carvings cast shadows across lively ochra, turquoise and white walls and every piece of furniture has been perfectly chosen. The central courtyard is as Eden might have been; Joerg built the hotel around a vast vine-and-frangipani-clad rain tree. Creeping green vanilla climbs up whitewashed walls, and the lovely, petal-sprinkled plunge pool sits beneath a hanging roof. Tables from the veranda'd restaurant spill out under the trees, bamboo overhangs the open-sided courtyard brushed by sea breezes. Joerg's Spanish wife Txuku concocts the food, a delicate, delectable harmony of east and west. Colonial four-poster teak beds stand opposite vast Keralan masks, subtly lit works of contemporary art mix with ancient ones. The roof garden suites are the largest, lightest and the most private. Most of the building is new, yet every inch reflects Joerg's commitment to the Keralan vernacular. Old and new seamlessly combine and the luxury is perfectly simple. A calm oasis in this historic harbour city.

rooms	17: 13 doubles, 4 suites.
price	€150–€195. Suites €170–€325. Plus 15% tax. Peak season: October–May.
meals	Lunch & dinner from €15 each.
closed	Rarely.
directions	Signed from seaside Kochi. Do not get taken to Taj Malabar! Airport: Kochi (1 hour).

Hotel

	Mr Mervin Isaac (Manager)
tel	+91 (0)4842 216 666
fax	+91 (0)4842 217 777
email	info@malabarhouse.com
web	www.malabarhouse.com

E 📖 🍷 ⚱ 🏊

Map 8 Entry 171

Fort House
2/6A Calvetty Road, Fort Kochi, Kochi, 682 001 Kerala

Kochi harbour, one of the grand sights of Kerala, is right there, lapping against the edge of the hotel's jetty. All that remains of the trading company building where Fort House now stands are the whitewashed walls of the jetty and the grand old wooden front door. Scattered between, where traders used to haul their wares from boat to roadside, is a wild garden of trees, plants, sculptures and bright blooms. Don't expect luxury: the huts (some bamboo, some brick) are basic, spotless and wonderfully free of hotel frippery. Just a big bed, crisp white sheets, a clothes rail – all you need and nothing more. Each hut shares part of a wide connecting veranda that overlooks the garden. Watch flocks of sparrows taking a bath in the sandy path that wends its way down to the the jetty where boats bob about. With great views over the harbour entrance, and a much-loved restaurant serving some of the best food and cakes in Fort Kochi, Fort House is a simple but truly charming place to stay.

rooms	9 doubles.
price	Rs950-Rs1,800. Peak season: September-February.
meals	Lunch & dinner from Rs200 each.
closed	Never.
directions	In Fort Kochi, between coast guard & jetty. Airport: Kochi (45km). Train: Ernakulam South (13km).

Guest house

	Mrs Joanita Thomas (Manager)
tel	+91 (0)4842 217 103
res. no	+91 (0)4842 215 125
mobile	+91 (0)9349 146 880
email	fort_hs@yahoo.com

A ㄱ

Map 8 Entry 172

Anthraper Gardens
Chertala, Kochi, Kerala

In parts Kerala feels so exotic, so 'other', thanks to the rich palate of colours that were used when this slender tranche of India was first laid down. Along came humankind, with its white daub, and the picture was complete: the most brilliant of greens and alluring of blues set against Grecian whites. Anthraper Gardens has all of this in abundance. It's the sort of Keralan scene that you begin to take for granted – a veranda dinner of the freshest fish, and serene backwater shallows at the bottom of the garden, across which sit dense green palm forests. Yet memories of such moments are an important weapon against dreary European winters. The Anthraper family have been here for over a hundred years next to the tiny backwaters village of Chertala. Their gracious home typifies the new breed of Keralan homestay, where old world charm holds hands with modernity, but isn't led by it. They are accomplished and passionate cooks (much of their food is homegrown) and easy, convivial hosts. The beaches of Chertala are around the corner, as are temples, churches and, beyond, the rest of Kerala.

Homestay

rooms	2 doubles.
price	Full-board $100-$180. Peak season: October-March; 20 December-10 January.
meals	Full-board only.
closed	Rarely.
directions	Airport: Kochi (60km, 1.5 hours). Train: Chertala (5km, 15 mins).

	Mrs Rani Bachani, Mrs Omana Thomas
tel	+91 (0)4842 351 219
res. no	+91 (0)4782 813 211
mobile	+91 (0)9846 061 219
email	vicetravels@vsnl.com

C ☀ ⚡ ⛷ 🚲 👟

Map 8 Entry 173

Philip Kutty's Farm

Pallivathukal, Ambika Market P.O., Vechoor, Kottayam District, 686 144 Kerala

Come to be marooned, in comfort, on an island. Each of these waterfront cottages is solidly built along old architectural lines using tiled overhanging roofs and shuttered windows. One has an open-plan layout with a veranda running around it, others have separate bedroom and sitting area and 'sit outs' in front of the water; two are new this year. The coconut and spice plantation is criss-crossed by hundreds of water channels – enchanting. All is simplicity and serenity inside: dark wooden ceilings, white walls, some antique furniture. Bedrooms are small but delightful, their heavy wooden doors opening out to water; showers are westernised and luxurious; tiled living areas are open to catch the breeze. The 750-acre island of Puthenkayal was created from land reclaimed by this Syrian Christian family in the 1950s. Gentle Anu and her mother run cookery courses, their food is delicious and meals are communal occasions under the outdoor pavilion. You can be alone or involved, take out punts or just lie back and read. Very much the comfortable homestay. *Cooking & painting holidays.*

rooms	6 cottages for 2.
price	Full-board $135-$200. Peak season: October-May.
meals	Full-board only.
closed	Rarely.
directions	From Ambika Market, Church Road for 1km. Boat collects from jetty. 1 hour from Kochi. Train: Kottayam (25km). Airport: Kochi (75km).

Anu Mathew

tel	+91 (0)4829 276 529
res. no	+91 (0)4829 276 530
mobile	+91 (0)9895 075 130
email	mail@philipkuttysfarm.com
web	www.philipkuttysfarm.com

Homestay

C

Map 8 Entry 174

Coconut Lagoon

Kumakarom, Kottayam, Kottayam District, 686 563 Kerala

Tourism has a stormy relationship with the environment, yet here is an example of eco-ingenuity that doesn't cut corners. Dung fuel *biogas*, water recycling, organic rice paddies – all are in place, yet no comfort is lacking. Rare-breed Vechur cows graze tethered between the cottages and a butterfly garden juts into the paddies. You may experience a frisson of grandeur as you arrive by boat through a small channel crossed by bridges, then step into a low-slung, veranda'd reception to be greeted graciously with a coconut and jasmine garland. The quaint heritage bungalows have been crafted from the remnants of ruined Keralan palaces, all wooden carvings and brasswork. Simple dark wooden furniture, plain cotton bedthrows and cool, red-tiled floors may be discovered through tiny but heavy wooden doors, while the suites, with a pool each, are deliciously private. The days may be busy, yet there is ample time to swing in a hammock. Coconut Lagoon is, undeniably, a resort, yet one that strives to make a difference. It is calm, easy-going and fun – and wonderful if you're travelling with children.

Resort

rooms	50: 42 doubles, 8 suites.
price	$149–$171. Suite $319. Plus 25% tax. Peak season: 21 December–20 January.
meals	Breakfast $5. Lunch & dinner from $10 each.
closed	Rarely.
directions	Only accessible by boat from Kumakarom. Contact hotel to arrange pick-up.

	Mr P Subrahmanian
tel	+91 (0)4812 524 491
fax	+91 (0)4812 524 495
email	contactus@casinogroup.com
web	www.casinogroup.com

Map 8 Entry 175

Kumarakom Lake Resort

Kumarakom North, Kottayam, Kottayam District, 686 566 Kerala

Despite being a new resort employing many of the 'heritage' techniques of the backwaters, this one we include for its bold and even fanciful luxury. As you recline by the infinity pool you might imagine you are in a stylish photo shoot: natural cloth umbrellas cast shade over heavy teak sun loungers, coconut trees rustle in the breeze and hushed pool attendants ready themselves with towels. The cottages are raftered and positively ornate. Painted temple drawings look down onto generous beds and double doors open to a plant-rich garden into which is sunk a vast mosaic bathtub. The restaurant is a 300-year-old Keralan royal house through which one of the canals passes – and the 'women's balcony', from which regal ladies would watch courtly goings-on, still remains. The whole feel is one of polished history; no cracks apparent. The meandering pool villas are the most resort-like, and, with extra beds for children, ideal for families; the suites have their own pools. Watching the sun go down from the tea garden is a treat.

rooms	50: 22 cottages, 26 villas, 2 suites.
price	Cottages Rs10,225–Rs12,075. Villas Rs14,375–Rs20,125. Suites Rs40,250. Plus 15% tax. Peak season: October–April.
meals	Lunch Rs800. Dinner Rs1,000.
closed	Rarely.
directions	90 minutes from Kochi airport via Chertala. 3km from Kumarakom on backwaters. Free transfers from Kottayam train station (20 mins) or Muhamma jetty.

Resort

Mr Paul John

tel	+91 (0)4812 524 900
res. no	+91 (0)16004 255 030
fax	+91 (0)4812 524 987
email	gm@klresort.com
web	www.klresort.com

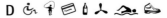

Map 8 Entry 176

Vanilla County

Vagamon Road, Mavady Estate, Teekoy, Kottayam, 686 580 Kerala

A purple jacaranda tree swathes the front garden in colour and the rich scent of vanilla hangs in the breeze. This is an intimate homestay, where gentle Rani and Baby welcome you like friends and involve you in family and plantation life. A thousand acres of this land were given to your host's grandfather by the local maharaja; the house was built 60 years ago. The new generation are running this vanilla, coffee and rubber plantation organically and delight in showing guests how it all works. Spotless bedrooms are simple not stylish, with concrete floors, patterned Indian bed sheets on wooden beds, and lampshades and coat stands crafted from polished coffee roots. One family room connects via a large private balcony; the rest share verandas. Rani is an excellent cook so you'll enjoy an exquisite chicken biriani with other guests round the yellow and white checked dining table. Tourist board pictures adorn the walls and there's a small Christian family shrine. This is wonderful, warm, family home so bring the children, cool off in the natural pools and make the most of living on a remote, lush plantation.

rooms	4: 2 doubles, 2 family rooms.
price	Full-board $125. Peak season: October–March.
meals	Full-board only.
closed	Rarely.
directions	From Erattupetta, head towards Vagamon (13km). Turn left at Mavady. Airport: Kochi (100km, 2.5 hours). Train: Kottayam (56 miles, 1.5 hours).

Homestay

	Baby Mathew & Rani Baby Vallikappen
tel	+91 (0)4822 281 225
email	vanillacounty@yahoo.com
web	www.vanillacounty.in

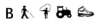

Map 8 Entry 177

Privacy at Sanctuary Bay

TP111/185 Kannamkara P.O., Muhamma, Thaneermukkom, Kerala

Huge sliding screens give onto the veranda with its bamboo blinds and views across the lake. This must be one of the most heavenly spots in Kerala – and, with its two double bedrooms, the thatched bungalow is all yours while you're here. There can be few more idyllic spots in which to enjoy an evening meal – candlelit, cooked for you, and close enough to the shimmering lake to be able to dip one's toes in the water. The interiors are colourfully minimalist, representative of the Malabar House design ethos that renovates old Keralan buildings with a bold simplicity. Nothing is here that is not pleasing to the eye, and harmony and symmetry underpin the placing of the few choice ethno-graphic collectables. Your own chef is present but never overbearing; the focus is on privacy. Food is delicious – delicate curries and fresh juices served as and when you want. You'll see no-one bar the odd passing fisherman, and be disturbed by little other than the cawing of crows. Stay for a place to call your own, in one of the most exquisite settings on the Vembanad Lake.

rooms	Cottage for 4-6.
price	€180-€250 per night. Peak season: October-May.
meals	Lunch & dinner $30 each.
closed	Rarely.
directions	10-minute drive from Cherthala.

Catered cottage

	Mr Mervin Isaac (Manager)
tel	+91 (0)4782 582 794
res. no	+91 (0)4842 216 666
fax	+91 (0)4842 217 777
email	info@malabarhouse.com
web	www.malabarhouse.com

B

Map 8 Entry 178

Kayaloram Lake Resort

Avalookunnu PO, Punnamada, Alappuzha (Alleppey), 688 006 Kerala

The gardens run down to water that stretches for silvery kilometers: Kayaloram is in one of the most stunning spots on the western side of the Vembanad Lake. The resort is low-key but has an easy feel that can only exist in such a small place. This is the original backwater resort, and the first to make use of deconstructed Keralan houses. Each low-slung house has several rooms, their shower rooms open to the sky, and stands in well-tended open gardens landscaped around a small pool. Postcard-perfect sights are two-a-penny in the Keralan backwaters, but the views from the lake-facing rooms here, through coconut trees palms and across the luminous water, are especially lovely. It's gorgeous in a low-key way, and perfect for those who are after something a little less resort-like than similar Keralan haunts. They have rice barges for backwaters sunset cruises, table tennis, a fine ayurvedic centre and a small, attractive, open-sided restaurant at which you have to place orders at least an hour in advance: slightly eccentric, worth the wait. *Air-conditioning at night only.*

Resort

rooms	12 doubles.
price	$70-$150. Plus 15% tax. Peak seaon: 15 December-15 January.
meals	Breakfast $4. Lunch & dinner $7 each.
closed	Rarely.
directions	Access by pre-arranged boat from Alappuzha. Airport: Kochi (90km, 1.5 hours).

	Mr Antony George
tel	+91 (0)4772 231 572/3
fax	+91 (0)4772 231 571
email	kayaloram@satyam.net.in
web	www.kayaloram.com

Map 8 Entry 179

Keraleeyam Ayurvedic Resort

Thathampally, Alappuzha (Alleppey), 688 006 Kerala

The owner group, SD Pharmacy, has 60 years of experience in ayurvedic health – one excellent reason to include this small resort. Keraleeyam isn't just clinging to the coat tails of the Keralan cash cow: it offers the real thing. The 'heritage', air-conditioned cottages have dark ornate wooden doors and bathrooms so pristine you can almost see your reflection in the gleaming white tiles. Other cottages are constructed entirely of coconut thatching (the locals re-thatch every month) and are great fun, the views from the top-storey verandas reaching over the gentle backwaters. Tradition meets modernity in the open-air bathrooms – the view to the stars will have you singing an extra verse as you shower. The double rooms in the house are equally good: fresh simple furnishings and not an ounce of 'tat'. In the cool, dark, chunkily furnished dining room you may indulge in the great Indian tradition of 'tea and snacks' – and retreat from the heat. Continental and Chinese food is served too. An idyllic place, ayurveda to trust in and excellent value.

rooms	5 + 9: 5 doubles. 9 cottages: 2 for 4, 3 for 6, 4 for 8.
price	Rs1,425. Singles Rs1,140. Cottages Rs1,710–Rs2,280. Peak season: October–March.
meals	Breakfast Rs171. Lunch & dinner Rs285 each.
closed	Rarely.
directions	On the backwaters, 3km from Alappuzha station. Airport: Kochi (85km, 1.5 hours).

Resort

	Mr K Ramesh
tel	+91 (0)4772 231 468
res. no	+91 (0)4772 254 501/502
mobile	+91 (0)9847 050 711
email	mail@keraleeyam.com
web	www.keraleeyam.com

Map 8 Entry 180

Tharavad Heritage Resort

West of North Police Station, Sea View Ward, Alappuzha (Alleppey), 688 012 Kerala

A stroll around the house feels like a tour of a lived-in museum: many fascinating things and everything beautifully polished. An antique rosewood gramophone and a brass and wooden *para* for measuring rice are just two of the discoveries, and the vast rotund brass pot used by Madhu's great-grandfather for mixing ayurvedic oils squats on a gleaming veranda. Each of the bedrooms has its own antique *objet*: a huge metal safe in one, a set of ornate trinket boxes in another. Madhu is calm and smiling, perhaps less hands-on than other homestay hosts, but as involved as you wish him to be. This is his grandfather's house, now shared with his brother and mother. Occasionally your hosts take meals with their guests – fish curries and other local dishes served in a stone-floored dining room that opens to the garden. Sit out here in the shade of the ancient mango tree. The fishing town of Alappuzha (Alleppey) isn't far – Madhu will help to organise boating from there – but far enough away to feel free of urban hum. Brilliant value.

Homestay

rooms	7: 3 doubles, 1 single, 2 apartments for 4.
price	Rs750-Rs1,500. Single Rs500. Apartment Rs1,500-Rs2,500 for 2. Peak season: October-January.
meals	Breakfast Rs75. Lunch & dinner Rs200-Rs300 each.
closed	Rarely.
directions	1km from Alappuzha station near North Police Station Road. Pick-up can be arranged from Kochi or Trivandrum airports.

Biju & Madhu Mohan

tel	+91 (0)4772 244 599
mobile	+91 (0)9846 144 599 or (0)9349 440 406
email	alleppeytharavad@sify.com
web	www.tharavadheritageresort.com

A ♦ 人

Map 8 Entry 181

Motty's Homestay

Murickanadiyil, Kidangamparambu Road, Thathampally, Alappuzha (Alleppey), 688 013 Kerala

The first thing you'll notice is Motty's deep infectious chuckle; the second, his eye for beautiful things. Motty and Lali's home is crammed with objets d'art from India and beyond, yet his interior designer instinct has made the most of the space – nothing looks too busy. With beautiful plant-strewn verandas at both front and back you have as much communal space ouside as in. Smooth teak pillars hold the front veranda while the one at the back is arched and has a carved jackwood trestle table. The bedrooms, each with its own entrance, are big and private; one has a splendid four-poster and an intriguing collection of walking sticks that splay out at the foot of the bed. Lali's cooking is Keralan and very good, and she is delighted to share her recipes. Motty can organise rice-barge cruises on the Keralan backwaters (book in advance during the peak season) and will ensure you make the most of your time. Charming Alappuzha, or Alleppey, is a five-minute rickshaw away, but you'd never know it.

rooms	2: 1 double, 1 twin/double.
price	Rs4,000-Rs6,000. Singles 20% reduction. Peak season: November–May.
meals	Lunch £4. Dinner £5.
closed	Never.
directions	5 minutes from cental Alappuzha. Airport: Kochi (90km, 2 hours). Train: Alappuzha (4km, 10 minutes).

Homestay

	Motty & Lali Matthew
tel	+91 (0)4772 243 535
mobile	+91 (0)9847 032 836
fax	+91 (0)4772 260 573
email	motty1@satyam.net.in
web	www.mararibeachhomes.com

C 🚶🏠

Map 8 Entry 182

Marari Beach Homes

Marari Beach, Alappuzha (Alleppey), Kerala

In a country that prides itself on its hospitality, here is somewhere where you can look after yourself and live at your own pace. Five fishermen's shacks have been cleverly converted into classily simple beach cottages, some with kitchenettes. A terracotta and yellow wash decorates the walls, there's coir matting underfoot and vibrant bedspreads to encourage siestas from the sun. Each cottage has its own shady veranda dotted with lazy chairs and there are uninterrupted views to the sea; it laps yards from the door. Some cottages have shower rooms open to the sky and there's plenty of space, thanks to generous verandas. Kitchens are well-equipped but you're not bound to them; you can give a shopping list to the staff if you don't want to explore the markets yourself – rickshaws and buses are nearby. And arrange to have a chef if you are staying for more than a week (authentic Keralan food from fresh vegetables and the catch of the day). The Marari Beach restaurant is a few sandy paces along the coast. White sandy beaches, no crowds and an independent feel: engagingly different for India. *Cookery courses available.*

Catered cottage

rooms	5 cottages: 4 for 2, 1 for 4.
price	$80–$250. Plus 15% tax. Peak season: November–April.
meals	Breakfast $5. Lunch & dinner $10 each. Self-catering option.
closed	Rarely.
directions	Kochi-Alappuzha highway; turn west at Marari junction. 15km from Alappuzha.

	Mr M K Mathew
tel	+91 (0)4772 243 535
email	motty1@satyam.net.in
web	www.mararibeachhomes.com

D ㅅ

Map 8 Entry 183

Arakal Heritage

Chethy P.O., Alappuzha (Alleppey), 688 530 Kerala

Carved elephants squat on the sand-scattered steps of the heritage cottage — a Keralan sign of welcome. You're a world away from cosseted hotel living here: no frills, just real, rural India. Duck through an intricately carved antique door to discover a four-poster bed, a cosy dressing room hung with Abi's great-grandmother's tapestry work, and an outdoor bathroom decked in leaf-print tiles. Things may be snug inside but there is a veranda to lounge on; you enjoy your meals there, served on banana leaves, or in the family dining room. Apart from the cottages there are two very basic double rooms, but family miscellany may have to be shifted to give you space. Best to book a cottage; if you're a group, you'll appreciate the space. Abi and Mini are warm and engaging hosts who gently introduce you to their family life and will do everything to make your stay special. It's a short wander through sandy coconut plantations to the sea and a pleasant one: pass fishermen's huts and locals making coir and tapping toddy.

rooms	4 cottages: 3 for 2, 1 for 3-4.
price	Full-board from Rs3,500 for 2. Peak season: August-March.
meals	Full-board only.
closed	Rarely.
directions	18km from Alappuzha, 11km from Cherthala, near Marari Beach Resort. Airport: Kochi (55km, 2 hours). Train: Alappuzha (12km, 30 mins).

Homestay

	Abi & Mini Arakal
tel	+91 (0)4782 865 545
mobile	+91 (0)9847 268 661
fax	+91 (0)4782 865 659
email	abiarakal@sify.com

Map 8 Entry 184

Emerald Isle

Kanjooparambil-Manimalathara, Chathurthiakary P.O., Alappuzha (Alleppey), 688 511 Kerala

You are swathed in romance from the word go. A dug-out canoe glides you across the Pamba river to the historic, low-slung wooden bungalow that hides on a little island in the backwaters. A sprawling veranda dotted with wicker chairs hugs the contours of what one guest described as the "mother of all bungalows"; settle in with a book and cup of sweet, milky *chai*. This is a place just to 'be'. The furniture is dark and heavy and much of it is original; even the hinges of the carved teak doors are wooden. Vinod's great-grandfather renovated the place years ago, and property deeds etched into 250-year-old palm leaves hang in the cool dark living room. Vinod is genuine and friendly, keen to share the history of this dreamy place – and unintrusive. He will organise overnight backwater boat trips, or point you towards a gentle amble through the maze of canals to the paddy and coconut fields of the ten-acre estate. Hammocks have been strategically placed en route, making this a delightfully soporific way to spend your time in India. *Cookery classes. Country boat available for pick up at any time.*

Guest house

rooms	5 doubles.
price	Full-board £30–£60. Peak season: August–April.
meals	Full-board only.
closed	Rarely.
directions	10km from Alappuzha. Road access until opp. property; collection by boat from 'Chathurthyakary Kadav'. Directions on booking. Airport: Kochi (95km, 2 hours). Train: Alappuzha (12km, 25 mins).

	Mr Vinod Job
tel	+91 (0)4772 703 899
res. no	+91 (0)4773 290 577
mobile	+91 (0)9447 077 555
email	info@emeraldislekerala.com
web	www.emeraldislekerala.com

B 🚜 🧍

Map 8 Entry 185

Raheem Residency

Beach Road, Alappuzha (Alleppey), 688 012 Kerala

All is wonderfully serene. Facing the ocean on a quiet Keralan beach, this oasis in Alleppey softens the spirit. The elegant colonial house was built in 1868 and became the home of the Raheems – Muslim/Gujarati traders with links to Gandhi. Today generous Bibi, Irish ex-journalist, and her Indian business partner Flemin, have transformed it into a relaxing, spoiling retreat. Inside, find cool high-ceilinged rooms, pretty antique beds with crisp linen, carvedsofas with burnt orange cushions and inlaid coloured glass, and bathrooms that open to the stars. Pad across tiled floors to the courtyard pool after a divineayurvedic massage; select a book from the library. Guests' privacy isrespected and with only seven rooms, it feels intimate. The restaurant isopen to non-hotel guests and serves exquisite fresh fish, crab andseafood, Malabar chicken and coconut-flavoured vegetarian dishes. Fromhere, gaze at the waves rolling in or take in the cricket. Experience realIndian life – Bibi knows the best places to shop for silk, spices, cottonand gold. Understated luxury and good taste prevail.

rooms	7: 6 doubles, 1 family suite.
price	€90–€190. Suite €160–€250. Plus 15% tax. Peak season: October–March.
meals	Breakfast €6. Lunch €7. Dinner €12.
closed	Rarely.
directions	Airport: Kochi (88km, 1.5 hours). Train: Alappuzha (6km, 10 mins).

Hotel

	Mr Flemin Welben
tel	+91 (0)4772 239 767
fax	+91 (0)4772 230 767
email	contact@raheemresidency.com
web	www.raheemresidency.com

Map 8 Entry 186

Shalimar Spice Garden

Murikkady P.O., Kumily, Idukki District, 685 535 Kerala

Thatched luxury teak-clad huts are dotted among the trees and the interiors smack of those tiny hill top Greek temples, all whitewashed doorways and fine cotton curtains blowing in the breeze. Inside, red and blue checked bedspreads, coloured glass windows, patterned hangings on white walls, fresh flowers on comfy beds. Beautiful bathrooms have an array of potions. There is a touch of zen about the place: beams of sunlight illuminate the oldspice tree in the lobby that lies across a wooden bridge; Garnesh the elephant God wears a garland of flowers. Wander through the ornamental spice gardens, take a book to the peaceful treehouse. The hotel has been under new management since its German founder retired. Breakfast on fresh mango, grape or pineapple juice and scrambled eggs at rough granite-topped tables outside. Dine at tables for two, or order snacks by the pool – or on your bedroom veranda. The low-slung, thatched ayurveda centre beckons – enjoy a massage in front of the open fire. A tranquil place. *5km from Periyar Tiger Reserve.*

Hotel

rooms	20: 10 doubles, 10 cottages for 2.
price	€70-€120. Cottages €80-€300. Plus 10% tax. Peak season: October-March; 20 Dec-10 Jan.
meals	Lunch & dinner from €17 each. Plus 12.5% tax. Restaurants 5km.
closed	Rarely.
directions	5km from Kumily bus stand. Airports: Kochi/Trivandrum (4/5 hours).

	Mr Abdul Gafoor (Manager)
tel	+91 (0)4869 222 132
fax	+91 (0)4869 223 022
email	shalimar_resort@vsnl.com
web	www.shalimarkerala.com

Map 8 Entry 187

Paradisa Plantation Retreat

Murinjapuzha P O, Idukki District, Murinjapuzha, 685 532 Kerala

Find peace and tranquility in the Periyar Wildlife Sanctuary at this remote, friendly village guest house on the point of a tree-rich valley. Your attentive host, Simon, took on this challenging project in 1994; the 40-acre site now has an access road but the property is still not connected to mains electricity – that's part of the charm. Set around the property are several private cottages with panelled walls and ceilings in rich red and brown teak; traditional Chettinad-style antique pillars add grandeur to the entrances. With low-level lighting and lots of dark wood, the rooms feel a little sombre – and you may fall asleep early here as the generator is turned off at 11pm. (Candles and torches are provided.) Savour delicious, home-cooked food in the open-sided, view-filled thatched restaurant; on some evenings, classical performers dance out a story in stunning costume. Treks searching for wild elephants can be arranged, there are snacks by the pool and ayurvedic massages to enjoy. Or climb to the top of the hill and watch the eagles soar off towards the sea.

rooms	13 doubles.
price	€145–€165. Singles 10% discount. Plus 15% tax. Peak season: September–April.
meals	Lunch & dinner €15 each.
closed	Mid–May–mid–July.
directions	On the Kottyam/Kumilly road at Murinjapuzha; signed. Airport: Kochi (140km, 3.5 hours). Train: Kottayam (80km, 2 hours).

Guest house

Mr Simon Paulose

tel	+91 (0)4692 701 311
mobile	+91 (0)9447 088 119
fax	+91 (0)4692 602 828
email	paradisa@rediffmail.com
web	www.paradisaretreat.com

Map 8 Entry 188

Kanjirapally Estate
K.K. Road, Vandiperiyar P.O., Vandiperiyar, 685 533 Kerala

An unusual homestay, and an atypical farmhouse. Built on a cardamom and coffee plantation bordering the Periyar Tiger Reserve, this angular, 30-year-old building is cool and colourful, all bright terrazzo floors and modern art. It's funky yet restrained, smart yet informal. Gita and Mathew are young, sophisticated, interested and involved. Both are passionate conservationists and nature lovers and can take you for long bird-spotting walks around the plantation that spreads its forested tentacles across kilometres of steep hillside. (It also plays occasional host to the wandering furry, hooved or feathered residents from the next-door reserve.) Having cut their teeth in the hotel world, Gita and Mathew are sticklers for detail – yet the house has an easy style that belies the time and thought that has gone into perfecting every corner. And they can cook up a storm in the kitchen! Come here for the birdlife and the people. Readers love this place. *Guided trekking, rafting, plantation walks & cardamon auctions.*

Homestay

rooms	3: 2 doubles, 1 single.
price	Full-board Rs6,500. Singles Rs5,000. Peak season: October-February.
meals	Full-board only.
closed	Rarely.
directions	The estate borders the Periyar Tiger Reserve. Directions on booking. Airport: Kochi (128km, 4 hours). Train: Kottayam (65km, 2 hours).

	Gita & Mathew Eapen
tel	+91 (0)4869 252 278
mobile	+91 (0)91989 5042278
email	kanjirapallyestate@hotmail.com

Map 8 Entry 189

Green Mansions

Kerala Forest Development Corporation, Gavi, Vandiperiyar, Idukki District, 685 533 Kerala

Rarely does a government-run spot feel so cared for and so dynamic, or revive you as much as Green Mansions. Getting there is half the fun; the three-and-a-half-hour scenic route jeep ride rattles even the most well-travelled bones – and sets the soul soaring. Travel through blankets of tropical forest, neat plantations and stark grassland hilltops – this is some of the most awe-inspiring scenery in the country. On its own little hillock overlooking Gavi Lake, the building is snug and unassuming, and the bedrooms simple but not unhospitable; indeed, perfect for those with fond memories of youth-hostelling days. Vegetarian meals are served outside: breakfasts in the lakeside straw gazebo after a sunrise trek, campfire dinners under the stars. It's reassuring to feel miles from nowhere, in the knowledge that a man as passionate as Mr Bashir is in charge. His vision has made Green Mansions a centre for local employment and organic smallholdings. This is an unbeatable spot run by inspiring people. *Wonderful for trekking & wildlife sighting.*

rooms	3 doubles.
price	Full-board $70.
meals	Full-board only.
closed	Rarely.
directions	30km from Vandiperiyar. Or 120km scenic drive from Kottayam (prior permission from Forest Department required). Airport: Kochi (128km, 4 hours). Train: Kottayam (65km, 2 hours).

Safari lodge

	C A Ardul Bashir (Manager)
tel	+91 (0)4869 252 118
res. no	+91 (0)4812 581 205
fax	+91 (0)4812 581 338
email	tourism@periyartigerreserve.org
web	www.kfdcgavi.com

A

Map 8 Entry 190

Serenity at Kanam Estate

c/o P.V. George, Payikad, Kanam P.O., Vazhoor, 686 515 Kerala

A young and fittingly luxurious sibling to Malabar House in Fort Kochi, where, again, a modern minimalism highlights the simple grandeur of Keralan architecture. The peaceful 1920s plantation house is enclosed by trees – a grand white edifice with open sides that allows the air to take the edge off summer's humidity. Darkish spaces with high ceilings and slate-tiled floors, the communal rooms open to the breeze. The windows are wooden-shuttered and unglazed, while the main living area has latticed screens not walls. Indeed, the whole building is designed to bring the outside in. The bedrooms are serene and restrained affairs, the coir matting, cotton curtains and gentle hues softening the austerity of the wooden beds. This is more house than hotel and can be hired in its entirety – a beautiful home over which you can briefly reign. Everyone gets their own space on one of the wide wooden verandas, while meals may be shared with other guests. Staff are young and enthusiastic. A wonderful stop-off between the Periyar Tiger Reserve and the backwaters. *On-site elephant takes guests for rides.*

Guest house

rooms	5: 3 doubles, 2 twins.
price	$160. Plus 10% tax. Peak season: October–April.
meals	Lunch & dinner $30 each.
closed	Rarely.
directions	On Kanam Estate between Kottayam & Kumily. Do not attempt to get here on your own!

	Mr Mervin Issac (Manager)
tel	+91 (0)4842 216 666
fax	+91 (0)4842 217 777
email	escapes@malabarhouse.com
web	www.malabarhouse.com

D 💳 🚜 ⚒

Map 8 Entry 191

Friday's Place

Poovar Island, Uchekkada PO, Thiruvananthapuram (Trivandrum), Kerala

Quirky wooden eco cottages in the quiet backwaters of Kerala. From the moment you are greeted at the jetty with jasmine garlands and melon juice you know you have chosen well. Mark, a self-styled engineer, his Sri Lankan wife Sujeewa, a teacher in alternative healing, and their local staff do their most to make sure you have a memorable stay. The thatched and beautifully crafted teak and mahogany cottages are raised on granite steddle stones and surrounded by coconut palms and tall tropical plants. Cotton sheets drape over generous beds with sturdy kaya/rubber mattresses (excellent for the back!); baby-blue and purple mosquito nets add a flash of colour. The cottages are solar-powered and ayurvedic soap is provided in the (blissful!) rainwater shower room and detached communal bathroom. Sujeewa uses southern India organic recipes for fresh fish and river crabs. Dine with other guests in the dining area that doubles up as a yoga sanctuary, or on your own veranda listening to the sounds of rainforest birds and the distant call to prayer in the nearby villages. *Minimum stay three nights.*

rooms	4 cottages for 2.
price	Full-board £100-£150. Singles £50. Peak season October-March.
meals	Full-board only.
closed	April-mid-October.
directions	Head to Poovar Island Resort jetty. Airport: Trivandrum (40 mins).

Resort

Mark & Sujeewa Reynolds

tel	+91 (0)4712 133 292
email	amphibious_robinson_crusoe@hotmail.com
web	www.fridaysplace.biz

C 👟

Map 8 Entry 192

The Varikatt Heritage

Poonnen Road, Thiruvananthapuram (Trivandrum), 695 001 Kerala

Minutes from the busy streets of Trivandrum, step through the door and back in time to the British Raj. Sundowners on the veranda, hunting trophies on the wall, whirring ceiling fans overhead. You half-expect a young Victorian, Miss Blanket, to appear (she fell in love with an English tea-planter and followed her heart to Travancore to find him, building this bungalow in the 1850s). Ever since they left, the house has remained with the same Indian family — and the sense of history remains. Antique rosewood furniture and family pieces sit beneath wood panelled ceilings, and big bedrooms have a genteel air, like the guest rooms in a favourite uncle's house. Rugs are scattered on tiled floors, cabinets gleam with china, curious *objets* catch the eye. It's very much 'look and touch'. Colonel Kuncheira (retired, Ghurkha Rifles) will delight in telling you their stories. Explore the city, then return to an ayurvedic massage or badminton beneath tropical trees. After dinner with the Colonel and his wife, find a rocking chair on the veranda and drink to the legacy of Miss Blanket.

Homestay

rooms	2 doubles.
price	Rs3,500-Rs4,500.
	Peak season: November-February.
meals	Lunch & dinner from Rs300 each.
closed	Never.
directions	50m from Cantonment Police Station, near the Secretariat. On corner with big brown gates. Airport: Trivandrum (6km, 20 mins). Train: Trivandrum (3km, 10 mins).

	Col. Roy Kuncheira
tel	+91 (0)4712 336 057
mobile	+91 (0)9895 239 055
fax	+91 (0)4712 725 164
email	sales@varikattheritage.com
web	www.varikattheritage.com

C ⚹ 👟

Map 8 Entry 193

Graceful Homestay

PHRA No. 20-21 Philip's Hill, Pothujanam Rd, Kumarapuram, Trivandrum, 695 011 Kerala

Sylvia is high energy and smiley, a self-confessed workaholic and dotty about cats. Through her work with the humanitarian organisation CARE she has travelled widely, gathering tales and knick-knacks along the way. A whitewashed mass of arches and verandas give her modern house a colonial air, and Sylvia's collection of handicrafts – from Tanzanian wood carvings to metal work from Kosovo – cover the walls. Artefacts from Tajikistan are a recent addition. Meals are wonderfully relaxed affairs on the big balcony, but when Sylvia is off on her travels her brother Giles, who lives in the original family home on the other side of the lush garden, takes over. Accept an invitation to eat at his place, or wander into the kitchen and invite his family over to yours. Things are truly relaxed here, and the great thing is, you can be as independent as you like. The bustling centre of Trivandrum may be minutes away, but gazing out across a carpet of palms to the thin blue line of the Arabian Sea, you'd never know it. *Air conditioning on request.*

rooms	4 doubles.
price	$30–$45.
meals	Lunch & dinner $5 each.
closed	Rarely.
directions	From Trivandrum, taxi to Kumarapuram. Then Pothujanam road (opp. community centre A J Hall); 400m to sign for Philip's Hill; house within compound. Airport/train: Trivandrum.

Homestay

	Ms Sylvia Francis
tel	+91 (0)4712 444 358/429
fax	+91 (0)4712 552 891
email	southernsafaris@yahoo.co.in
web	www.gracefulhomestay.com

A

Map 8 Entry 194

Wild Palms Guesthouse

Mathrubhoomi Road, Vanchiyoor, Thiruvananthapuram (Trivandrum), 695 035 Kerala

Hilda and Justin lived and worked for 30 years in London, but always knew they'd return to their roots. Wild Palms is their retirement dream – a large, rather grand townhouse in a leafy suburb of Trivandrum, ten minutes from the sea. More formal than a homestay (there's 24-hour room service and cable TV), the house is an eclectic mix of 'designer' and 'ethnic'. The elegant dining room chair was poached from a Charles Rennie Mackintosh design, the beds are traditional Keralan. The house is modern, and indulges a miscellany of architectural fancies. The central atrium has an almost church-like resonance, wide marble spaces, a sweeping wooden staircase and leaded windows. Downstairs, an ornamental fountain tinkles in the hallway; upstairs, bedrooms have more space than you need and the suite has a balcony over the garden. The atmosphere is relaxed, you come and go as you please and eat with the family around an expanse of dining table. The restaurants of Kerala's capital Trivandrum, where ancient meets bustling modern, is a ten-minute walk away.

Guest house

rooms	6: 5 doubles, 1 suite.
price	Rs945-Rs1,395. Suite Rs1,695. Singles Rs745-Rs1,395. Plus 7.5 %-15% (suite) tax. Peak season: August-January.
meals	Lunch & dinner from Rs125 each.
closed	Rarely.
directions	Next to Mathrubhoomi newspaper office & close to Holy Angels convent; 20-minute walk from MG Road. Airport: Trivandrum (6km).

	Hilda & Justin Pereira
tel	+91 (0)4712 471 175
fax	+91 (0)4712 461 971
email	wildpalm@md3.vsnl.net.in
web	www.wildpalmsguesthouse.com

A 🗇 入

Map 8 Entry 195

Lagoona Davina

Pachalloor Village, Thiruvananthapuram (Trivandrum), 695 027 Kerala

After a charming trip through the backwaters, a charming place to stay. Seduced by the raucous colours and textiles of India, Davina has created a mood of barefoot chic. Guests' personal room boys ensure their every need is tended to, from arranging bookings to serving fresh, healthy food. Bedrooms are named after Indian animals and bathrooms share the theme; under thatched roofs the whole place feels handmade. Cream and gold Kerala saris drape windows, walls are hand-painted pale terracotta, beds are four-posters prettily mosquito-netted. Some open onto the sandy waterfront garden, others are tucked around the back, with small gardens. Watch the fishermen from the lagoon edge, and the waves crashing on the beach. Guests come to practise yoga or reiki with the masters, to enjoy ayurveda massage or just laze; books are read on wall beds overlooking the lagoon. The sea's currents make the beach unsuitable for swims but there's a small pool here. A fine destination for laid-back honeymooners – and for anyone escaping the madness of city life. *Weddings organised.*

rooms	18 twins/doubles.
price	$84-$133. Plus 10% tax. Peak season: November-April.
meals	Breakfast $8. Lunch $10. Dinner $16.
closed	Rarely.
directions	4km before Kovalam on the road south of Trivandrum. Airport: Trivandrum (20 minutes).

	Ms Davina Taylor
tel	+91 (0)4712 380 049
fax	+91 (0)4712 462 935
email	lagoonadavina@hotmail.com
web	www.lagoonadavina.com

Hotel

Map 8 Entry 196

Karikkathi Beach House

Mulloor, Thottam, Pulinkudi, Thiruvananthapuram (Trivandrum), Kerala

Foreign diplomats come here for a break from the social whirl. It is secluded and beautiful yet wonderfully simple. Mr Sajjad's Beach House is an unusual concept in the Indian travel scene. It sits on a stunning part of terraced shoreline, looking out over the Arabian Sea, the small shared beach shaded by swaying coconut trees. Perfection! Yet this is only one small house, with two double bedrooms and a sitting room in between; you may book just one room or the house. The project was fuelled by Sajjad's despair at the burgeoning concrete desecration of Kerala's coastal beauty; the one-storey building, designed by Swiss architect Karl Damschen, uses local materials and natural colours. The roof is palm thatch on lashed wooden poles, the floors are country-red tiles and the shuttered windows open to the blue horizon. The beds are of cane and comfortable, with linen sheets and cotton throws, the bathrooms are spacious and white-tiled and the sea breezes cool. A chef comes to cook when and what you want, and there's a 'boy' on call. Pure escapism. *Wooden canoe & snorkel hire next door.*

Catered cottage

rooms	House for 2-4.
price	$150. Peak season: November-April.
meals	Full-board extra $20 p.p.
closed	June.
directions	Just before Surya Samudra Beach Garden, on main road 6km south of Kovalam. 5-min walk among palm groves from temple at Mulloor.

Mr Shaina Sajjad

tel	+91 (0)4712 400 956
email	karikkathi@yahoo.co.in
web	www.karikkathibeachhouse.com

Map 8 Entry 197

Somatheeram Ayurvedic Health Resort

Chowara P.O., South of Kovalam, Thiruvananthapuram (Trivandrum), 695 501 Kerala

A favourite, with rambling green gardens that tumble down to the clifftop, and cottages that feel more genuine than most. This is the original ayurvedic resort, and continues to win prizes for its medicinal and body treatments. Every cottage dotted up the steep slope has its own little grassy terrace with hammock or table and chairs; some have one or four bedrooms, most have two (one 'simple', one a suite, rented separately); the sea-facing ones have views along the glorious crescent beach. The steep, stepped gardens have palm-shaded mini-lawns, colourful climbers and bursting flower pots through which the paths wind. Thatched roofs, wooden poles and recycled bricks and tiles blend seamlessly into the surroundings. The restaurant perches at the top of the resort, a bustling candlelit nest from where you can see a procession of fishermen's lights snaking along the coast. At sun rise, the beach is alive with activity as the early haul is accompanied by Keralan chants. A well-run resort with a fine reputation, overseen by the friendliest people. *House boats can be booked. Ayurvedic packages available.*

rooms	40: 39 doubles, 1 suite.
price	€30-€182. Singles €27-€164.
	Suite €104-€410.
	Peak season: 15 Dec-15 Jan.
meals	Breakfast €6.
	Lunch & dinner €11 each.
closed	Never.
directions	On main road south of Kovalam towards Balarampuram. Airport/ train: Trivandrum (21km).

Mr Polly Mathew Arampankudy

tel	+91 (0)4712 269 702
res. no	+91 (0)4712 266 501
fax	+91 (0)4712 266 505
email	info@somatheeram.org
web	www.somatheeram.org

Resort

Map 8 Entry 198

Surya Samudra Beach Garden

Pulinkudi, Mullur P.O., Thiruvananthapuram (Trivandrum), 695 521 Kerala

One of the first 'heritage' retreats in Kerala, Surya Samudra was originally the creation of a German professor from Madras University. His 'octagon' house, a beach retreat from city life, is now this resort-hotel's best room, its glass doors opening to give you a bird's-eye view of rocky promontory and lashing waves. Wide stone steps flanked by ancient carved lions from Tamil temples lead one grandly down through the sandy garden from the reception to the cottages, delightfully restructured from old Keralan houses. All have verandas and lazy chairs, while those facing the sea (worth the extra) have stunning views through wide shuttered windows from the bed. The natural swimming pool built into the rocks overlooking the cliffs is spectacular, the beach is dreamy, and the restaurant, a granite-pillared, veranda'd semi-circle with panoramic views over the horizon, is one of the most heavenly places to dine on this stretch of coast. The mood is hushed and exclusive, the guests are mature, the coconut palms sway and the food's very good and very fresh. A luxurious, barefoot retreat.

rooms	21 cottages.
price	€80–€350. Plus 15% tax. Peak season: October–March; Christmas & New Year.
meals	Lunch €17. Dinner €17. Plus 12.5% tax.
closed	Never.
directions	8km south of Kovalam; signed.

Hotel

	Manish C. Palicha (Manager)
tel	+91 (0)4712 267 333
fax	+91 (0)4712 267 124
email	reservations@suryasamudra.com or suryasamudra@vsnl.com
web	www.suryasamudra.com

C ▭ ◊ ≈

Map 8 Entry 199

Karnataka

Karnataka stretches from the white sand beaches of the Arabian Sea to the tree-covered steeps of the Western Ghats where coffee, spices and fruit flourish – and also the dusty plains of the Deccan Plateau. Most of its 53 million inhabitants speak Kannada. Bangalore, the capital, is the brash software and computer centre of India where the middle classes eat in fast-food restaurants, shop in malls and dance in night clubs. Nevertheless, Karnataka is well known for its performing arts including Yakshagana, an all-night male folk dance with incredible costumes, headdresses and make up. These mimetic stories are based on the great epics. Leather puppets are used in shadow theatre.

Not to be missed is the World Heritage Site of Hampi. It is worth every inch of the backbreaking journey to see this golden, boulder-strewn, riverside site whose ancient complex has hand-carved pavilions, temples and elephant stables. Spend some time, too, in Gokarna – a pretty Hindu holy fishing town with white sand crescent beaches. In the Kodagu (or Coorg) area you will meet the friendly people from this distinct ethnic group who worship the River Cauvery as a godmother. Their weddings involve complex dances and mock stick fights. Men dress in black gowns with sashes and daggers; women wear chunky gold jewellery and a pinned and pleated sari. They delight in sharing their unique culture, and their delicious tangy pork-rich cuisine. In Mysore you can buy silks and sandalwood or visit the traditional Amba Vilas Palace. There is so much to see and do here: the temples of Belur and Halebid, the caves at Badami and Aihole, the sacred complex at Pattadakal, the tomb at Bijapur and the Muslim shrine at Gulbarga. The Nilgiri Biosphere Reserve has six wildlife sanctuaries that span the states of Karnataka, Kerala and Tamil Nadu.

Best time to visit
Karnataka: September-February

Photos Laura Kinch

Karnataka

Villa Pottipati

Neemrana Hotel, No.142, 4th Main, 8th Cross, Malleswaram, Bangalore, 560 003 Karnataka

A 'home from home', as the staff proudly call it, minutes from the centre of the Garden (or 'Silicon') City. Built in 1873 this is a wonderfully restored heritage property with an impressive entrance porch, elegant verandas and a tranquil country-house feel. Yet there is no shortage of enticements for the business traveller; you have laundry service, air conditioning and broadband in every room. Lunch is traditional Indian, served under the giant shivalinga tree; dinner is French, prepared by the chef from Pondicherry. Each serenely elegant room feels like the master bedroom of a private house yet each is unique: a sitting area here, a mezzanine there, a private veranda; warm brown tones, local cottons, spotless deep baths, perhaps direct access to the new outdoor pool. And there's no end to the wooden furniture – beautiful colonial pieces that came with the house or were shipped in from the other Neemrana hotels. The gardens feel wooded and keep city hum (and lunchtime chirrup from the local primary school) at bay. Comfortable, beautiful, welcoming – the Villa Pottipati is a joy.

Hotel

rooms	8: 6 doubles, 2 triples.
price	Rs2,500–Rs4,000. Triples Rs4,000. Plus 12% tax.
meals	Lunch & dinner Rs350 each. Plus 5% tax.
closed	Rarely.
directions	Hotel is in Malleswaram district. Airport: Bangalore (15km, 45 mins). Train: Bangalore (4km, 15 mins).

	Mr Kannan (Manager)
tel	+91 (0)8023 360 777
fax	+91 (0)8041 280 835
email	villapottipati@yahoo.com
web	www.neemranahotels.com

B 🏷 🍶 ⚰ 🏊

Map 8 Entry 200

Gitanjali Farm

PB No 6, Siddarthanagar, Mysore, 570 011 Karnataka

Such a warm, lovely family who give you a genuine welcome and make you comfortable. Yamuna looks after guests while her parents, Dalu and Muthu, are on hand for lively conversation and a drink before dinner in the sitting room. The family comes from the Coorg region and can tell you all about that fascinating tribal culture. Their modern home is just outside Mysore town with the backdrop of the grand Palace Hotel – you're close enough to see the sites, yet are surrounded by trees, flowers and tranquillity. The homemade traditional Kodave dinners are delicious: wild boar curry, bamboo salad and wild-mango spice dishes. Muthu also makes an excellent English marmalade so you'll feel quite at home. Your bedroom is old-fashioned and homely: hand-stitched bedcovers sewn at the local convent; a glass-topped dressing table with lace; flowery curtains. One room has a stool fashioned from an elephant's foot, another opens onto a little terrace. Yamuna can take you on cultural day trips, and can arrange Ganjita painting, yoga and meditation classes.

rooms	3 doubles.
price	Full-board from €120.
	Peak season: October-March.
meals	Full-board only.
closed	Rarely.
directions	From heritage arch of Lalita Palace Hotel & before end of Lalita Mahal Road, right to Indus Valley Ayurveda Centre; 0.5km, on right.
	Airport: Bangalore (160km, 3 hours).
	Train: Mysore (6km, 30 mins).

Homestay

	Yamuna Achaiah
tel	+91 (0)8212 473 779
mobile	+91 (0)9886 117 919
	or (0)9448 353 779
email	info@gitanjalifarm.com
web	www.gitanjalifarm.com

C 大 🍴 🛏 👟

Map 8 Entry 201

Rainforest Retreat

Kaloor Road, Galkibeedu Village, Madikeri, Mysore, Kodagu District, Karnataka

Stay deep in the rainforest and discover what it means to live in an ecologically-sound enviroment. Sujata, a botanist, and Anurag, a molecular biologist, are passionate about their eco retreat and their enthusiasm rubs off on you. Sujata takes guests on free guided walks around the three-valley organic spice plantation (cardamom, coffee, pepper, vanilla, medicinal plants), explaining the benefits of bio-diversity and the methods employed to preserve it. The project was initiated with a grant from the NGS in 1997 and the proceeds of the guest house go towards an NGO working on the restoration of ecological diversity. They also teach local farmers about organic farming. These three cottages have two (independent) bedrooms each, not luxurious but lovely, with colourful bedspeads, wall hangings and open fires. For privacy and simplicity choose Plantation Cottage in its own valley. There are photo-voltaic panels for electricity and woodburners for hot morning bucket showers. Star-lit dinners, much home-grown, are served around the camp fire. Wonderful. *Excellent trekking.*

Guesthouse

rooms	3 cottages, each with two doubles. Hot bucket showers.
price	Full-board £32–£45. Peak season: October–January; April–May.
meals	Full-board only.
closed	July/August.
directions	Airport: Mangalore (150km, 4 hours). Train: Mysore (135km, 3 hours).

SPECIAL GREEN ENTRY see page 18

	Drs. Anurag & Sujata Goel
tel	+91 (0)8272 265 636/638
fax	+91 (0)8272 265 636/638
email	wapred.india@vsnl.com or anugoel@blr.vsnl.net.in
web	www.rainforestours.com

B 👤 🚜 👟

Map 8 Entry 202

The Green Hotel

Chittaranjan Palace, 2270 Vinoba Road, Jayalakshmipuram, Mysore, 570 012 Karnataka

Once used as a film set, this palace on the outskirts of Mysore was built around 1910 by the Maharaja for his unmarried sisters. And very nice it is too – not too big, but with space and character. Rooms in the main house are easily the best, from the small Writer's Room to the large Maharani suite with four-poster and antiques. The ground-floor 'Bollywood' rooms feature framed panels of Indian film stars. The modern rooms in the garden annexe are pleasantly but plainly furnished and overlook the lawns. Bright with marigolds and bougainvillea, the garden is most fragrant and lovely at breakfast time and after dark – mind the monkeys don't get your bananas! In the shaded restaurant area, candlelit at night, the delicious food is Indian, Chinese or continental. Relax on the veranda or pick a window seat; there are books and games to dip into. There's also a travel desk manned by delightful staff. The hotel aims to be a model of sustainable tourism – hence the name – and all profits go to Indian charities and environmental projects. *Ranganathittu Bird Sanctuary nearby.*

rooms	31: 6 doubles, 1 suite. Annexe: 19 doubles, 5 suites.
price	Rs2,750-Rs5,250. Annexe: Rs1,800-Rs2,300. Plus 12.5% tax. Peak season: October-March.
meals	Lunch & dinner Rs250-Rs500 each.
closed	Rarely.
directions	From Mysore on Madikeri road, hotel signed on right, 75m after Basappa Memorial Hosp. Your landmark is old Premier Film Studios.

Mr J Hilel Manohar

tel	+91 (0)8214 255 000
fax	+91 (0)8212 516 139
email	thegreenhotel@airtelbroadband.in
web	www.greenhotelindia.com

Hotel

Map 8 Entry 203

Sandbanks

Polaycad Estate, Ammathi P.O. 30, Ammathi, District Kodagu, 571 211 Karnataka

A feast for mind, body and spirit – in the bend of the Cauvery river and with hills just to the west. It is often the people who make a place special and Micky and his family, generous and kind, are rooted in this place and treat you as friends. On arrival you may be invited into the thatched gazebo for a chat; the peacefulness of the place will wash over you. The family's own bungalow on the gentle green slopes of the garden is elegant and beautiful. You sleep in a purpose-designed gazebo with a bedroom, bathroom and veranda, and space for casual eating. The furnishings are warm, not opulent. It is simple, beautifully decorated, with high ceilings, plenty of light, cream walls, orange bedspreads, all mod cons. There is also a very large tent pitched under a thatched gazebo, with a double bed and a private shower block close by – fun for anyone but especially children. Prakesh, the serving-man, is always to hand but never intrusive (as can sometimes be the case). Serenity in gorgeous surroundings. *Good trekking around the estate & further afield.*

Guest house

rooms	4 cottages for 2. Tents available.
price	Rs1,750-Rs2,000. Peak season: October-May. 15 Dec-5 Jan 2,750-Rs3,000.
meals	Lunch & dinner from Rs110 each.
closed	Rarely.
directions	110km from Mysore; 185km from Mangalore.

	Mr Micky Kalappa
tel	+91 (0)8274 252 130 or (0)8274 264 130
email	kalaps@sancharnet.in or info@sand-banks.com
web	www.sand-banks.com

B 🚜

Map 8 Entry 204

Alath Cad Estate

Ammathi P.B. No. 7, Ammathi, District Kodagu, 571 211 Karnataka

Sixty-five lush acres of coffee plantation envelop the bungalow; distant mountain views peep through a million shades of green. You are in splendid isolation from the world – but not from the bird life or the butterflies. The setting is beautiful. The Muddaiah family has been here for generations and have done great things with the building and the gardens. There is a delightful red-tiled courtyard area and the bedrooms are charming: blue and white chiffon curtains, pale walls, perhaps views onto the garden. There is also a cottage with two further rooms, in similar style but with big beamed ceilings. All is done in simple and imaginative good taste, and the family are delightful… amusing, energetic, friendly and kind. They live in separate quarters but are always on hand, happy to organise treks, bike rides, fishing trips, golf, birdwatching and picnics by the river. In short, a fine place to which to retreat, perhaps with a group of friends. And you are a day trip away from Mysore, the most amenable of Indian cities.
Cycling, birdwatching, fishing.

rooms	9: 6 doubles, 1 suite, 1 suite for 4, 1 cottage for 4.
price	Half-board Rs2,000.
meals	Half-board only. Lunch Rs240.
closed	Rarely.
directions	2km from Ammathi; well-signed. Bus station: Virajpet (12km). Airport: Mysore (110km).

Guest house

	Mrs Kannu Muddaiah
tel	+91 (0)8274 452 190
res. no	+91 (0)8036 832 747
email	mudhus@rediffmail.com
web	www.alathcadcoorg.com

A 🚜 🚲

Map 8 Entry 205

The School Estate

Sidapur, District Kodagu, Karnataka

A rare treat: pretty, floral, birdsung gardens, an ancient mango tree, plantation views and the loveliest hostess, Rani. The comfort will be a blessing after the drive here – and is worth the effort. This big attractive house, originally built by a German missionary, has enormous, old-fashioned, carpeted bedrooms and a homely feel. Expect antique rosewood beds with embroidered floral bedspreads, themed colours, perhaps a small writing dresser, some garden flowers and horticultural pictures. Large bathrooms are a little antiquated but perfectly fine. The two garden rooms have a covered veranda with a sofa – drink in the sights and sounds as you read – while there are plenty of shady seats outside. Rani wears the traditional pinned sari and can recount many a Coorg yarn; Mr Aiyapa will take you on plantation walks or to the elephant camp nearby. Meals, mostly meat-centric, are truly delicious; eat in the formal dining room with the ancestors or in the conservatory with the birds. A truly comfortable and civilised place to stay, with more than a touch of refined English B&B about it.

Homestay

rooms	4: 3 doubles, 1 family room.
price	Full-board £100. Peak season: September–June.
meals	Full-board only.
closed	Rarely.
directions	From Mysore to Periyapatna. Just after Periyapatna crossing, left to Sidapur town. At Engilkere, take road on right, left at fork; tarmac road to bungalow. Airport: (228km, 5 hours). Train: Mysore (90km, 2 hours).

	Mrs Rani Aiyapa
tel	+91 (0)8274 258 358
mobile	+91 (0)9448 647 559
email	school1@sancharnet.in

Map 8 Entry 206

Four Winds Estate

Mysore Road, Madikeri, Kodagu, 571 201 Karnataka

The Colonel's enthusiasm for India and Kodagu (or Coorg – the 'Scotland of India') is infectious and enchanting. He is a remarkable, kind and well-educated man, and easy company – the main reason for including his house in this book. The modern bungalow is simple but comfortable and cosy, with pleasant views to the distant hills and few rules. Your double bed is a good size, you have a window onto the garden, brightly coloured curtains, good lighting and plenty of books to read. The sitting room is shared with Pradeep, as your host likes to be called; it is a cosily traditional room with wooden sofas and light checked covers, a dark red floor and a traditional rug. If you prefer to go out to lunch or dinner the Colonel will take you into town; there's stacks to do in the area and he can organise anything – even himself (with car) if you are lucky. He will also collect you if you arrive by bus. This is no contrived tourist machine, just a delightful and very human encounter with the best of modern India. *Trekking, golf, angling, birdwatching.*

rooms	1 double.
price	Rs1,500. Single Rs500. Peak season: November-May.
meals	Lunch & dinner Rs250 each.
closed	Rarely.
directions	2km from Madikeri centre on road to Mysore. The Colonel will pick up, or direct you in more detail.

Homestay

	Lt Col K G Uthaya
tel	+91 (0)8272 225 720
mobile	+91 (0)9448 167 400
email	speedy8@rediffmail.com
web	www.gurudongma.com

Map 8 Entry 207

Serenity Homestay

Krishnaraj Villa, Post Box 76, Madikeri, District Kodagu, 571 201 Karnataka

Leave behind the town, the roads and your troubles for this gracious 1920s villa – a haven of clean living and contemplation. Three dalmatians greet you and their artistic owner Monique – a smiling, calming presence – settles you in. Come to paint, walk, read, retreat or take part in a creativity or Vipassana meditation workshop. Your hostess and her helpers, who offer you fresh fruit juices, salads and Indian and continental food, are caring but unobtrusive. The airy double has oodles of colourful paintings and a Mediterranean feel, brushed peach walls and turquoise doors. Terracotta floors, dark wooden furniture, open fires – it's simple but homely. All rooms open to a private outside area – one double has a lovely garden filled with birdsong. There are also two simpler rooms: a large studio space with mattresses on the floor and a very basic twin with fabulous views – perfect for those on a tight budget. The place is owned by a group of friends and run as a charitable retreat; they also have an organic coffee estate and a swimming hole nearby for guests to use. *No children or alcohol.*

Guest house

rooms	7: 2 doubles, 1 twin, 2 singles, 2 family cottages for 2-10.
price	£29. Singles £7-£25. Cottages £25-£100. Peak season: October-May.
meals	Breakfast £3. Lunch £8. Dinner £5-£10. Vegetarian meals available.
closed	Rarely.
directions	Ask for details on booking. Airport: Mangalore (140km, 3hours) & Bangalore (260km, 7 hours). Train: Mysore (128km, 3 hours).

	Monique Somaya
res. no	+91 (0)8272 224 976
mobile	+91 (0)9845 724 885
email	monique@sancharnet.in
web	www.serenityhomestay.com

B

Map 8 Entry 208

Tamil Nadu, Pondicherry & the Andaman Islands

The heartland of southern India, Tamil Nadu is culturally and physically beautiful, extremely friendly and relatively unspoilt. Three powerful dynasties have dominated the south: the Cholas, the Pallavas and the Pandyans, and their creations were largely untouched by marauding Muslims. They created original religions, political institutions, and temples with incredible giant rainbow-coloured towers – many of which are ancient pilgrimage sites. Visit Kanchipuram (also known for its sensational silk saris), Chidambaram, Tiruchirappalli (Trichy), Madurai and Thanjavor (Tanjore). Cool off in the hill-stations of Ooty and Kodaikanal on the way to busier Kerala and have fun in Chennai (Madras), the stupefyingly busy state capital and home of the politically motivated 'Tolly'wood cinema. The world-heritage Mamallapurum (Mahabalipuram) Shore Temple is well worth a short trek and is satisfyingly close to the beach where sari-clad bathers frolic in the waves. Hike in the Nilgiris Hills, home to the Todas, a unique tribal group. The Chettinad region, where the wealthy Chettiars built ornate mansions, is absolutely fascinating.

Francois Martin, the first director of the French East India Company, established Pondicherry as a French enclave and capital of all the French territories in India in 1674. It has tree-lined boulevards, colonial mansions, funky bars and chic cafes. Stroll along the 3km seafront, the St Tropez of southern India, and admire the Gandhi statue. The famous Sri Aurobindo Ashram is here and the new-age centre at nearby Auroville grows organic produce for the area. There are Catholic churches, an interesting museum and shady botanical gardens.

Snorkel through the mangroves on Havelock Island, scuba dive in the crystal-clear waters in the serene Mahatma Gandhi Marine Park and bliss out on the white-sand, tree-fringed beaches in the extraordinary Andaman Islands.

Best time to visit
Tamil Nadu and Pondicherry: December-February
Andaman Islands: December-April

Photos Laura Kinch

Jungle Retreat
Bokkapuram, Nilgiri District, Masinagudi, 643 223 Tamil Nadu

The 35-acre estate rolls down to the foot of the Nilgiri hills. The countryside is lushly beautiful, especially in the rainy season. To perch in the bamboo treehouse and take in the view must be one of the world's most seductive holiday experiences. It is wild, remote and irresistible – and Hermie and her son Rohan are remarkable, too. Their cottages of stone and wood come with tiled bathrooms, air con and fridges, and are beautifully decorated with rosewood, batik and teak. There are 'regular' cottages too, and bamboo-and-thatch ones – these are particularly charming – and now a tree house with hot water, a loo and a view! Entirely constructed from natural materials, the bamboo structures sit a foot above the ground on stilts and have outside shower rooms that half-open to the sky. The communal bar/dining room, with snooker table, has a relaxed mood, in keeping with the owners who thoroughly enjoy looking after their guests. There is a tented children's camp here in the summer holidays, so check dates if you want to join in or avoid. *Camping, trekking & toda tribal village visits.*

Resort

rooms	13: 12 cottages for 2-3, 1 tree house. Tents also available.
price	Rs1,000-Rs2,000. Plus 12.5% tax. Peak season: mid-April-mid-June.
meals	Breakfast Rs150. Lunch Rs200. Dinner Rs250.
closed	Rarely.
directions	6km from Masinagudi on the Bokkapuram road. Right at the temple & follow signs.

	Rohan & Hermie Mathias
tel	+91 (0)4232 526 469
email	bookings@jungleretreat.com
web	www.jungleretreat.com

B

Map 8 Entry 209

The Tryst

Carolina Tea Estate, P.O. Box 6, Coonoor, Nilgiris, 643 102 Tamil Nadu

An Aladdin's cave of 'things': antique, interesting, odd or baffling. What to make of the old telephones and toy cars, the gramophones and the biscuit tins? And then there are Ann's tapestries and embroideries, framed jigsaw puzzles, lace table covers and homemade fire-screens. It is a wild and energetic clutter in a house stuffed with personality. So, not for the steel-and-teak minimalist but there *is* something engaging about the unexpectedness of it all. You could spend many happy rainy days in the library, games room, music room (two pianos), billiard room and exercise room. The Tryst has the loveliest possible position among the tea plantations, with rolling views and great walks and Coonoor out of sight behind a hill. Sathya worked for 17 years as a doctor in Liverpool before he met Ann and brought her here. They are eccentric and imaginative: be prepared for some provocative humour. And they are generous: the bedroom set aside for drivers has hot water and TV. They may even organise your whole holiday if you give them half a chance. *Owners run Salutary Trust (for sustainable development).*

rooms	6 + 1: 4 doubles, 2 twins. Cottage for 10.
price	Half-board Rs3,900. Cottage Rs9,000. Peak season: September-March.
meals	Half-board only. Lunch Rs150-Rs250.
closed	June-August.
directions	2km from Coonoor bus stand, up road opposite railway crossing. After 1km, signs to Carolina Tea Estate down left fork for 1.5km.

Homestay

	Dr Sathya & Ann Rao
tel	+91 (0)4232 207 057
fax	+91 (0)4232 207 057
email	tryst@vsnl.com
web	www.trystindia.com

B ⋏ ⌂ 🚜 👟

Map 8 Entry 210

Cardamom House

Athoor Village, Dindigul, Dindigul District, 624 701 Tamil Nadu

Chris is a foodie, a traveller, a gentleman and a comic. A retired British doctor, he has poured energy into creating his utopia. His humour and zest infuse the place, the staff wear the broadest smiles and the whole place sweeps you into a warm embrace. The house stands at the foot of a steep hill, huddled in a horseshoe of scrub hills with views from the pretty garden across the lake to the Western Ghats. Divided between three buildings, the bedrooms are a picture of taste and restraint – tiled floors, crisp white linen, solar-powered showers, fresh flowers on beds. Verandas crouch beneath bougainvillea cascading in every colour, creating hidden spots in which to escape into a book; the rooftop terrace sits beneath a nocturnal frenzy of Indian stars. Ultimately, the feeling is of conviviality, of sharing the treat of discovering a moment of true happiness in the remote heart of rural India. Chris is passionate about the environment and social responsibility, his staff are in charge of the developing organic vegetable garden and guided trips to the village support the local community. *Minimum stay two nights.*

rooms	7: 6 doubles, 1 suite.
price	Rs3,600. Suite Rs4,400. Peak season: December–March.
meals	Breakfast Rs150. Lunch Rs250. Dinner Rs350.
closed	Rarely.
directions	From Sembatti crossroad, on Madurai-Coimbatore road, signs to Coimbatore/Palani. 2km, left. Signed. Airport: Madurai (70km, 2 hours). Train: Dindigul (27km, 45 minutes).

Homestay

SPECIAL GREEN ENTRY see page 18

	Dr Chris Lucas
tel	+91 (0)4512 556 765/766
mobile	+91 (0)9360 691 793
email	chrislucas@cardamomhouse.com or cardamomhouse@yahoo.com
web	www.cardamomhouse.com

B 🍴 🚜 🚲 👟

Map 8 Entry 211

Cinnabar

Chettiar Rd, Kodaikanal, 624 101 Tamil Nadu

Come to be cosseted – ever-cheerful Bala and Vasu adore looking after guests and sharing their home. He is an organic fruit and vegetable farmer and also makes the most wonderful cheese – a rarity in India. They designed and built their modern home themselves, and have added on two self-contained bedrooms behind the main house. Australian blackwood floors are insulated with coconut coir to keep feet warm – this area gets chilly at night. There are pine ceilings, appliqué beige and white bedcovers, Vasu's watercolours and sweet touches: homemade chocolates, fresh flowers, a booklet about the fruit trees in the garden. You share the family lounge and may meet daughter Vidya and the three-legged dog Hero. A log fire smoulders in the evenings. Vasu cooks mainly European food served in the family dining room; delicious breakfasts will set you up for the day and include their own bread, coffee, honey and milk. Bala can take you on walks, drop in on the local quiltmaker and show you another side to this busy hill station.

rooms	2 doubles.
price	£29-£35. Peak season: May.
meals	Dinner £3.
closed	June & 1-15 December.
directions	From Kodaikanal lake, along Convent Road, right onto Kurunji Temple Road, fork left; 300m on right. Airport: Madurai (129km, 3 hours). Train: Kodai Road (80km, 2 hours).

Homestay

Bala Krishnan

tel +91 (0)4542 240 220

mobile +91 (0)9842 145 220

email cinnabarfarm@yahoo.com

web www.geocities.com/cinnabarfarm

B

Bison Wells

'Camp George', Oberservatory P.O., Kodaikanal, 624 103 Tamil Nadu

One well provides water for washing and another for the kitchen; the third is for the bison that come out of the forest to drink. The forest teems with life and giant squirrels and at night the noises are exhilarating. Your view is across a shallow, wooded valley to dense hills on the edge of a natural reserve – this remoteness is the reason George built his clay-and-wood lodge. He is a serious ecologist and you can learn much from him. He lives in Kodaikanal but likes to spend time with guests, so he sleeps down the hill in a hut. Your own space is basic and unremarkable, in natural earthy shades of yellow and green: strictly no frills! The modest bathroom is equally rustic and simple, with buckets to empty down the loo. But it all works. The helper, Williams, prepares your meals in a little kitchen and you eat out on the veranda, a wonderful place to while away the hours. A few yards from the house and you are in deep nature; the best way to set off on a walk is with a guide. An unusual and rich experience. *Trekking, bird watching & jungle trails.*

Catered cottage

rooms	Cottage for 2-3.
price	Full-board £30.
	Peak season: January-May.
meals	Full-board only.
closed	Rarely.
directions	90-minute drive from Kodaikanal; contact George before you leave for provisions & transport.
	Airport: Madurai (150km, 5 hours).
	Train: Kodai Road (110km, 4 hours).

	Mr George Roshan
tel	+91 (0)4542 240 566
email	bisonwells@rediffmail.com
web	www.wilderness-explorer.in

A 👟

Map 8 Entry 213

Elephant Valley

Ganesh Puram, Vilpatti, Kumpoor Vayal (PO), Kodaikanal, 624 104 Tamil Nadu

After a long, bumpy journey, sip lemongrass tea in the adobe-style restaurant; over breakfast you may spot an elephant drinking by the gently-flowing river. Go on a guided trek across the hills to the waterfall or take one of the beautiful horses out and ride among bison. This is a stylish fun place with a European twist. Funky cottages are set around the grounds for maximum privacy and peace. Inside: open-brick walls, woodburning stoves, some antique wooden furniture, fresh bright bed linen – maybe orange or vibrant turquoise – and private terraces with comfy chairs. Comic elephant paintings and silver painted shutters and doors add fun; bathrooms have composting sawdust loos, rainwater or bucket showers and organic neem smellies; electricity is solar. French owners have brought Gallic flair to their organic plantation and are growing vegetables and roasting their own fragrant coffee. A great place to relax, get stuck into a good book and let nature wash over you. *The best time for elephant spotting is from April to September.*

rooms	9 cottages: 8 for 2, 1 for 4.
price	Rs2,000–Rs5,500.
meals	Lunch & dinner Rs250 each.
closed	Rarely.
directions	At Perumal Malai junc., on Dindigul/Kodaikanal road, turn right towards Palani. After 1.5km, left to Garnesh Puram; follow for 6.5km; at junc., signed.

Guest house

Mr Stephen Fayon

tel	+91 (0)4542 230 399
res. no	+91 (0)4132 655 751
email	booking@elephantvalley.com
web	www.elephantvalley.com

Map 8 Entry 214

Mayuram Lodge

Kallarackal Farm, Govindaperri Village, Kadayam, Ambassamudram Taluk, Tirunelveli District

Paddy fields dotted with palms meet the Western Ghats — this is a beautiful place. Rajesh is a bubbling source of ideas on rainwater harvesting and other environmental issues and is re-establishing an indigenous forest on his estate. Close at hand are walks in wooded hills and among lakes — and the joy of swimming in mountain streams. Come when the rains have cooled the plains. The wide variety of habitat makes this a superb place for birdwatchers. Rajesh, US-educated, used his skills as an architect to design his guest house around a court with an ornamental pool, in keeping with the architectural vernacular, and has the bedrooms opening onto a generous balcony that overlooks the estate. The farm is some distance from a main road so you do need to be certain you know where you are going. If Rajesh is not going to be there himself he will pass special pre-requests on to the servants; they may not speak much English but should look after you well. They also provide excellent Indian food served in the small library. Serenely simple.

rooms	4 doubles.
price	Full-board Rs3,350.
	Peak season: November-15 March.
meals	Full-board only.
closed	Rarely.
directions	135km from Trivandrum; 235km from Kochi. Directions on booking.

Guest house

	Mr Rajesh George
tel	+91 (0)4634 240 715
res. no	+91 (0)4842 706 475
email	prakrti@vsnl.com
web	www.mayuramlodge.com

B 🚲 👟

Map 8 Entry 215

Chettinadu Mansion

S.A.R.M. House (Behind Raja's Palace), T.K.R. Street, Kanadukathan, Nr. Karakudi, Tamil Nadu

Slip through the gated entrance, under the white portico and into a bygone era of afternoon tea and gracious living. This staggering, 126-room mansion, built by a wealthy Chettiar trader, took ten years to complete at the beginning of the last century. In Russian-doll fashion, double doors open to reveal yet another marbled hall, yet another courtyard. Size is everything. The Marriage Hall, with its Italianate floor and inky marble pillars, is 70-feet long. You could spend half a day marvelling at ornamental ceilings, graceful archways, teak furnishings and decorative tiled floors. Bedrooms overlook the central courtyard on one side, with a street-side balcony on the other – a delightful spot for watching village life before retreating to the grandeur of a teak-carved bed. Ceilings disappear heavenwards, walls are painted and tiled in jewel-bright colours. White sheets, glass-topped tables, cascades of fruit and Edwardian-style telephones complete the elegant picture. Dine on authentic Chettinad food before enjoying the sunset from the roof terrace. Mr Chandramouli is a true gentleman.

rooms	7: 4 doubles, 3 twins.
price	Rs4,400. Singles Rs3,300.
meals	Breakfast Rs200. Lunch Rs400. Dinner Rs400.
closed	Rarely.
directions	Airport: Trichy (80km, 2 hours). Train 2km, 5 minutes.

	Mr Chandramouli
tel	+91 (0)4565 273 080
res. no	+91 (0)4842 312 678
mobile	+91 (0)9443 495 598
email	info@deshadan.com
web	www.chettinadumansion.com

Guest house

Map 9 Entry 216

The Bangala

Devakottai Road, Senjai, Karaikudi, Chettinad, 630 001 Tamil Nadu

After bumping across miles of scarred road to get here you may have begun to wonder why. But stepping out of the car and into the gardens of this heritage hotel soon banishes memories of dust and heat. Karaikudi has other secrets, too. This is the centre of the Chettiars, a small coterie of families who wielded immense commercial influence under the Raj. Their 'palaces' are thick on the ground in a scattering of small villages in and around Karaikudi. Imagine turning the corner in a dusty village to be confronted by an avenue lined with an assorted collection of villas, mansions, manors and mini-palaces from every conceivable era and every European country. The Chettiars poured their riches — made from trade and banking in South East Asia — into these homes and their temples, and the results are astonishing. The Bangala, more villa than hotel, is one of the rare places that serves genuine Chettinad food — as is the custom, on banana leaves — and is run with kindness and discretion. It is charming, elegant, stylish and comfortable, like a country house whose owner, though absent, is there in spirit.

rooms	12 doubles.
price	Full-board Rs6,200.
meals	Full-board only.
closed	Rarely.
directions	At the beginning of Devakottai Road, in the Senjai area. Airport/ train: Trichy & Madurai (90km).

Hotel

	Mrs Meenaksh Meyyappan
tel	+91 (0)4565 220 221
res. no	+91 (0)4424 934 851
fax	+91 (0)4424 934 543
email	bangala@vsnl.com
web	www.thebangala.com

B 🍴 💳 🧍 👞

Map 9 Entry 217

Sterling Swamimalai

6/30 B Timmakudi Agiraharam, Baburajapuram P.O., Swamimalai, Kumbakonam, 612 302

Ayurveda is the essence of the place – few hotels are so genuinely devoted to the practice and you will be magnificently treated; on arrival, they massage your feet with oils and sound a welcome bell. The heart of the hotel is an 1896 villa – admire the curious antique collection that lies in six acres of land and coconut groves. On the banks of the river Cauvery, this place is designed like a typical Indian village – enjoy games in the Urmayam, the village centre. Sculptures dot the grounds, free-range fowl and deer wander and the buildings are designed with an eye to eco-awareness and authenticity. Bedrooms are sober and old-fashioned but pleasing, with soft beige walls, wooden beds and Tanjore silver-inlay paintings. And there's masses to indulge in here: herbal oil massage, classic and folk theatre, pottery, swimming, yoga – experience harmony for body, mind and soul. The manager and staff are delightful and the vegetarian food utterly delicious. This is very much a resort hotel – albeit with a strong difference – and you will encounter groups here.

rooms	27: 22 doubles, 5 suites.
price	$94. Suites $130. Peak season: October-February.
meals	Breakfast $4. Lunch & dinner $8 each.
closed	Never.
directions	Airports: Trichy (91km), Madurai (211km), Chennai (300km). Train: Kumbakonam (4km, 10 minutes).

Resort

Mr Steve Borgia

tel	+91 (0)4352 480 044
res. no	+91 (0)4424 890 194
mobile	+91 (0)9444 410 396
email	sterling_kmb@sancharnet.in
web	www.sterlingswamimalai.net

Map 9 Entry 218

Bungalow on the Beach

24 King Street, Tharangambadi, District Nagapattinam, 609 313 Tamil Nadu

The coastal views are extraordinary: breathe in the balmy air from your balcony and watch the fishermen in their colourful boats. On one side is the impressive Danish Fort, on the other a very pretty crumbling Hindu temple. Tranquebar, as it was called, is a quiet, beautiful and rather desolate place. The restoration of the 'bungalow' is remarkable – constructed in part by the Danish in the 16th century, it was finished in the 1830s and handed to the British mayor in the 1840s. The entrance hall is cavernous and the new teak staircase leads to a blue and white panelled drawing room. Enormous bedrooms, individually decorated, are named after Danish ships that stopped here; some are a little musty until aired. Very pretty patterned bedcovers set the theme in each room, where pastel pink, turquoise and yellow stripes accompany white walls, dark-wood four-posters and stripped floors. Upstairs rooms have wraparound views from balconies, and privacy. There is a set menu in the little restaurant (no other good choices nearby) and continental breakfast can be served on the terrace. A good stopover.

Hotel

rooms	8 doubles.
price	Rs4,000–Rs5,000. Plus 12.5% tax.
meals	Breakfast Rs150. Lunch & dinner RS350 each.
closed	Rarely.
directions	Head inside the Danish Fort; hotel next to Fort by the sea. Airport: Chennai (300km, 6 hours). Train: Nagapattinam (24km, 45 mins).

	Suresh (Manager)
tel	+91 (0)4364 288 065
res. no	+91 (0)1124 356 145
fax	+91 (0)4364 289 038
email	bungalowonthebeach_tqbr@yahoo.com
web	www.neemranahotels.com

C Ⓚ 🛏 ⚓ 👟

Map 9 Entry 219

Sterling Beach Resort

Shore Temple Road, Mahabalipuram, 603 104 Tamil Nadu

Steve Borgia is hugely energetic – a man of vision who likes a challenge, he converted this former British camp in 30 days, with 30 people and 30,000 rupees. It is quite an achievement to create such a special space. A giant hanger-style, breezy reception area is where you'll be greeted with a fresh coconut drink and a foot massage. Then drift through lush and shady gardens where delicious vegetarian meals are seved, or eat in the cool interior. A pongamia tree peeps out of the roof of the restaurant, and there are lovely stained glass suns and antiques gathered from the local villages – many women were sweethearts to the British. In six clusters of buildings, rooms are simple and fresh with green slatted headboards, yellow cushions and natural materials. Or stay in the luxurious domed 'pod'! The hotel has conference facilities and will generally not take individual bookings when they are being used. The authentic ayurvedic massages are given in simple rooms on neem tables; the beach, with its famous 7th-century Shore Temple and colourful sari-bathers, is a stroll away.

rooms	30 twins/doubles.
price	Full-board $110. Plus tax.
meals	Full-board only.
closed	Rarely.
directions	In Mahabalipuram, close to the Shore Temple; signed.

	Mr Steve Borgia
tel	+91 (0)4427 442 287
fax	+91 (0)4427 443 916
email	sterling_kmb@sancharnet.in
web	www.sterlingmahabalipuram.net

Hotel

Map 9 Entry 220

The Park

601 Anna Salai, Chennai (Madras), 600 006 Tamil Nadu

Feel like a 'Tolly'wood star in this former film studio where India's first picture, *Chandralekha*, was recorded in 1948. It now oozes glamour and ultra-modern style. Fat chocolate sofas, dotty cushions, tall bamboos and falling water in the atrium reception and a leather floor in the funky bar – Bhangra music creates the vibe. This is *the* place to be seen in Chennai. Try Malabar spice-fried soft shell crab or a raw mango curry in the minimal Six 'o' One restaurant or pop in for a 'midnight biriani' later on. Linger over Mediterranean dishes by the roof-top pool or Thai in the lotus-flower room. Tropical architectural flowers add drama, movies enthrall in the crushed-silk lift. Bedrooms are suprisingly understated and calming. Fresh, cream bed linen and rich cinammon or sage cushions, suede headboards, fat feather duvets and state-of-the-art beds – this is the ideal place to recuperate. Experience mood lighting, glass-walled bathrooms, ayurvedic honey lotions. And then there's the spa, with dazzling treatments… A fun find in a cosmopolitan city – and worth every dollar.

rooms	214: 161 doubles, 9 suites.
price	$205-$215. Suites $350-$400. Plus 12.5% tax.
meals	Lunch £2-£12.
closed	Rarely.
directions	Opposite the Gemini flyover, centre of town. Airport: Chennai (15km, 35 mins). Train: Chennai (8km, 20 mins).

Hotel

	V. V. Giri (Manager)
tel	+91 (0)4442 144 000
fax	+91 (0)4442 144 000
email	resv.che@theparkhotels.com
web	www.theparkhotels.com

D 🍴 📖 🍶 ⅄ 🏊

Map 9 Entry 221

Kailash Beach Resort

Poornankuppam Village, Ariankuppam Commune, 605 007 Pondicherry

A place of learning and reflection amid fragrant gardens... come to retreat, practise yoga, learn Hindi, write and unwind. Three large new pink buidings inspired by Sikkim houses, with wide terraces and large courtyards, rest on typical Chettinad teak pillars. There's an Asian/French twist here – Raj, a publisher, is Indian and has spent much of his life in Asia, Elisabete is French and has a brilliant eye for colour. Discover golden carved doorways, a frangipani tree in the courtyard, bowls of flower petals and good outdoor seating areas with rattan furniture and crisp white cushions. Bedrooms have various Asian styles while simple yet effective touches like Chinese black and red cushions and Keraykudi painted wooden dolls add to the magic. Wander through the floral semi-formal gardens past the Chinese pagoda to the beach or swim in the lovely pool. There's pretty pottery for a cup of tea and a simple evening meal – fresh fish is always available. The service is a touch slow and large groups come here but no matter: if you're not in a hurry there are plenty of blissful corners to enjoy.

rooms	37 doubles.
price	Rs2,900. Triples Rs3,600. Singles Rs2,300. Plus 8% tax. Peak season: mid November–March.
meals	Breakfast £2. Lunch & dinner £5 each.
closed	Never.
directions	Airport: Chennai (155km, 2.5 hours). Train: Pondicherry (12km, 20 mins).

Hotel

	Mr Raj de Condappa
tel	+91 (0)4132 619 700/01/02/03
fax	+91 (0)4132 619 704
email	kailashbeachresort@dataone.in
web	www.kailashbeachhotel.com

Map 9 Entry 222

Hotel de L'Orient

17 Rue Romain Rolland, 605 001 Pondicherry

In the pastel charm that is colonial Pondicherry you could forget this is India. The hotel, formerly the French Department of Education, is an elegant pink-and-white 18th-century mansion whose recently decorated rooms are dotted with antiques, statuettes, rhinestone-studded oleographs and Savonnerie-style dhurries from the looms of Jaipur. From the vast and superior Chandernagore Suite to the crow's nest of Gingy (reached via a steep, ladder-like stair), each room is rich in individual character and the dull essentials of life secreted away in teak cupboards and dowry chests. For a private terrace with pillared recess and terracotta-tiled floor, choose the Karikal Suite, while some of the lofty, beam-ceilinged, window-shuttered rooms overlook the internal courtyard where Creole food – a blend of French and Tamil – is served. Breakfasts are a feast of fresh tropical juices and Neemrana jams; buy some to take home. It's an elegant, wonderful place – and at night you may drift off to sleep to the ripples of the Bay of Bengal lapping against the shore two streets away.

Hotel

rooms	16: 3 doubles, 10 twins, 3 suites.
price	Rs2,500–Rs4,500.
	Peak season: September–March.
meals	Breakfast Rs100. Lunch Rs250.
	Dinner Rs350.
closed	Rarely.
directions	In central Pondicherry.
	Airport: Chennai (160km).
	Train: Pondicherry (2km).

	Mr Anthony Gabriel Thomas
tel	+91 (0)4132 343 067
res. no	+91 (0)1124 356 145
fax	+91 (0)4132 227 829
email	sales@neemranahotels.com
web	www.neemranahotels.com

B 🖃 🌡

Map 9 Entry 223

The Promenade

Beach Road (next to Old Lighthouse), Pondicherry

Take a handbag designer, a new building in the neoclassical style and a dose of creative licence... and you get a hip, playful beach hangout that feels more St Tropez than Pondy. Dilip Kapur and his German wife own a smart leatherware company, Hidesign, and have created an affordable contemporary hotel to match. They've used leather, huge swathes of it, for the softest headboards; elephant-grey and red seats in the restaurant; a gorgeous pink, yellow and blue leather lift. Textural contrasts tempt: teak floors and windows and raw silk bedcovers, sumptuous leather chairs and floor-to-ceiling mosaic'd bathrooms. Throw open the French windows and let the sea breezes in – some rooms have a sea view from the bed. Luxuriate with melon and green tea bath products; sip tea in your soft dressing gown; indulge in lazy long lunches on the sun-blazed terrace or barbecued wild prawns – fresh and tasty – on the rooftop. And there's all-night dining in the coffee shop. Pose by the sunken café-side plunge pool, stroll along the sea front to the Gandhi statue, shop in the old town.

rooms	27: 25 doubles, 2 suites.
price	Rs2,800–Rs3,500. Suites Rs7,000.
meals	Rs250–Rs350.
	Upstairs restaurant Rs300–Rs400.
closed	Never.
directions	On the Beach Road, near Gandhi statue, next to Old Lighthouse. Airport: Chennai (160km, 2.5 hours). Train: Pondicherry (2km, 5 mins).

Hotel

Mr Dilip Kapur, Mr Akash Kapur, Mrs Jacqueline Kapur

tel	+91 (0)4132 227 750
fax	+91 (0)4132 227 141
email	promenade@sarovarhotels.com
web	www.sarovarhotels.com

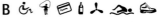

Map 9 Entry 224

Le Dupleix
5, rue de la Caserne, 605 001 Pondicherry

The oldest and probably the most gorgeous villa in town, it was once the 18th-century home of Nawab and General Marquis Joseph Francois Dupleix, the former French governor of Pondicherry. It sits in a remarkably quiet street where mango trees flourish – one shades the courtyard restaurant. Food is the passion of this place, and chef Kumar will tailor-make your dish once he knows your favourite flavours. The ingredients are super fresh, organic and locally-sourced; everything, including the jam, is homemade. But it's not just the food that makes this place stand out – the interiors are heavenly, too. There are French windows, wide balconies, sweet-smelling teak, exquisite antique carved pillars and hugely high ceilings. Add modern touches – glass walkways, structural tropical flowers, silver-painted wrought-iron balconies, a stone waterfall – and original bedrooms: a four-poster bed on a chessboard floor, a glass-walled rooftop, a cream canopy bed with the crispest linen and the lightest voile. Modern meets old and it's fabulous.

rooms	14: 11 doubles, 3 suites.
price	Rs2,700–Rs5,000.
meals	Lunch & dinner from Rs500 each.
closed	Never.
directions	In the centre of Pondicherry Old Town, on the corner of Rue Suffren & Rue de la Caserne. Airport: Chennai (160km, 2.5 hours). Train: Pondicherry (2km, 5 mins).

Hotel

Mr Dilip Kapur, Mr Akash Kapur, Mr Dimitri Klein

tel	+91 (0)4132 226 999
fax	+91 (0)4132 335 278
email	ledupleix@sarovarhotels.com

C 🛏 📧 🕯 🧘

Map 9 Entry 225

Barefoot at Havelock

Beach No 7, Radhangar Village, Havelock Island, 744 101 Andaman Islands

Good things come to those that persevere! Here is a remote retreat that sustains the unwritten rule that the best places are the hardest to reach. Forget clichéd coconuts and palms, listen instead to forest-bird ballad in eight acres of gardens and mahua trees minutes from a long, white and curvaceous beach. No TV or phone, just stunning sunsets over the Andaman Sea. These beautifully designed, conically thatched cottages are locally made from bamboo, wood and palm leaves, and draw their water from the camp's own spring. The slightly more luxurious hardwood villas have floor-to-ceiling windows on three sides, shady balconies and opaque jungle-shower roofs to pull light in from the forest canopy. Relax by candlelight and cool jazz in the oriental living area before your next meal; the fusion food is local, organic, delicious and they cook your own catch. Susheel, a native islander who built the resort with the help of local friends, now oversees it all with Samit — who arrived as a backpacker and has never left. Easy to see why. *Iyengar yoga; snorkelling; ocean swimming with elephants.*

rooms	18 cottages & villas for 2-4.
price	$63-$125.
meals	Lunch & dinner $12 each.
closed	Rarely.
directions	Flight to Port Blair Airport. Ask for details of boat transfers when booking.

	Mr Samit Sawhny
tel	+91 (0)3192 236 008
res	+91 (0)3192 245 070
email	reservations@barefootindia.com
web	www.barefootindia.com

Resort

Map 9 Entry 226

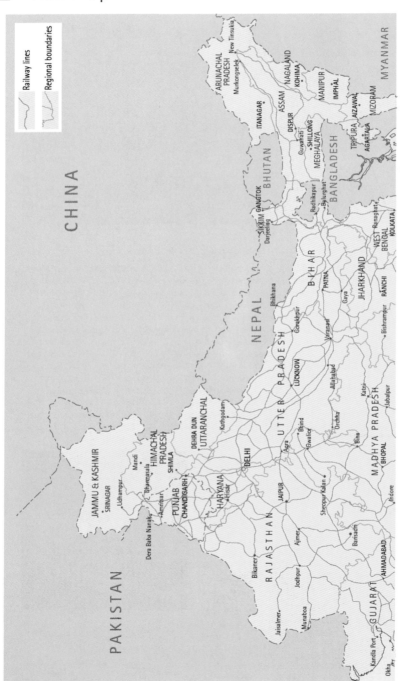

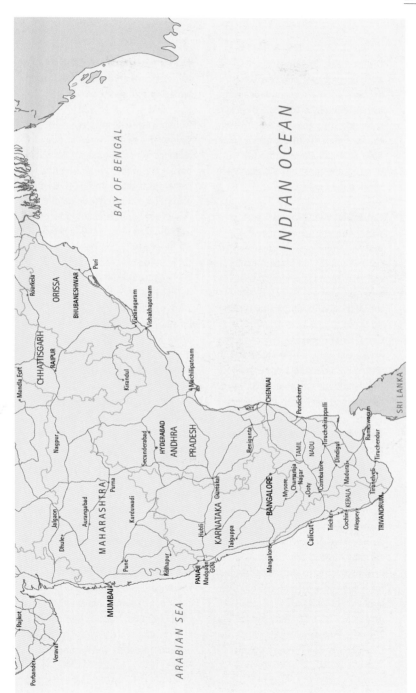

Direct Room Bookings
It's quicker, easier and cheaper to arrange your own accommodation rather than pay a tour operator to do it for you. This guide makes it easy: the vast majority of our special places have an email address or a fax number, and most owners/managers speak good English.

Organising your own transport is pretty straightforward, too. Train journeys in India are a great way to see the country and meet people. You can also organise a car and a driver, or a taxi, and you can make use of the vast network of internal flights.

Car & driver versus taxi
A tour operator can be invaluable in arranging a car and a driver for your trip. Find details of tour operators we recommend further on in this section.

The owners in this guide are also a great resource when booking a car and driver. They often know the best local companies and get good prices.

Drivers can be excellent and knowledgeable. Note, many hotels do not have drivers' facilities so the car may have to double up as the driver's bedroom. The costs per day for a car and a driver vary, but you may expect to pay:
A/c Jeep: £20-£30 a day (under 200km); Non-a/c Ambassador: £15-£25 per day (under 200km).

Taxis are much cheaper and let's not forget the trusty rickshaw – ideal for whizzing round cities.

Booking train tickets from the UK
One of the easiest ways to book in advance is to organise an 'Indrail' pass – this allows you unlimited travel for a set period. SD Enterprises also book train routes in advance; this is advisable, as many routes get fully-booked, especially at weekends. SD Enterprises, 103 Wembley Park Drive, Middlesex, London
Tel: +44 (0)208 903 3411
Indrail Pass (pre-bookings only)
7 days £82; 15 days £112.
Email: info@indiarail.co.uk
Web: www.indiarail.co.uk
Alternatively, book your train tickets with an Indian tour operator.

Booking train tickets online
You can book train tickets online using the government-sponsored service at www.irctc.co.in

You can book up to four journeys a month. Tickets are sent to an Indian address so you should arrange for these to be sent to your hotel (ask the hotel in advance).

Train timetable Information
www.seat61.com/India.htm is an excellent beginner's guide to train travel in India. Information about all aspects of train travel are given, including how to understand the

Indian Government Railway Information (see below).

Indian Government Railway Information www.indianrail.gov.in This is a good web site for train times and information. There are very good International Tourist Bureau for direct bookings at the following railway stations: New Delhi, Mumbai (Bombay), Kolkata (Calcutta), Agra, Jaipur, Varanasi.

Booking flights
Flights to and around India can be booked online or via a UK or Indian travel agent. The airline industry had been recently privatised so there are plenty of cheap deals.

Jet Airways www.jetairways.com
Click on the link for Special Offers. 'Visit India' (unlimited travel on their routes): 15 days $630; 21 days $895; 7 days regional (north, south, east or west India) $320.

Air India www.airindia.com
'Discover India' – unlimited travel for 15 days $750 (no single route twice). 'India Wonderfare' – 7 days travel in one region $300.

New airlines, similar to the European low-cost airlines, include:
Sahara Airways www.airsahara.net
Kingfisher www.flykingfisher.com
Air Deccan www.airdeccan.net
Spice Jet www.spicejet.com

Travel agents & tour operators
There are hundreds of travel agents and tour operators in India and we list the few we know. Quite often the best source of up-to-date information on the best tour operators comes from the owners themselves. Tour operators can book train tickets, organise a car and a driver for you, or a completely tailor-made tour.

Kerala Connections
www.keralaconnections.com
A small British-based outfit run by a husband and wife team that arranges trips to the southern coastal state.
Tel: 01892 722440
Email: info@keralaconnect.co.uk

Some of our owners run their own travel companies, which we mention in italics under the entry write-ups. Here are others that you might contact:

Aana Holidays, Kochi, Kerala
www.aanaholidays.com
Run by a knowledgeable team, Leric Reeches and Dilip Vasudevan. They can organise all types of trips all over India, from a car and a driver to train tickets or a tailor-made guided tour.
Tel: +91 (0)4843 020369
or +91 (0)4843 2203669
Email: mail@aanaholidays.com

Getting there and getting around

Banyan Tours & Travels Private Ltd, Delhi (plus regional offices) can organise all manner of luxury travel within India. They cover cars, trains, hotel bookings, flights and the fiddly aspects of getting around India.
Tel: +91 (0)11 2435 0435
Email: banyan.delhi@vsnl.com

Choomti Travellers, Delhi
www.choomti.com
Simon Bazely specialises in tailor-made package tours for individuals and small groups (mid-range and upmarket travellers).
Tel: +91 (0)11 2331 1194
Email: choomti@vsnl.com

Explore Culture & Tours, Delhi
www.exploreculturetours.com
Specialists in northern Indian travel, trekking and mountaineering with a strong focus on low-impact travel.
Tel: +91 (0)11 2335 8711
Email: ect@bol.net.in

Sundale Tours, Kochi, Kerala
www.sundale.com
A charming outfit that organises homestays, cookery holidays and backwater cruises and can help with any travel arrangements in southern India.
Tel: +91 (0)48 4238 0127
Email: tropical@vsnl.com

Though we are happy to recommend the above companies, we cannot be held responsible for their choices and recommendations.

Post-independence place name changes

- Alleppey is now Allappuzha
- Bombay is now Mumbai
- Calcutta is now Kolkata
- Calicut is now Kozhikode
- Cannanore is now Kannur
- Cochin is now Kochi
- Coorg is now Kodagu
- Madras is now Chennai
- Ooty is now Udhagamandalam
- Palghat is now Palakkad
- Quilon is now Kollam
- Simla is now Shimla
- Trivandrum is now Thiruvananthapuram

Photo Indian Tourist Board

Where on the web?

The World Wide Web is big – very big. So big, in fact, that it can be a fruitless search if you don't know where to find reliable, trustworthy, up-to-date information about fantastic places to stay in Europe, India, Morocco and beyond....

Fortunately, there's www.specialplacestostay.com, where you can dip into all of our guides, find special offers from owners, catch up on news about the series and tell us about the special places you've been to.

www.specialplacestostay.com

Discover your perfect self-catering escape in Britain... With the same punch and attitude as all our printed guides, Special Escapes celebrates only those places we have visited and genuinely like.

www.special-escapes.co.uk

Order form

All these books are available in major bookshops or you may order them direct.
Post and packaging are FREE within the UK.

Bed & Breakfast for Garden Lovers	£14.99
British Hotels, Inns & Other Places	£13.99
British Bed & Breakfast	£14.99
French Bed & Breakfast	£15.99
French Hotels, Châteaux & Other Places	£14.99
French Holiday Homes	£12.99
Greece	£11.99
India	£11.99
Ireland	£12.99
Italy	£14.99
London	£9.99
Morocco	£11.99
Mountains of Europe	£9.99
Paris Hotels	£9.99
Portugal	£10.99
Pubs & Inns of England & Wales	£13.99
Spain	£14.99
Turkey	£11.99
The Little Earth Book	£6.99
The Little Food Book	£6.99
The Little Money Book	£6.99
Six Days	£12.99

Please make cheques payable to Alastair Sawday Publishing   Total £ _____

Please send cheques to: Alastair Sawday Publishing, The Old Farmyard, Yanley
Lane, Long Ashton, Bristol BS41 9LR. For credit card orders call 01275 395431
or order directly from our web site www.specialplacestostay.com

Title   First name   Surname

Address

Postcode   Tel

IND2

If you do not wish to receive mail from other like-minded companies, please tick here ☐
If you would prefer not to receive information about special offers on our books, please tick here ☐

Report form

If you have any comments on entries in this guide, please let us have them. If you have a favourite house, hotel, inn or other new discovery, please let us know abou it. You can return this form, email info@sawdays.co.uk, or visit www.specialplacestostay.com and click on 'contact'.

Existing entry
Property name:_____

Entry number: _____ Date of visit: ___ / ___ / ___

New recommendation
Property name:_____

Address: _____

_____

Tel: _____

Your comments

What did you like (or dislike) about this place? Were the people friendly? What was the location like? What sort of food did they serve?

_____

_____

_____

_____

_____

_____

_____

_____

Your details

Name: _____

Address: _____

Postcode: _____ Tel: _____

IND2

Please send completed form to ASP, The Old Farmyard, Yanley Lane, Long Ashton, Bristol BS41 9LR

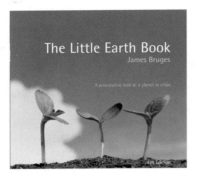

The Little Earth Book
Edition 4, £6.99
By James Bruges

A little book that has proved both hugely popular – and provocative. This new edition has chapters on Islam, Climate Change and The Tyranny of Corporations.

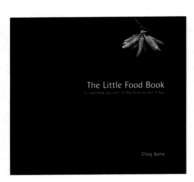

The Little Food Book
Edition 1, £6.99
By Craig Sams, Chairman of the Soil Association

An explosive account of the food we eat today. Never have we been at such risk – from our food. This book will help clarify what's at stake.

The Little Money Book
Edition 1, £6.99
By David Boyle, an associate of the New Economics Foundation

This pithy, wry little guide will tell you where money comes from, what it means, what it's doing to the planet and what we might be able to do about it.

www.fragile-earth.com

Quick reference indices

Quick reference indices

Index by property name

Index by place

Photo Laura Kinch

1 Haryana

Tikli Bottom

Manender Farm, Gairatpur Bas, P.O. Tikli, Gurgaon, 122 001 Haryana

2 The perfect soft landing into India. Martin and Annie are true Delhi-ites, having been here for 20 years. Both have a profound knowledge of India and its machinations, and are immensely affable and generous hosts. Finished in 2000, their Lutyens-style farmhouse, an hour outside the craziness of Delhi, displays impeccable taste. It is at once English and Indian – in winter a roaring fire blazes in the study; in summer, relax in the cosy living room where only the dormant fan above is a reminder of one's whereabouts. In summer you can sleep on the rope-strung beds (*charpois*) in either garden, or in one of the elegant bedrooms, each of which opens onto the veranda'd courtyard. The gardens, encircled by the only real hills around the capital, have been a labour of love – tiered lawns and flowerbeds bursting with colour, a discreet sunken pool hewn from rural mustard fields. Martin will walk you round his organic farmstead, where citrus fruits flourish and kitchen vegetables grow in neat rows. They keep pigs and buffalos (for milk) too. Peace, good conversation, beautiful food and the warmest of welcomes.

rooms	4: 2 doubles, 2 twins.	**3**
price	Full-board £115. Singles £75.	**4**
meals	Full-board only.	**5**
closed	20 April-30 June.	**6**
directions	Airport: Delhi (33km, 45 mins). Train: Delhi (50km, 1.25 hours). They will pick you up from Delhi station or airport.	**7**

10 Hotel

11 **12**

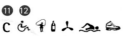

9 Map 2 Entry 54

Martin & Annie Howard **8**
tel +91 (0)1242 766 556
mobile +91 (0)9899 459 123
fax +91 (0)1123 351 272
email honiwala@vsnl.com
web www.tiklibottom.com